Harry Thurston Peck, Robert Arrowsmith

Roman Life in Latin Prose and Verse

Illustrative Readings From Latin Literature

Harry Thurston Peck, Robert Arrowsmith

Roman Life in Latin Prose and Verse
Illustrative Readings From Latin Literature

ISBN/EAN: 9783337021078

Printed in Europe, USA, Canada, Australia, Japan

Cover: Foto ©Thomas Meinert / pixelio.de

More available books at **www.hansebooks.com**

ROMAN LIFE

IN

LATIN PROSE AND VERSE

*ILLUSTRATIVE READINGS FROM LATIN
LITERATURE*

SELECTED AND EDITED BY

HARRY THURSTON PECK, Ph.D.

PROFESSOR OF THE LATIN LANGUAGE AND LITERATURE, COLUMBIA COLLEGE

AND

ROBERT ARROWSMITH, Ph.D.

PROFESSOR OF GREEK AND LATIN, TEACHERS COLLEGE, NEW YORK

NEW YORK ∴ CINCINNATI ∴ CHICAGO

AMERICAN BOOK COMPANY

Printed by
William Ivison
New York, U. S. A.

INTRODUCTORY NOTE.

In the preparation of this volume the needs of three classes of students have been kept constantly in mind. Primarily, it is intended for the use of those whose plan of work makes it impossible for them to devote to the study of Latin more than a limited amount of time, yet who are nevertheless desirous of becoming familiar with what is most famous in the literature of the language, and of gaining incidentally some general knowledge of the life and thought of ancient Rome. It is intended also to provide for school and college classes, in the sight-reading of Latin, a wider, more interesting, and more instructive course than is offered by any existing volume designed for rapid reading. Finally, it aims to be a history of Latin letters, giving in concise and practical form an outline of the development of Roman literature from its earliest days, as illustrated in the most characteristic and striking passages that have descended to us. It is, therefore, meant either to be read as supplementary to a regular course in Latin literature, or to be made itself the fundamental work in such a course.

The general plan of the book is to give, in chronological order, and grouped under the author's names, so far as these are known, such selections as will not only show the individuality of the writer and the quality of his literary style, but also reveal something of the life, manners, and opinions of the age in which he wrote. Thus, the first selection in the book is made, not from purely literary sources, but from the Roman folk-songs, the popular rhymes, and the verses sung by children in their play — all antedating the beginnings of written literature. In like manner, the editors have given, in their proper chronological order, other material of a popular nature, such as the advertisements found upon the walls of Pompeii, lampoons and parodies, theatrical and gladiatorial notices, announcements of ball-games, epitaphs upon tombstones, and old saws and maxims, all of which, though not themselves literature, throw a flood of light upon much that is found in literature and upon the life and customs of those for whom the literature was written.

In the purely literary extracts, the editors have ranged over a wide field, so as to make the collection a thoroughly representative one. The selections cover the early dramatists, the historians, orators, and philosophers, the writers of satire and epigram, the lyric and epic poets, the collectors of anecdotes, the letter-writers, and the authors of prose fiction. The last reading in the book is one of the early Christian hymns.

To the selections from each author is prefixed a concise account of his life, his works, and his place in the history of Latin literature, with a notice of the best editions of the text, the best commentary, and the best literary translations. These, taken together, give a conspectus of the development of the literature and a working bibliography of the most recent classical publications. This bibliography aims only to direct the reader to the best works easily accessible to him in any good public or college library; and the references are in most instances only to works in the English language.

To facilitate the use of the book in classes formed for the reading of Latin at sight, the more difficult words are translated at the bottom of each page. Fuller notes relating to special points are given at the end of the book. Several of the selections thus annotated have never before been published with an English commentary, so that the volume may be of interest to advanced students of Latin, as well as to those for whom the book is primarily intended. The commentary is designed to afford only such assistance as is necessary to the understanding of the selections as parts of literature, and not at all as material for drill in parsing. There are, therefore, no grammatical references and few discussions of grammatical points. The notes are intended to treat only the matters of allusion, style, and construction which would naturally come up for notice in the classroom.

It has been the plan of the editors throughout, in making the selections, to choose only such passages as are in themselves complete, embodying an entire episode or a finished thought. The collection is, therefore, not a collection of fragments, but a group of literary gems, selected and arranged upon a definite plan and with a distinct purpose kept steadily in view. It is believed that a book of this character will be welcome to those teachers who have vainly sought for a relief from the commonplace; and that it will, in making the study of Latin more attractive, create and stimulate in the student a desire for a still wider course of reading.

HARRY THURSTON PECK.
ROBERT ARROWSMITH.

August, 1894.

TABLE OF CONTENTS.

CONTENTS.

LIST OF ILLUSTRATIONS.

11

I. POPULAR SONGS, CHARMS, ETC.

Comparatively few of the Roman popular songs of classical times have descended to us. Such as exist are in the main preserved by casual quotations in such authors as Plautus, Cato, and Varro, in inscriptions and in the scholiasts. The fact that Roman literature, as we have it, is so largely influenced by Greek models, gives it a certain artificiality and restraint that prevent it from assimilating the crude material found in the earlier popular compositions which the over-refined writers of the Augustan Age regarded as vulgar. Such specimens of the folk-songs, proverbs, spells, and language as are known to us can be found collected by Bährens in his *Fragmenta Poetarum Romanorum* (Leipzig, 1886). Reference may be made to Du Méril's *Poésies Populaires Latines* (Paris, 1843). Cf. the introductions on pp. 18, 154 and 181.

Nursery Song.

Lalla,[1] lalla, lalla, aut dormi aut lacta.

A Charm against Foot-ache.

Terra pestem teneto, salus[2] hic maneto.

Verse for a Race.

Habeat scabiem[3] quisquis ad me venerit novissimus.[4]

A Charm against Sprains.

Huat, hanat, huat,[5] ista pista sista.[6]

---

[1] bye-bye. [2] health. [3] the pest. [4] last of all. [5] hocus-pocus. [6] = *istam pestem sistam.*

Weather Wisdom.

Hiberno pulvere verno luto,[1]
Grandia farra,[2] camille,[3] metes.

To a Miser.

Quod habes ne habeas et illuc[4] quod non habes, habeas, malum :
Quando equidem nec tibi bene esse pote pati neque alteri.

Boating Song.

Heia,[5] viri, nostrum reboans echo sonet heia !
    Arbiter[6] effusi late maris ore sereno
    Placatum stravit pelagus posuitque procellam,[7]
    Edomitique vago sederunt pondere fluctus.
5   Heia, viri, nostrum reboans echo sonet heia !
    Annisu[8] parili tremat ictibus acta carina.
    Nunc dabit arridens pelago concordia caeli
    Ventorum motu praegnanti[9] currere velo.
    Heia, viri, nostrum reboans echo sonet heia !
10   Aequora prora secet delphinis aemula saltu
    Atque gemat largum, promat seseque lacertis,
    Pone trahens canum deducat et orbita[10] sulcum.
    Heia, viri, nostrum reboans echo sonet heia !
    Aequore flet corus :[11] vocitemus nos tamen heia !
15   Convulsum remis spumet mare : nos tamen heia !
    Vocibus adsiduis litus resonet : tamen heia !

The Nightingale; or, The Language of Birds and Beasts.

Dulcis amica veni, noctis solatia praestans ;
    Inter aves et enim nulla tui similis.

---

[1] mire. [2] crops. [3] my boy. [4] = illud. [5] yoho! [6] the lord. [7] blast. [8] pull. [9] swelling.
[10] track. [11] north wind.

Tu, philomela, potes vocum discrimina mille,
    Mille vales varios rite referre modos.
Nam quamvis aliae volucres modulamina temptent,   5
    Nulla potest modulos aequiperare tuos.
Insuper est avium spatiis garrire diurnis :
    Tu cantare simul nocte dieque potes.
Parrus [1] enim quamquam per noctem tinnipet omnem,
    Stridula vox nulli iure placere potest.   10
Dulce per ora sonat, dicunt quam nomine droscam, [2]
    Sed fugiente die illa quieta silet.
Et merulus [3] modulans tam pulchris zinzitat odis,
    Nocte ruente tamen cantica nulla canit.
Vere calente novo componit acredula [4] cantus   15
    Matutinali tempore rurirulans.
Tunc turdus [5] trucilat, sturnus [6] tunc pusitat ore ;
    Sed quod mane canunt, vespere non recolunt.
Caccabat hinc perdix [7] et graccitat improbus anser,
    Et castus turtur atque columba gemunt.   20
Pausitat arboreā clamans de fronde palumbes
    In fluviisque natans forte tetrinnit anas. [8]
Grus [9] gruit in grumis, cygni prope flumina drensant,
    Accipitres [10] pipant milvus [11] hiansque lupit.
Cucurrire solet gallus, gallina cacillat,   25
    Paupulat et pavo, trissat hirundo [12] vaga.
Dum clangunt aquilae, vultur pulpare probatur,
    Et crocitat corvus, fringulit et graculus. [13]
Glottorat immenso maerens ciconia [14] rostro,
    Pessimus et passer [15] sons titiare solet.   30
Psittacus [16] humanas depromit voce loquellas
    Atque suo domino *chaere* sonat uel ave.
Pica [17] loquax varias concinnat gutture voces,

---

[1] jay.   [2] throstle.   [3] blackbird.   [4] owl.   [5] thrush.   [6] starling.   [7] partridge.   [8] duck.   [9] crane.
[10] hawks.   [11] kite.   [12] swallow.   [13] jackdaw.   [14] stork.   [15] sparrow.   [16] parrot.   [17] magpie.

Scurrili strepitu omne quod audit ait.
35   Et cuculi cuculant et rauca cicada fritinnit.
    Bombilat ore legens munera mellis apis.
Bubilat horrendum ferali murmure bubo
    Humano generi tristia fata ferens.
Strix[1] nocturna sonans et uespertilio[2] stridunt,
40   Noctua[3] lucifugax cucubit in tenebris.
Ast ululant ululae lugubri uoce canentes
    Inque paludiferis butio[4] butit aquis.
Regulus[5] atque merops[6] et rubro pectore prognis[7]
    Consimili modulo zinzilulare sciunt.
45   Scribere me voces avium philomela coegit,
    Quae cantu cunctas exsuperat volucres.
Sed iam quadrupedum fari discrimina vocum
    Nemine cogente nunc ego sponte sequar.
Tigrides indomitae raccant rugiuntque leones,
50   Panther caurit amans, pardus[8] hiando felit.
Dum lynces urcando fremunt, ursus ferus uncat,
    Atque lupus ululat, frendit agrestis aper.
Et barrus[9] barrit, cervi clocitant et onagri;
    Ac taurus mugit, et celer hinnit equus.
55   Quirritat et verres[10] setosus et oncat asellus,
    Blatterat hinc aries et pia balat ovis.
Sordida sus subiens ruris per gramina grunnit,
    At miccire caprae, hirce petulce,[11] soles.
Rite canes latrant, fallax vulpecula gannit,
60   Glattitat et catulus ac lepores vagiunt.
Mus avidus mintrit, velox mustelaque[12] drindat,
    Et grillus[13] grillat, desticat inde sorex.[14]
Ecce venenosus serpendo sibilat anguis,
    Garrula limosis rana coaxat aquis.

---

[1] screech owl. [2] bat. [3] night owl. [4] bittern. [5] wren. [6] bee-eater. [7] swallow
elephant. [10] boar. [11] butting. [12] weasel. [13] cricket. [14] shrewmouse.

Has volucrum voces describens quadrupedumque   65
Cautus discrimen cuique suum dederam.

Serenade.   (Plautus, *Curculio*, i. 2, 60 foll.)

Pessuli,[1] heus, pessuli, vos saluto lubens,
Vos amo, vos volo, vos peto atque obsecro,
Gerite amanti mihi morem[2] amoenissumi :
Fite causā meā[3] ludii barbari,
Subsilite, obsecro, et mittite istanc[4] foras   5
Quae mihi misero amanti ebibit sanguinem.
Hoc vide! ut dormiunt pessuli pessumi!
Nec meā gratiā commovent se ocius.
Respicio nihili meam vos gratiam facere.[5]

Triumphal Song of the Roman Army.   (Vopiscus, *Aurel.* 6.)

ROMAN TRIUMPH.

Unus homo[6] mille mille mille decollavimus![7]
Mille mille mille mille bibat qui mille occidit;
Tantum vini nemo habet quantum fudit sanguinis!

---

[1] bolts, i.e. of the lady's door.   [2] *gerite morem,* oblige me.   [3] for my sake.   [4] her, i.e. my love.   [5] *nihili facere,* don't care for my good will.   [6] as a single man.   [7] beheaded.

II. TOMB INSCRIPTIONS.

Inscriptions upon tombs are among the earliest remains of Roman literature, and are of importance in the study of the development of the language. They are frequently written in the rough accentual verse (versus Saturninus) which the Romans employed before the introduction of the more formal Greek prosody. Numbers of them are collected in the *Corpus Inscriptionum Latinarum* (Berlin, 1862 ff.), especially in the first volume. See also Wordsworth's *Fragments and Specimens of Early Latin* (Oxford, 1874), and for the epitaphs in the Catacombs, De Rossi's *Inscriptiones Christianae* (Rome, 1857–61). *An Introduction to the Study of Latin Inscriptions*, by J. C. Egbert, Jr. ; in press (N. Y., 1895).

Epitaph of Lucius Cornelius Scipio.

Epitaph of a Roman Matron.   (*C. I. L.* i. 1007.)

Hospes,[1] quod dico paullum est; asta ac perlege.
Hic est sepulcrum hau pulcrum pulcrae feminae:
Nomen parentes nominârunt Claudiam;
Suum maritum corde dilexit suo.

---

[1] stranger.

18

Natos duos creavit:[1] horunc[2] alterum   5
In terra[3] linquit, alium sub terra locat.
Sermone lepido[4] tum autem incessu commodo,[5]
Domum servavit, lanam fecit: dixi. Abi.[6]

Epitaph on a Soldier's Tomb.   (*C. I. L.* iii. 293.)

Dum vixi bibi libenter: bibite vos qui vivitis.

Epitaph of a Roman Freedwoman.   (*C. I. L.* i. 1010.)

Primae[7] Pompeiae ossua[8] heic.
Fortuna spondet[9] multa multis, praestat nemini.
Vive in dies et horas,[10] nam proprium[11] est nihil.
Salvius et Eros dant.

Epitaph of a Roman Boy.

Lagge fili bene quiescas.
Mater tua rogat te
Ut me ad te recipias:
Vale!

Inscriptions from the Catacombs.

1. Vivas in Deo.
2. Cum sanctis.
3. Vivas inter sanctos.
4. Refrigera cum spiritibus sanctis.
5. Accersitus[12] ab angelis.   5
6. Dulcis anima.
7. Sophronia, Sophronia dulcis, vivas in Deo!

---

[1] she bore.   [2] = *horum.*   [3] on earth.   [4] winning.   [5] with gentle mien.   [6] farewell.   [7] eldest daughter.   [8] = *ossa.*   [9] promises.   [10] for the day and the hour.   [11] one's own.   [12] called away.

III. QUINTUS ENNIUS.

Quintus Ennius (239-169 B.C.), the father of Roman poetry, was born at Rudiae in Calabria, and became a Roman citizen in 184. His chief work was an epic poem, *Annales*, in eighteen books, treating the history of Rome from the coming of Aeneas to the poet's time. In it the Greek hexameter was first employed in Roman literature, and it remained the national epic of Rome until superseded by Vergil's *Aeneid*. Ennius also wrote trage-dies and comedies, on Greek models, of which about twenty are known through titles and fragments.

The importance of Ennius in the history of Roman litera-ture is very great. He definitely, and with authority, gave to Latin writers Greek models and Greek standards, and also led the way in polishing and refining the Latin language so as to adapt it to elegant literary composition.

Collections of the epic fragments are those of Vahlen (Leipzig, 1854), and Lucian Müller (St. Petersburg, 1885); the dramatic portions in Ribbeck, *Scae-nicae Romanorum Poesis Fragmenta* (Leipzig, 1871-73). For literary criticism, see Sellar, *Roman Poets of the Republic* (Oxford, 1881).

The Fortune Tellers.   (*Tr. Frag.* 272 foll. Ribbeck.)

Sed superstitiosi vates impudentesque arioli,[1]
Aut inertes[2] aut insani aut quibus egestas imperat,
Qui sibi semitam[3] non sapiunt alteri[4] monstrant viam;
Quibus divitias pollicentur, ab eis dracumam ipsi petunt:
5   De his divitiis sibi deducant[5] dracumam, reddant cetera.

The Poet's Picture of Himself.   (*Annales*, viii. 194, Bährens.)

Haece locutus vocat, quocum bene saepe libenter
Mensam sermonesque suos rerumque suarum
Materiem[6] partit, magnam cum lassus diei
Partem trivisset[7] de summis rebus regundis

---

[1] conjurers.   [2] dullards.   [3] path.   [4] dative case.   [5] take out.   [6] knowledge.   [7] gone through.

Consilio lato, indu[1] foro sanctoque senatu ;   5
Cui res audacter[2] magnas parvasque iocumque
Eloqueretur et ut certo malaque et bona dictu
Evomeret,[3] si qui vellet, tutoque[4] locaret ;
Quocum multa volutat grandia clamque palamque,
Prudenter qui dicta loquive tacereve posset   10
Ingenuos, cui nulla malum sententia suâsset
Ut faceret facinus levis[5] aut malus ; doctus, fidelis,
Suavis homo, facundus, suo contentus, beatus,
Scitus,[6] secunda loquens in tempore, commodus, verbûm
Paucûm, multa tenens antiqua sepulta,[7] vetustas   15
Maiorum veterum leges divomque hominumque,
Quae faciunt mores veteresque novosque notantem.

   Alliterative Line.   (*Annales*, i. 65, Bährens.)

O Tite tute Tati tibi tanta, tyranne, tulisti !

   Pyrrhus to the Romans.   (*Annales*, i. 143, Bährens.)

Nec mi aurum posco nec mi pretium dederitis :
Nec cauponantes bellum,[8] sed belligerantes,
Ferro non auro vitam cernamus[9] utrique !
Vosne velit an me regnare era[10] quidve ferat Fors,
Virtute experiamur ; et hoc simul acpite[11] dictum :   5
Quorum virtuti belli fortuna pepercit,
Eorundem libertati me parcere certumst.[12]
Dono, ducite, doque volentibus cum magnis dis.

   The Poet's Epitaph.

Nemo me decoret dacrumis[13] neque funera fletu[14]
Faxit.[15]   Cur ?   Volito vivus per ora virûm.

---

[1] = *in*.   [2] confidently.   [3] pour forth.   [4] safely.   [5] wanton.   [6] shrewd.   [7] hidden.   [8] not playing the huckster in war.   [9] let us contend.   [10] queen.   [11] = *accipite*.   [12] I am resolved.
[13] = *lacrimis*.   [14] lamentation.   [15] = *faciat*.

IV. TITUS MACCIUS PLAUTUS.

Titus Maccius Plautus was born at Sarsina in Umbria 254 B.C., and died in 184. He was of humble parentage. While serving as a theatrical assistant in Rome, he composed some comedies, which met with so favorable a reception that he devoted himself to comic writing. Varro found about one hundred and thirty pieces bearing the name of Plautus, of which only twenty-one were surely authentic. Of these, twenty are still extant, and present the oldest complete works of Roman literature. His plays, intended only for the momentary amusement of the public, are full of comic situations, lively dialogue, and striking pictures of Roman conditions; but the boundaries of probability and decency are often overstepped. These comedies held their place on the Roman stage until the end of the Republic. The greatest edition of the text of Plautus is that of Ritschl (Bonn, 1848-54), revised by Löwe, Goetz, and Schöll (1894), but there is no complete edition with English notes. The plays were translated into English prose by Thornton (London, 1767-74), and there is a poor version, by Riley, in the Bohn Classical Library (1880). The Plautine comedy *Menaechmi* is the original source of Shakespeare's *Comedy of Errors;* and the *Aulularia*, of Molière's *L'Avare.*

COMIC MASKS.

A Roman Drinking Bout.   (*Mostellaria*, i. 4.)

CALLIDAMATES, a gay young man. DELPHIUM, a girl. PHILOLACHES, friend of Callidamates. PHILEMATIUM, a girl.

CA. Advorsum venire mihi ad Philolachem
Volo temperi;[1] audi; hem, tibi imperatum est.
Nam illi[2] ubi fui, inde effugi foras:
Ita me ibi male convivi sermonisque taesum[3] est.
5 Nunc comissatum[4] ibo ad Philolachetem,
Ubi nos hilari ingenio et lepide accipiet.

---

[1] In good season.   [2] there.   [3] bored.   [4] to have a bout.

Ecquid tibi videor ma-ma-madere ?[1]

DE. Semper istoc modo moratus,[2] vita, debebas —

CA. Visne ego te ac tu me amplectare?

DE. Si tibi cordi est facere,[3] licet. CA. Lepida es.[4]   10

Duce me, amabo.[5] DE. Cave ne cadas. Asta.

CA. Oh! oh! Ocellus es meus ; tuus sum alumnus, mel meum.[6]

DE. Cave modo, ne prius in viâ[7] accumbas,

Quam illi, ubi lectus est stratus, coimus.

CA. Sine sine cadere me. DE. Sino. CA. Sed et hoc,[8] quod 15
    mihi in manu est.

DE. Si cades, non cades, quin cadam[9] tecum.

Iacentis tollet postea nos ambos aliquis.

Madet homo. CA. Tun' me ais ma-ma-madere ?

DE. Cedo[10] manum : nolo equidem te adfligi.

CA. Hem, tene. DE. Age, i i simul. CA. Quo ego eam, an scis ? 20

DE. Scio. CA. In mentem venit modo: nempe domum eo —

Comissatum. DE. Immo[11] — CA. Istuc quidem iam memini.

PHILOL. Num non vis me obviam his ire, anime mi ?

Illi ego ex omnibus optume volo.

Iam revortar. PHILEM. Diu 'iam' id mihi.   25

CA. Ecquis hic est ? PHILOL. Adest. CA. En, Philolaches,

Salve, amicissume mihi omnium hominum.

PHILOL. Di te ament.[12] Accuba, Callidamates.

Unde agis te ? CA. Unde homo ebrius.

PHILOL. Probe.[13] Quin,[14] amabo, accubas, Delphium mea?   30

CA. Da illi, quod bibat ; dormiam ego iam.

PHILOL. Num mirum aut novum quippiam facit ?

Quid ego hoc faciam postea, mea ? DE. Sic sine eumpse.[15]

PHILOL. Age tu, interim da ab[16] Delphio cito cantharum circum.

---

[1] d-d-drunk. [2] as this is your usual state. [3] if you want to. [4] you're a nice girl. [5] please.
[6] darling. [7] in the street. [8] (sine) et hoc (cadere), i.e. her arm. [9] Without my falling down too.
[10] give me ; old emphatic form of *da*. [11] not at all. [12] God bless you ! [13] good ! [14] = *cur
non*. [15] = *ipsum*, by himself. [16] beginning with.

SCENE FROM A COMEDY.

The Young Man and the Extravagant Girl.   (*Trinummus*, ii. 1.)

LUSITELES.

Multas res simitu[1] in meo corde vorso,
Multum in cogitando dolorem indipiscor.[2]
Egomet me coquo[3] et macero[4] et defetigo:[5]
Magister mihi exercitor[6] animus nunc est.
5   Set hoc non liquet[7] nec satis cogitatumst,
Utram potius harum mihi artem expetessam,[8]
Utram aetati agundae[9] arbitrer firmiorem:
Amorin me an rei[10] opsequi potius par sit,
Utra in parte plus sit voluptatis vitae
10   Ad aetatem agundam.
  De hac re mihi satis hau liquet: nisi hoc sic faciam, opinor,
  Ut utramque rem semul exputem, iudex sim reusque[11] ad eam rem.

---

[1] at the same time.   [2] get.   [3] put myself in a stew.   [4] fret.   [5] vex.   [6] taskmaster.   [7] clear.
[8] to desire.   [9] for living.   [10] wealth.   [11] culprit.

Sic faciam : sic placet. Omnium primum
Amoris artes eloquar, quemnam ad modum se expediant.[1]
Numquam amor quemquam nisi cupidum postulat[2] se hominem 15
    in plagas[3]
Conicere: eos petit, eos sectatur, subdole[4] ab re[5] consulit :
    Blandiloquentulust, harpago,[6] mendax, cuppes,
    Despoliator, latebricolarum[7] hominum corrumptor,
        Celatûm indagator.[8]
Nam qui habet quod amat quom extemplo saviis[9] perculsus est,   20
    Ilico res[10] foras labitur, liquitur.
    " Da mihi hoc, mel meum, si me amas, si audes."
    Ibi ille cuculus: " O ocelle mi, fiat :
    Et istuc et si amplius vis dari dabitur."
        Ibi illa pendentem ferit.[11]   25
        Jam amplius orat : non satis
        Id est mali, ni etiam ampliust,
    Quod bibit, quod comest, quod facit sumpti.
    Nox datur : ducitur familia tota,
Vestiplica, unctor, auri custos, flabelliferae, sandaligerulae,   30
Cantrices, cistellatrices,[12] nuntii, renuntii,
Raptores panis et peni. Fit ipse, dum illis comis est
    Amator, inops. Haec quom ago cum meo animo
    Et recolo, ubi qui eget, quam preti sit parvi, apage
        Amor, non places, te nil utor.   35

Two Married Men. (*Trinummus*, i. 2. 1-28.)

CALLICLES. MEGARONIDES.

CA. Larem coronâ nostrum decorari volo :
Uxor, venerare[13] ut nobis haec habitatio

---

[1] appear. [2] expects. [3] toils. [4] craftily. [5] to their disadvantage. [6] rapacious. [7] who lead double lives. [8] a regular Paul Pry. [9] kisses. [10] money. [11] she strikes him. [12] maids. [13] pray.

Bona fausta felix fortunataque evenat[1] —

(*aside*) Teque ut quam primum possim videam emortuam.

5 ME. Adgrediar hominem.   CA. Quoia[2] hic prope me vox sonat?

ME. Tui benevolentis,[3] si ita's ut ego te volo:

Sin aliter es, inimici atque irati tibi.

CA. O amice, salve.

ME. Et tu edepol salve, Callicles.

10 Valen? valuistin?   CA. Valeo et valui rectius.

ME. Quid tua agit uxor? ut valet?   CA. Plus quam ego volo.

ME. Bene herclest illam tibi valere et vivere.

CA. Credo hercle te gaudere, siquid mihi malist.

ME. Omnibus amicis quod mihist cupio esse item.

15 CA. Eho tu, tua uxor quid agit?   ME. Inmortalis est:

Vivit victuraquest.   CA. Bene hercle nuntias,

Deosque oro ut vitae tuae superstes suppetat.

ME. Dum quidem hercle tecum nupta sit, sane velim.

CA. Vin conmutemus? tuam ego ducam et tu meam?

20 Faxo[4] haud tantillum[5] dederis verborum[6] mihi.

ME. Nempe enim tu, credo, me inprudentem obrepseris.[7]

CA. Ne[8] tu hercle faxo hau nescias quam rem egeris.

ME. Habeas ut nanctu's: nota mala res optumast.

Nam ego nunc si ignotam capiam, quid agam nesciam.

25 CA. Edepol proinde ut diu vivitur, bene vivitur.

ME. Set hoc[9] animum advorte atque aufer ridicularia.[10]

---

[1] = *eveniat.*   [2] whose.   [3] good friend.   [4] = *faciam.*   [5] the least bit.   [6] *verba dare* = cheat, deceive.   [7] steal a march on me.   [8] verily.   [9] What I'm going to say.   [10] stop jesting.

V. CATO THE CENSOR.

Marcus Porcius Cato (234-149 B.C.) was the typical Roman of the Republican era. A shrewd, hard-headed, obstinate, energetic man, a sturdy soldier, a pungent and powerful orator, he resisted during his life all the tendencies that were transforming Rome into a centre of Hellenic culture, and ever after typified to the nation the "good old times" when men of the highest rank labored in the fields, ate at the same table with their slaves, and despised learning. Cato was the father of Roman prose as Ennius was the father of Roman verse, and was a very prolific writer, publishing more than one hundred and fifty of his orations now lost, letters, suggestions on oratory, practical instructions on agriculture, and a great work in seven books, *Origines*, the first historical volume ever written in Latin prose, and dealing with the ethnology and antiquities of Italy. The only work of Cato's now remaining entire is the treatise *De Agri Cultura*, in sixty-two chapters. It is a sort of farmer's note-book in which are jotted down in the most off-hand style all sorts of practical directions for the care of a farm, rules for housekeeping, forms for sales and leases, and recipes for domestic medicine. It has been edited by Keil (Leipzig, 1884-94).

How to treat Slaves. (*De Agri Cultura*, 5, 56, 57, 58, 59.)

Haec erunt vilici[1] officia. Disciplinā bonā utatur. Feriae serventur. Alieno manum abstineat, sua servat diligenter. Litibus[2] familiā supersedeat; siquis quid deliquerit, pro noxā bono modo vindicet. Familiae[3] male ne sit, ne algeat, ne esuriat: opere bene exerceat, facilius malo et alieno prohibebit. Vilicus si nolet 5 male facere, non faciat. Si passus erit, dominus impune ne sinat esse. Pro beneficio gratiam referat, ut aliis recte facere libeat. Vilicus ne sit ambulator, sobrius siet[4] semper, ad cenam nequo eat. Familiam exerceat, considerct quae dominus imperaverit fiant. Ne plus censeat sapere se quam dominum. Amicos domini eos 10 habeat sibi amicos. Cui iussus siet,[4] auscultet.[5] Rem divinam nisi Compitalibus in compito[6] aut in foco ne faciat.

Iniussu domini credat nemini: quod dominus crediderit, exigat.

---

[1] overseer.　[2] quarrels.　[3] the slaves.　[4] = sit.　[5] pay attention.　[6] the crossways.

Satui[1] semen, cibaria, far, vinum, oleum mutuum[2] dederit nemini.
15 Duas aut tres familias habeat, unde utenda roget et quibus det,
praeterea nemini. Rationem[3] cum domino crebro putet.[4] Opera-
rium, mercennarium, politorem diutius eundem ne habeat die.
Nequid emisse velit insciente domino, neu quid dominum celavisse
velit. Parasitum ne quem habeat. Haruspicem, augurem, hario-
20 lum, Chaldaeum ne quem consuluisse velit. Segetem ne defru-
det:[5] nam id infelix est. Opus rusticum omne uti sciat facere,
et id faciat saepe, dum ne lassus fiat: si fecerit, scibit[6] in mente
familiae quid sit, et illi animo aequiore facient, si hoc faciet,
minus libebit ambulare et valebit rectius et dormibit[7] libentius.
25 Primus cubitu[8] surgat, postremus cubitum eat. Prius villam
videat clausa uti siet, et uti suo quisque loco cubet et uti iumenta[9]
pabulum habeant.

Familiae cibaria. Qui opus facient per hiemem tritici[10] modios
IIII., per aestatem modios IIII S., vilico, vilicae, epistatae,[11] opi-
30 lioni[12] modios III., conpeditis per hiemem panis P.[13] IIII. ubi
vineam fodere[14] coeperint, panis P. V. usque adeo dum ficos esse
coeperint, deinde ad P. IIII. redito.

Vinum familiae. Ubi vindemia[15] facta erit, loram[16] bibant
menses tres: mense quarto heminas[17] in dies, id est in mense
35 congios[18] II S: mense quinto, sexto, septimo, octavo in dies sex-
tarios,[19] id est in mense congios quinque: nono, decimo, undecimo,
duodecimo in dies heminas ternas, id est in mense amphoram:[20]
hoc amplius Saturnalibus et Conpitalibus in singulos homines
congios: summa vini in homines singulos inter annum Q.[21] VIII.
40 Conpeditis, uti quidquid operis facient, pro portione addito: eos
non est nimium in annos singulos vini Q. X ebibere.

Pulmentarium[22] familiae. Oleae caducae quam plurimum condito. Postea oleas tempestivas, unde minimum olei fieri poterit,

---

[1] crop. [2] as a loan. [3] account. [4] make up. [5] = *defraudet*. [6] = *sciet*. [7] = *dormiet*. [8] from
sleep. [9] cattle. [10] wheat. [11] steward. [12] shepherd. [13] *pondo*, pounds. [14] dig. [15] vintage.
[16] lees. [17] half-pints. [18] gallons. [19] pints. [20] six gallons. [21] = *quadrantalia*. [22] relishes.

eas condito, parcito, uti quam diutissime durent. Ubi oleae comesae erunt, hallecem [1] et acetum [2] dato. Oleum dato in menses 45 uni cuique S. I. Salis uni cuique in anno modium satis est.

Vestimenta familiae. Tunicam P. III S., saga [3] alternis annis: quotiens cuique tunicam aut sagum dabis, prius veterem accipito, unde centones [4] fiant: sculponeas [5] bonas alternis annis dare oportet. 50

---

[1] brine. [2] vinegar. [3] cloaks. [4] patch-work. [5] wooden shoes.

VI. TITUS LUCRETIUS CARUS.

Titus Lucretius Carus was born in the year 96 B.C. and died in the year 55. According to the legend preserved by St. Jerome, his wife gave him a love potion which deprived him of his reason, — a story which forms the subject of a beautiful poem by Tennyson. His great work on the nature of the universe (*De Rerum Natura*) is in six books, but was never finished. In it he sets forth the Epicurean system of philosophy, which is one of pure materialism. He teaches (1) that nothing exists except matter and empty space ; (2) that the soul, being material as well as the body, dies when the body dies ; and (3) that the world is not governed by the gods, but by the fixed law of Nature, to which he gives the name Necessity. Macaulay has characterized this work as "the noblest poem ever written, in behalf of the meanest system of philosophy."

The best commentary on the whole of Lucretius is that of H. A. J. Munro (4th ed., Cambridge, 1886), which is accompanied by a fine translation into idiomatic English prose. Good accounts of the Lucretian philosophy are J. Masson's *Atomic Theory of Lucretius* (London, 1884), Wallace's *Epicureanism* (London, 1880), and that of Lange in his *History of Materialism* (London, 1881).

Death is not to be Dreaded.   (iii. 830-869.)

Nil igitur mors est ad nos neque pertinet hilum,[1]
Quandoquidem natura animi mortalis habetur.
Et velut ante acto nil tempore sensimus aegri,[2]
Ad confligendum venientibus undique Poenis,
5   Omnia cum belli trepido concussa tumultu
Horrida contremuere sub altis aetheris oris,
In dubioque fuere utrorum ad regna cadendum
Omnibus humanis esset terrāque marique,
Sic, ubi non erimus, cum corporis atque animai
10   Discidium[3] fuerit, quibus e[4] sumus uniter[5] apti,
Scilicet haud nobis quicquam, qui non erimus tum,
Accidere omnino poterit sensumque movere,
Non si terra mari miscebitur et mare caelo.

---

[1] a whit.   [2] suffering.   [3] *separation*.   [4] = *e quibus*.   [5] into one.

Et si iam nostro sentit de corpore postquam
Distractast animi natura animaeque potestas,   15
Nil tamen est ad nos, qui comptu[1] coniugioque
Corporis atque animae consistimus uniter apti.
Nec, si materiem nostram collegerit aetas
Post obitum rursumque redegerit ut sita nunc est,
Atque iterum nobis fuerint data lumina vitae,   20
Pertineat quicquam tamen ad nos id quoque factum,
Interrupta semel cum sit retinentia[2] nostri.
Et nunc nil ad nos de nobis attinet, ante
Qui fuimus, neque iam de illis nos adficit angor.
Nam cum respicias inmensi temporis omne   25
Praeteritum spatium, tum motus materiai
Multimodis[3] quam sint, facile hoc adcredere possis,
Semina saepe in eodem, ut nunc sunt, ordine posta[4]
Haec eadem, quibus e nunc nos sumus, ante fuisse.
Nec memori tamen id quimus reprehendere mente: 30
Inter enim iectast vitai pausa, vageque
Deerrârunt passim motus ab sensibus omnes.
Debet enim, misere si forte aegreque futurumst,
Ipse quoque esse in eo tum tempore, cui male possit
Accidere: id quoniam mors eximit, esseque probet   35
Illum cui possint incommoda conciliari,
Scire licet nobis nil esse in morte timendum,
Nec miserum fieri qui non est posse, neque hilum
Differre anne ullo fuerit iam tempore natus,
Mortalem vitam mors cum inmortalis ademit.   40

The Early Days of the World.   (v. 925–1102.)

At genus humanum multo fuit illud in arvis
Durius,[5] ut decuit, tellus quod dura creâsset,

---

[1] combination.   [2] recollection.   [3] variously.   [4] = *posita*   [5] more rugged.

Et maioribus et solidis magis ossibus intus
Fundatum,[1] validis aptum per viscera nervis,
5   Nec facile ex aestu nec frigore quod caperetur,
Nec novitate cibi nec labi corporis[2] ulla.
Multaque per caelum solis volventia lustra[3]
Volgivago[4] vitam tractabant more ferarum.
Nec robustus erat curvi moderator aratri
10   Quisquam, nec scibat ferro molirier[5] arva
Nec nova defodere in terram virgulta[6] neque altis
Arboribus veteres decidere falcibus ramos.
Quod sol atque imbres dederant, quod terra creârat
Sponte suâ, satis id placabat pectora donum.
15   Glandiferas[7] inter curabant corpora quercus
Plerumque: et quae nunc hiberno tempore cernis
Arbita puniceo[8] fieri matura colore,
Plurima tum tellus etiam maiora ferebat.
Multaque praeterea novitas[9] tum florida mundi
20   Pabula dura tulit, miseris mortalibus ampla.
At sedare sitim fluvii fontesque vocabant,
Ut nunc montibus e magnis decursus aquai
Clarigitat[10] late sitientia saecla[11] ferarum.
Denique nota vagi silvestria templa tenebant
25   Nympharum, quibus e scibant umoris fluenta[12]
Lubrica proluvie largâ lavere umida saxa,
Umida saxa, super viridi stillantia[13] musco,
Et partim plano scatere[14] atque erumpere campo.
    Necdum res igni scibant tractare neque uti
30   Pellibus et spoliis corpus vestire ferarum,
Sed nemora atque cavos montes silvasque colebant,
Et frutices inter condebant squalida membra,
Verbera ventorum vitare imbrisque coacti.

---

[1] sustained.   [2] bodily defect.   [3] years.   [4] roving.   [5] worked.   [6] saplings.   [7] acorn-bearing.
[8] purple.   [9] youth.   [10] calls.   [11] broods.   [12] streams.   [13] dripping.   [14] leap out.

Nec commune bonum poterant spectare, neque ullis
Moribus inter se scibant nec legibus uti.   35
Quod cuique obtulerat praedae fortuna, ferebat
Sponte suā sibi quisque valere et vivere doctus.
Conciliabat enim vel mutua quamque cupido
Vel pretium, glandes atque arbita vel pira lecta.
Et manuum mirā freti virtute pedumque   40
Consectabantur silvestria saecla ferarum,
Missilibus saxis et magno pondere clavae;
Multaque vincebant, vitabant pauca latebris,
Saetigerisque pares subus sic silvestria membra
Nuda dabant terrae, nocturno tempore capti,[1]   45
Circum se foliis ac frondibus involventes.
Nec plangore [2] diem magno solemque per agros
Quaerebant pavidi palantes noctis in umbris,
Sed taciti respectabant somnoque sepulti,
Dum roseā face sol inferret lumina caelo.   50
A parvis quod enim consuerant cernere semper
Alterno tenebras et lucem tempore gigni,
Non erat ut fieri posset mirarier[3] umquam
Nec diffidere, ne terras aeterna teneret
Nox in perpetuum detracto lumine solis.   55
Sed magis illud erat curae, quod saecla ferarum
Infestam miseris faciebant saepe quietem:
Eiectique domo fugiebant saxea tecta
Spumigeri [4] suis adventu validive leonis,
Atque intempestā cedebant nocte paventes   60
Hospitibus saevis instrata cubilia fronde.
    Nec nimio tum plus quam nunc mortalia saecla
Dulcia linquebant labentis lumina vitae.
Unus enim tum quisque magis deprensus eorum

---

[1] overtaken.   [2] lamentation.   [3] = mirari.   [4] foaming.

65 Pabula viva feris praebebat, dentibus haustus,
    Et nemora ac montes gemitu silvasque replebat,
    Viva videns vivo sepeliri viscera busto.
    At quos effugium servârat corpore adeso,[1]
    Posterius tremulas super ulcera taetra tenentes
70 Palmas horriferis accibant[2] vocibus Orcum,
    Donique eos vitâ privârant vermina saeva,
    Expertes opis, ignaros quid volnera vellent.[3]
    At non multa virûm sub signis milia ducta
    Una dies dabat exitio, nec turbida ponti
75 Aequora fligebant[4] naves ad saxa virosque.
    Hic temere incassum[5] frustra mare saepe coortum
    Saevibat leviterque minas[6] ponebat inanes,
    Nec poterat quemquam placidi pellacia[7] ponti
    Subdola pellicere[8] in fraudem ridentibus undis.
80 [Improba navigii ratio tum caeca iacebat]
    Tum penuria deinde cibi languentia leto
    Membra dabat, contra nunc rerum copia mersat.
    Illi inprudentes ipsi sibi saepe venenum
    Vergebant, nunc dant aliis sollertius[9] ipsum.
85   Inde casas[10] postquam ac pelles ignemque parârunt,
    Et mulier coniuncta viro concessit in unum
    Coniugium, prolemque ex se videre creatam,
    Tum genus humanum primum mollescere coepit.
    Ignis enim curavit ut alsia[11] corpora frigus
90 Non ita iam possent caeli sub tegmine ferre,
    Et Venus inminuit vires, puerique parentum
    Blanditiis facile ingenium fregere superbum.
    Tunc et amicitiem coeperunt iungere aventes.
    Finitimi inter se nec laedere nec violari,
95 Et pueros commendârunt muliebreque saeclum,

---

[1] mangled. [2] invoked. [3] required. [4] smote. [5] fruitlessly. [6] threatenings. [7] blandishment. [8] lure. [9] more craftily. [10] huts. [11] chilled.

Vocibus et gestu cum balbe[1] significarent
Imbecillorum esse aequum misererier omnes.
Nec tamen omnimodis[2] poterat concordia gigni,
Sed bona magnaque pars servabat foedera caste:
Aut genus humanum iam tum foret omne peremptum,   100
Nec potuisset adhuc perducere saecla propago.
   At varios linguae sonitus natura subegit
Mittere, et utilitas[3] expressit nomina rerum,
Non aliā longe ratione atque ipsa videtur
Protrahere ad gestum pueros infantia linguae,   105
Cum facit ut digito quae sint praesentia monstrent.
Sentit enim vim quisque suam quoad possit abuti.
Cornua nata prius vitulo quam frontibus extent,
Illis iratus petit atque infestus inurget.
At catuli[4] pantherarum scymnique[5] leonum   110
Unguibus ac pedibus iam tum morsuque repugnant,
Vix etiam cum sunt dentes unguesque creati.
Alituum[6] porro genus alis omne videmus
Fidere et a pinnis tremulum petere auxiliatum.[7]
Proinde putare aliquem tum nomina distribuisse   115
Rebus, et inde homines didicisse vocabula prima,
Desiperest; nam cur hic posset cuncta notare
Vocibus et varios sonitus emittere linguae,
Tempore eodem alii facere id non quisse[8] putentur?
Praeterea si non alii quoque vocibus usi   120
Inter se fuerant, unde insita notities est
Utilitatis et unde data est huic prima potestas,
Quid vellet, facere ut scirent animoque viderent?
Cogere item plures unus victosque domare
Non poterat, rerum ut perdiscere nomina vellent.   125
Nec ratione docere ullā suadereque surdis,[9]

---

[1] stammeringly. [2] altogether. [3] convenience. [4] cubs. [5] whelps. [6] birds. [7] = *auxilium*.
[8] = *potuisse*. [9] deaf.

Quid sit opus facto, facilest: neque enim paterentur,
Nec ratione ullā sibi ferrent amplius aures
Vocis inauditos sonitus obtundere frustra.

130 Postremo quid in hac mirabile tantoperest re,
Si genus humanum, cui vox et lingua vigeret,
Pro vario sensu variā res voce notaret?
Cum pecudes mutae, cum denique saecla ferarum
Dissimiles soleant voces variasque ciere,[1]

135 Cum metus aut dolor est et cum iam gaudia gliscunt.[2]
Quippe etenim licet id rebus cognoscere apertis.
Inritata canum cum primum inmane Molossûm
Mollia ricta[3] fremunt duros nudantia dentes,
Longe alio sonitu rabie restricta minantur,

140 Et cum iam latrant et vocibus omnia complent:
Et catulos blande cum linguā lambere temptant,
Aut ubi eos iactant pedibus morsuque petentes
Suspensis teneros minitantur dentibus haustus.
Longe alio pacto gannitu[4] vocis adulant,

145 Et cum deserti baubantur[5] in aedibus, aut cum
Plorantes fugiunt summisso corpore plagas.
Denique non hinnitus[6] item differre videtur,
Inter equas ubi equus florenti aetate iuvencus
Pinnigeri saevit calcaribus[7] ictus amoris,

150 Et fremitum patulis ubi naribus edit ad arma,
Et cum sic alias concussis artibus hinnit?
Postremo genus alituum variaeque volucres,
Accipitres atque ossifragae[8] mergique[9] marinis
Fluctibus in salso victum vitamque petentes,

155 Longe alias alio iaciunt in tempore voces,
Et quom de victu certant praedaeque repugnant:
Et partim mutant cum tempestatibus una

---

[1] utter. [2] are rife. [3] jaws. [4] yelp. [5] bark. [6] neighing. [7] goads. [8] ospreys. [9] cormorants.

Raucisonos[1] cantus, cornicum ut saecla vetusta
Corvorumque greges ubi aquam dicuntur et imbris
Poscere et interdum ventos aurasque vocare.   160
Ergo si varii sensus animalia cogunt,
Muta tamen cum sint, varias emittere voces,
Quanto mortales magis aequumst tum potuisse
Dissimiles aliā atque aliā res voce notare!
   Illud in his rebus tacitus ne forte requiras,   165
Fulmen detulit in terram mortalibus ignem
Primitus,[2] inde omnis flammarum diditur ardor :
Multa videmus enim caelestibus inlita[3] flammis
Fulgere, cum caeli donavit plaga vapore.
Et ramosa tamen cum ventis pulsa vacillans   170
Aestuat in ramos incumbens arboris arbor,
Exprimitur validis extritus viribus ignis
Et micat[4] interdum flammai fervidus ardor,
Mutua dum inter se rami stirpesque teruntur.
Quorum utrumque dedisse potest mortalibus ignem.   175
Inde cibum coquere ac flammae mollire vapore[5]
Sol docuit quoniam mitescere multa videbant
Verberibus[6] radiorum atque aestu victa per agros.

The Plague at Athens.   (vi. 1138-1251.)

   Haec ratio quondam morborum et mortifer aestus
Finibus in Cecropis[7] funestos[8] reddidit agros
Vastavitque vias, exhausit[9] civibus urbem.
Nam penitus veniens Aegypti finibus morbus,
Aëra permensus multum camposque natantes,[10]   5
Incubuit tandem populo Pandionis omni.
Inde catervatim[11] morbo mortique dabantur.

---

[1] hoarse. [2] adverb. [3] touched. [4] glitter. [5] heat. [6] the smiting. [7] = Athens. [8] desolate.
[9] drain. [10] i.e. the seas. [11] in herds.

Principio caput incensum fervore gerebant
Et duplices oculos suffusā luce rubentes.
10 Sudabant[1] etiam fauces intrinsecus[2] atrae
Sanguine, et ulceribus vocis via saepta[3] coibat,
Atque animi interpres manabat lingua cruore,
Debilitata malis, motu gravis, aspera tactu.
Inde ubi per fauces pectus complērat et ipsum
15 Morbida vis in cor maestum confluxerat aegris,
Omnia tum vero vitai claustra[4] lababant.[5]
Spiritus ore foras taetrum[6] volvebat odorem,
Rancida[7] quo perolent[8] proiecta[9] cadavera ritu.
Atque animi prorsum tum vires totius, omne
20 Languebat corpus, leti[10] iam limine in ipso.
Intolerabilibusque malis erat anxius angor
Adsidue comes et gemitu commixta querella.
Singultusque[11] frequens noctem per saepe diemque
Corripere[12] adsidue nervos et membra coactans[13]
25 Dissolvebat eos, defessos ante, fatigans.
Nec nimio cuiquam posses ardore tueri
Corporis in summo summam fervescere partem,
Sed potius tepidum manibus proponere tactum
Et simul ulceribus quasi inustis[14] omne rubere
30 Corpus, ut est per membra sacer dum diditur[15] ignis.
Intima pars hominum vero flagrabat ad ossa,
Flagrabat stomacho flamma ut fornacibus intus.
Nil adeo posses cuiquam leve tenveque membris
Vertere in utilitatem, at ventum et frigora semper.
35 In fluvios partim, gelidos ardentia morbo
Membra dabant, nudum iacientes corpus in undas.
Multi praecipites lymphis putealibus[16] alte

---

[1] drip. [2] within. [3] obstruct. [4] barriers. [5] gave way. [6] foul. [7] loathsome. [8] stink, reek. [9] expose. [10] death. [11] gasp, hiccough. [12] attack. [13] convulsing. [14] burnt in. [15] spreads. [16] wells.

Inciderunt, ipso venientes ore patente:
Insedabiliter sitis arida, corpora inurens,
Aequabat multum parvis umoribus imbrem.   40
Nec requies erat ulla mali: defessa iacebant
Corpora. Mussabat[1] tacito medicina timore,
Quippe patentia cum totiens ac nuntia mortis
Lumina versarent oculorum expertia somno.
Multaque praeterea mortis tum signa dabantur,   45
Perturbata animi mens in maerore metuque,
Triste supercilium, furiosus voltus[2] et acer,
Sollicitae porro plenaeque sonoribus aures,
Creber spiritus[3] aut ingens raroque coörtus,
Sudorisque madens per collum splendidus[4] umor,   50
Tenvia sputa[5] minuta,[6] croci contacta colore
Salsaque, per fauces raucas vix edita tussi.[7]
In manibus vero nervi trahere et tremere artus
A pedibusque minutatim[8] succedere frigus
Non dubitabat: item ad supremum denique tempus   55
Conpressae nares, nasi primoris acumen
Tenve, cavati oculi, cava tempora, frigida pellis
Duraque, inhorrescens rictum,[9] frons tenta tumebat.[10]
Nec nimio rigidi post artus morte iacebant.
Octavoque fere candenti lumine solis   60
Aut etiam nonā reddebant lampade[11] vitam.
Quorum siquis vix vitārat funera leti,
Ulceribus taetris et nigrā proluvie[12] alvi
Posterius tamen hunc tabes[13] letumque manebat,
Aut etiam multus capitis cum saepe dolore   65
Corruptus sanguis expletis naribus ibat:
Huc hominis totae vires corpusque fluebat.
Profluvium porro qui taetri sanguinis acre

---

[1] spoke low. [2] look. [3] breath. [4] bright. [5] spittle. [6] diminished. [7] cough. [8] by degrees.
[9] mouth. [10] swelled. [11] torch, i.e. day. [12] excrement. [13] wasting.

Exierat,[1] tamen in nervos huic morbus et artus
70 Ibat et in partes genitales corporis ipsas.
Et manibus sine nonnulli pedibusque manebant
In vitã tamen, et perdebant lumina partim:
Usque adeo mortis metus his incesserat acer.
Atque etiam quosdam cepere oblivia rerum
75 Cunctarum, neque se possent cognoscere ut ipsi.
Multaque humi cum inhumata iacerent corpora supra
Corporibus, tamen alituum genus atque ferarum
Aut procul apsiliebat,[2] ut acrem exiret odorem,
Aut, ubi gustãrat, languebat morte propinquã.
80 Nec tamen omnino temere illis solibus ulla
Comparebat avis, nec tristia saecla[3] ferarum
Exibant silvis: languebant pleraque morbo
Et moriebantur. Cum primis fida canum vis
Strata viis animam ponebat in omnibus aegre:
85 Extorquebat enim vitam vis morbida membris.
Nec ratio remedi communis certa dabatur:
Nam quod ali dederat vitales aëris auras
Volvere in ore licere et caeli templa tueri,
Hoc aliis erat exitio letumque parabat.
90 Illud in his rebus miserandum magnopere unum
Aerumnabile erat,[4] quod ubi se quisque videbat
Implicitum morbo, morti damnatus ut esset.
Deficiens animo maesto cum corde iacebat,
Funera respectans animam amittebat ibidem.
95 Quippe etenim nullo cessabant tempore apisci[5]
Ex aliis alios avidi contagia[6] morbi,
Lanigeras tamquam pecudes et bucera[7] saecla.
Idque vel in primis cumulabat funere funus.
Nam quicumque suos fugitabant visere ad aegros,

---

[1] escape. [2] spring away. [3] breed. [4] wretched. [5] seize upon. [6] infection. [7] horned.

Vitai nimium cupidos mortisque timentes   100
Poenibat paulo post turpi morte malāque,
Desertos, opis expertes, incuria [1] mactans.[2]
Qui fuerant autem praesto,[3] contagibus ibant
Atque labore, pudor quem tum cogebat obire
Blandaque lassorum vox mixtā voce querellae.   105
Optimus hoc leti genus ergo quisque subibat.
Incomitata rapi [4] cernebant funera vasta,
Inque aliis alium populum sepelire [5] suorum
Certantes: lacrimis lassi luctuque redibant:
Inde bonam partem in lectum maerore dabantur.   110
Nec poterat quisquam reperiri, quem neque morbus
Nec mors nec luctus temptaret tempore tali.

---

[1] want of care.   [2] destroying.   [3] at hand.   [4] hurried along.   [5] bury.

VII. GAIUS VALERIUS CATULLUS.

Gaius Valerius Catullus was born at Verona in 87 B.C. and died in the year 54. He went to Rome at an early age, and spent the rest of his life there in the intimacy of the leading men of his time. He stands at the head of Roman lyric poets. The most prominent event of the poet's life was his infatuation for Clodia, the wife of Q. Caecilius Metellus Celer, to whom, under the pseudonym of Lesbia, most of his amatory verses are addressed. An ardent admirer of Greek poetry, some of his songs, especially the Marriage Hymns, are more Greek than Roman in spirit. His language is usually the speech of every-day life, and abounds in diminutives, foreign words, and alliteration.

The standard edition of Catullus with English notes is that of Robinson Ellis (2d ed., Oxford, 1889). There is a good translation into English by Ellis (London, 1871), and by Sir Theodore Martin, in verse (London, 1875).

Lesbia's Sparrow.   (ii.)

Passer, deliciae meae puellae
Quicum[1] ludere, quem in sinu tenere,
Cui primum digitum[2] dare adpetenti
Et acres solet incitare morsus,
5 Cum desiderio meo nitenti
Carum nescio quid libet iocari
(Et solaciolum sui doloris,
Credo, ut tum gravis adquiescat ardor),
Tecum ludere sicut ipsa possem
10 Et tristes animi levare curas!

The Kisses.   (v.)

Vivamus, mea Lesbia, atque amemus,
Rumoresque[3] senum severiorum
Omnes unius aestimemus assis.

---

[1] qui, abl.   [2] primum digitum, finger-tip.   [3] censure.

42

Soles occidere et redire possunt:
Nobis, cum semel occidit brevis lux,   5
Nox est perpetua una dormienda.
Da mi basia mille, deinde centum,
Dein mille altera, dein secunda centum,
Deinde usque altera mille, deinde centum,
Dein, cum milia multa fecerimus,   10
Conturbabimus[1] illa, ne sciamus,
Aut ne quis malus invidere[2] possit,
Cum tantum[3] sciat esse basiorum.

To Cicero. (xlix.)

Disertissime Romuli nepotum,
Quot sunt quotque fuere, Marce Tulli,
Quotque post aliis erunt in annis,
Gratias tibi maximas Catullus
Agit, pessimus omnium poeta,   5
Tanto pessimus omnium poeta
Quanto tu optimus omnium patronus.[4]

A Roman Wedding Song. (lxi.)

Collis O Heliconii
Cultor,[5] Uraniae genus,
Qui rapis teneram ad virum
Virginem, O Hymenaee Hymen,
O Hymen Hymenaee.   5

Cinge tempora floribus
Suave olentis amaraci[6]
Flammeum[7] cape, laetus huc,

---

[1] lose the reckoning.   [2] cast an evil eye.   [3] just so many.   [4] orator.   [5] dweller.   [6] sweet marjoram.   [7] marriage veil.

THE ALDOBRANDINI MARRIAGE.

(*Vatican.*)

Huc veni niveo gerens
10   Luteum [1] pede soccum,[2]

Excitusque hilari [3] die
Nuptialia concinens
Voce carmina tinnulā [4]
Pelle humum pedibus, manu
15   Pineam quate taedam.

Namque Vinia Manlio,
Qualis Idalium colens
Venit ad Phrygium Venus
Iudicem,[5] bona cum bonā
20   Nubet alite [6] virgo.

Floridis velut enitens
Myrtus Asia ramulis,
Quos hamadryades deae [7]
Ludicrum sibi [8] roscido [9]
25   Nutriunt umore.

Vosque item simul, integrae
Virgines. quibus advenit

1 yellow.   2 slipper.   3 cheerful.   4 clear.   5 i.e. Paris.   6 omen.   7 tree-nymphs.   8 with
Ludicrum.   9 dewy.

Par dies, agite, in modum[1]
Dicite 'O Hymenaee Hymen
O Hymen Hymenaee.'   30

Te suis tremulus parens
Invocat, tibi virgines
Zonulā soluunt sinus,[2]
Te timens cupidā novus
Captat aure maritus.   35

Tu fero[3] inveni in manus
Floridam ipse puellulam
Dedis a gremio suae
Matris, O Hymenaee Hymen,
O Hymen Hymenaee.   40

Claustra pandite ianuae,
Virgo adest.   Viden ut faces
Splendidas quatiunt comas?

Flere desine.   Non tibi, Au-
runculeia, periculum est   45
Ne qua femina pulchrior
Clarum ab Oceano diem
Viderit venientem.

Talis in vario[4] solet
Divitis domini hortulo   50
Stare flos hyacinthinus.
Sed moraris, abit dies:
Prodeas, nova nupta.

---

[1] measure.   [2] bosom.   [3] ardent.   [4] many-hued.

Prodeas, nova nupta, si
55   Iam videtur, et audias
Nostra verba. Viden faces
Aureas quatiunt comas ?
Prodeas, nova nupta.

Tollite, O pueri, faces :
60   Flammeum video venire.
Ite, concinite in modum
O Hymen Hymenaee io,
O Hymen Hymenaee.

O bonae senibus viris
65   Cognitae bene feminae,
Conlocate puellulam.
O Hymen Hymenaee io,
O Hymen Hymenaee.

Iam licet venias, marite :
70   Uxor in thalamo tibi est
Ore floridulo nitens
Alba parthenice [1] velut
Luteumve papaver. [2]

At, marite (ita me iuvent
75   Caelites), nihilo minus [3]
Pulcher es, neque te Venus
Neglegit. Sed abit dies:
Perge, ne remorare.

Non diu remoratus es,
80   Iam venis. Bona te Venus

---

[1] *Parthenice*, kind of artemisia.   [2] poppy.   [3] sc. than she.

Iuverit, quoniam palam
Quod cupis capis et bonum
Non abscondis [1] amorem.

———

Claudite ostia, virgines:
Lusimus satis. At, boni   85
Coniuges, bene vivite et
Munere adsiduo valentem
Exercete iuventam.

Marriage Hymn. (lxii.)

YOUTHS.

Vesper [2] adest: iuvenes, consurgite; [3] Vesper Olympo
Exspectata diu vix tandem lumina tollit.
Surgere iam tempus, iam pingues linquere mensas;
Iam veniet virgo, iam dicetur hymenaeus.
Hymen o Hymenaee, Hymen ades o Hymenaee.   5

MAIDENS.

Cernitis, innuptae, iuvenes? consurgite contra:
Nimirum Oetaeos [4] ostendit Noctifer ignes.
Sic certe est: viden ut perniciter [5] exsiluere?
Non temere exsiluere: canent quod vincere par [6] est.
Hymen o Hymenaee, Hymen ades o Hymenaee.   10

YOUTHS.

Non facilis nobis, aequales, palma parata est;
Adspicite, innuptae secum ut meditata [7] requirunt.
Non frustra meditantur; habent memorabile quod sit.
Nec mirum, penitus quae totā mente laborant.
Nos alio [8] mentes, alio divisimus aures: 15

---

[1] hide. [2] the evening star. [3] sc. *mensis.* [4] Thessalian. [5] eagerly. [6] sc. *nobis,* = it is our task. [7] studied (verses). [8] *alio . . . alio,* correlatives.

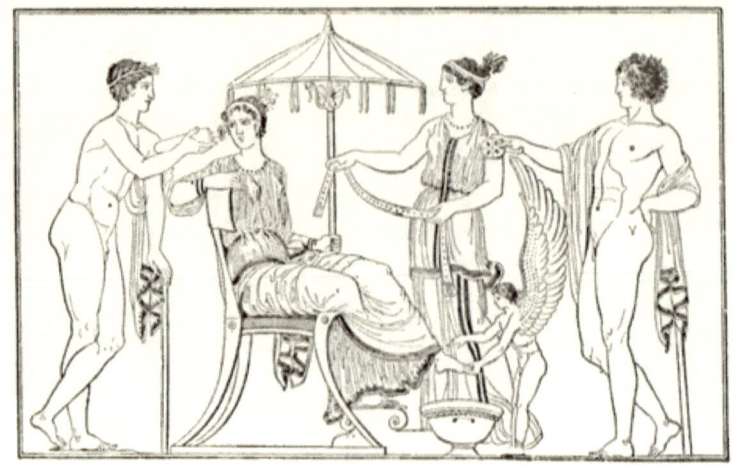

PREPARING THE BRIDE.
(*Von Falke.*)

Iure igitur vincemur; amat victoria curam.
Quare nunc animos saltem convertite vestros:
Dicere iam incipient, iam respondere decebit.
Hymen o Hymenaee, Hymen ades o Hymenaee.

MAIDENS.

20   Hespere, qui caelo fertur crudelior ignis?
Qui natam possis complexu avellere matris,
Complexu matris retinentem avellere natam
Et iuveni ardenti castam donare puellam?
Quid faciunt hostes captā crudelius urbe?
25   Hymen o Hymenaee, Hymen ades o Hymenaee.

YOUTHS.

Hespere, qui caelo lucet iucundior ignis?
Qui desponsa tuā firmes conubia flammā,
Quae pepigere[1] viri, pepigerunt ante parentes

---

[1] promised.

Nec iunxere prius quam se tuus extulit ardor,
Quid datur a divis felici optatius horā?   30
Hymen o Hymenaee, Hymen ades o Hymenaee.

MAIDENS.

Hesperus e nobis, aequales, abstulit unam.

YOUTHS.

Namque tuo adventu vigilat custodia semper.
Nocte latent fures, quos idem saepe revertens,
Hespere, mutato comprendis [1] nomine eosdem.   35
At libet innuptis ficto te carpere [2] questu.
Quid tum, si carpunt tacitā quem mente requirunt? [3]
Hymen o Hymenaee, Hymen ades o Hymenaee.

MAIDENS.

Ut flos in saeptis [4] secretus nascitur hortis,
Ignotus pecori, nullo convulsus aratro,   40
Quem mulcent aurae, firmat sol, educat imber,
Multi illum pueri, multae optavere puellae;
Idem cum tenui carptus defloruit ungui,
Nulli illum pueri, nullae optavere puellae:
Sic virgo, dum intacta manet, dum cara suis est,   45
Cum castum amisit polluto corpore florem,
Nec pueris iucunda manet. nec cara puellis.
Hymen o Hymenaee, Hymen ades o Hymenaee.

YOUTHS.

Ut vidua [5] in nudo vitis quae nascitur arvo
Nunquam se extollit, nunquam mitem [6] educat uvam,   50
Sed tenerum prono deflectens pondere corpus
Iam iam contingit summum radice flagellum,[7]

---

[1] surprise.   [2] rail at.   [3] long for.   [4] inclosed.   [5] = *caelebs*, solitary, not trained on a tree.
[6] ripe.   [7] shoot.

Hanc nulli agricolae, nulli accoluere iuvenci;
At si forte eadem est ulmo coniuncta marito,
55   Multi illam agricolae, multi accoluere iuvenci:
Sic virgo, dum intacta manet, dum inculta[1] senescit;
Cum par conubium maturo tempore adepta est,
Cara viro magis et minus est invisa parenti.

Et tu ne pugna cum tali coniuge, virgo,
60   Non aequum est pugnare, pater cui tradidit ipse,
Ipse pater cum matre quibus parere necesse est.
Virginitas non tota tua est, ex parte parentum est;
Tertia pars patri, pars est data tertia matri,
Tertia sola tua est. Noli pugnare duobus,
65   Qui genero suo iura simul cum dote dederunt.
Hymen o Hymenaee, Hymen ades o Hymenaee.

A Roman Swell. (lxxxiv.)

'Chommoda' dicebat, si quando 'commoda' vellet
  Dicere et 'insidias' Arrius 'hinsidias.'
Et tum mirifice sperabat se esse locutum,
  Cum, quantum poterat, dixerat 'hinsidias.'
5   Credo sic mater sic liber avunculus eius,
  Sic maternus avus dixerit atque avia.
Hoc misso in Syriam, requiêrant omnibus aures,
  Audibant eadem haec leniter[2] et leviter.
Nec sibi postilla[3] metuebant talia verba,
10   Cum subito adfertur nuntius horribilis:
Ionios fluctus, postquam illuc Arrius isset,
  Iam non 'Ionios' esse sed 'Hionios'!

---

[1] uncared-for.   [2] i.e., without aspiration.   [3] = *postea*.

VIII. GAIUS JULIUS CAESAR.

CAESAR.
(*Naples Museum.*)

Gaius Julius Caesar, whose family traced its origin back to the Trojan Aeneas, was born July 12th, 100 B.C. He received the usual education of a patrician youth, and at the same time a thorough training in affairs of war and statesmanship in the struggle between the patricians and plebeians, which was going on during his early years. He gradually identified himself with the democracy by his marriage in 83 B.C. with Cornelia, daughter of Cinna, who was at that time the leader of the Marian party. By this marriage he incurred the hostility of the dictator Sulla, who ordered him to divorce Cornelia, and Caesar remained away from Rome until Sulla's death in 78 B.C. On his return, after signal successes as an orator, he went to Rhodes to study rhetoric under Apollonius Molon. On his return to Rome in 74 B.C. he was elected successively pontiff, military tribune, and quaestor. His marriage with Pompeia, cousin of Pompey the Great, brought him into more intimate relations with the latter and with the people's party, and he was careful to strengthen his popularity by all possible means. In the conspiracy of Catiline he wisely kept himself in the background, but opposed the execution of the convicted conspirators. After serving as propraetor in Spain, Caesar was made consul (59 B.C.), and formed, with Pompey and Crassus, the First Triumvirate. His growing power excited the apprehension of the Senate, and, in order to keep him away from Rome, the Senate assigned to him as proconsul the provinces of Gaul and Illyricum for five years. It was in these campaigns (58-51 B.C.) that Caesar's generalship and successes gained for him the title of one of the greatest commanders of all time. Crassus died in battle (53 B.C.), when Caesar's successes in Gaul had excited the jealousy of Pompey. It had been agreed that Caesar's term of office in that province should be extended to ten years, but in 50 B.C. it was proposed in the Senate that Caesar should give up his command. In the following year, a resolution was passed, making him a public enemy unless he should disband his army. This was the beginning of civil war. Caesar advanced to Rome, receiving the submission of the cities through which he passed, and by his victory over Pompey at Pharsalus (Aug. 9, 48 B.C.) made himself master of Rome; and Pompey fled to Egypt, where he was murdered. Caesar's victory over his enemies, Cato and Scipio, at Thapsus

(April 6, 46 B.C.), ended the war, and he returned to Rome with supreme power. An insurrection in Spain, excited by the sons of Pompey, was suppressed in the battle of Munda (45 B.C.), and Caesar was free to carry out the work of reform. He corrected the calendar, and made wise plans for righting abuses in the laws and administration of the state, for adorning the city, and extending the Empire. These plans he was, however, unable to see completed, although many great changes were wrought in a very short time. His career was closed by his assassination on March 15th, 44 B.C.

DEATH OF CAESAR.
(*From the painting by Gérôme.*)

Caesar's literary reputation rests chiefly on his Commentaries on the Gallic War, the best known and most widely studied military note-book of all ages. In it he set down, in simple language, a straightforward narrative of his campaigns, remarkable for its concise descriptions of regions, peoples, and customs, and in its revelation of the character of the writer, — his personal courage, his mastery of tactics, his power of overcoming natural obstacles, his indomitable perseverance. The Commentaries are in eight books, the last of which is the work of Caesar's friend Hirtius. There remains also a treatise by Caesar on the Civil War in three books. Other works that pass under his name were not written by him.

An interesting life of Caesar is that of Froude (N. Y. 1884) and that of Anthony Trollope (London, 1870). A study of his campaigns is that of Col. T. A. Dodge (N. Y. 1892). His work as a statesman and organizer is analyzed by Fowler in his book *Julius Caesar and the Organization of the Roman Empire* (N. Y. 1892). There is a good edition of his *Gallic War* by Peskett in five volumes (Cambridge, 1878–82), and of the *Civil War* by the same scholar (1890). There is a special lexicon to Caesar by Mensel (Berlin, 1884 foll.). See an interesting article by Ropes, *The Likenesses of Julius Caesar*, in *Scribner's Monthly* for February, 1887.

The Customs and Religion of the Gauls. (*B. G.* vi. 13-20.)

HEAD OF GAUL.
(*Rome.*)

13. In omni Galliā eorum hominum, qui aliquo sunt numero atque honore, genera sunt duo. Nam plebes paene servorum habetur loco, quae nihil audet per se, nullo adhibetur consilio. Plerique, cum aut aere alieno aut 5 magnitudine tributorum aut iniuriā potentiorum premuntur, sese in servitutem dicant nobilibus; in hos eadem omnia sunt iura, quae dominis in servos. Sed de his duobus generibus alterum est Druidum, alterum equitum. Illi rebus divinis intersunt, sacrificia 10 publica ac privata procurant, religiones[1] interpretantur; ad eos magnus adulescentium numerus disciplinae causā concurrit. magnoque hi sunt apud eos honore. Nam fere de omnibus controversiis publicis privatisque constituunt, et si quod est admissum facinus, si caedes facta, si de hereditate, si de finibus 15 controversia est, idem decernunt, praemia poenasque constituunt; si qui aut privatus aut populus eorum decreto non stetit, sacrificiis interdicunt. Haec poena apud eos est gravissima Quibus ita est interdictum, hi numero impiorum ac sceleratorum

---

[1] religious rites.

20 habentur, his omnes decedunt, aditum sermonemque defugiunt,
ne quid ex contagione incommodi accipiant, neque his petentibus
ius redditur neque honos ullus communicatur. His autem omnibus Druidibus praeest unus, qui summam inter eos habet auctoritatem. Hoc mortuo aut, si qui ex reliquis excellit dignitate,
25 succedit, aut, si sunt plures pares, suffragio Druidum, nonnumquam etiam armis de principatu contendunt. Hi certo anni
tempore in finibus Carnutum, quae regio totius Galliae media
habetur, considunt in loco consecrato. Huc omnes undique, qui
controversias habent, conveniunt eorumque decretis iudiciisque
30 parent. Disciplina[1] in Britanniā reperta atque inde in Galliam
translata esse existimatur, et nunc, qui diligentius eam rem cognoscere volunt, plerumque illo discendi causā proficiscuntur.

14. Druides a bello abesse consuêrunt neque tributa una cum
reliquis pendunt, militiae vacationem omniumque rerum habent
35 immunitatem. Tantis excitati praemiis et suā sponte multi in
disciplinam conveniunt et a parentibus propinquisque mittuntur.
Magnum ibi numerum versuum ediscere[2] dicuntur. Itaque
annos nonnulli vicenos in disciplinā permanent. Neque fas esse
existimant ea litteris mandare, cum in reliquis fere rebus, publi-
40 cis privatisque rationibus, Graecis litteris utantur. Id mihi
duabus de causis instituisse videntur, quod neque in vulgum disciplinam efferri velint neque eos, qui discunt, litteris confisos
minus memoriae studere; quod fere plerisque accidit, ut praesidio
litterarum diligentiam in perdiscendo ac memoriam remittant.
45 Imprimis hoc volunt persuadere, non interire animas, sed ab aliis
post mortem transire ad alios, atque hoc maxime ad virtutem
excitari putant, metu mortis neglecto. Multa praeterea de sideri-
bus atque eorum motu, de mundi ac terrarum magnitudine, de
rerum naturā. de deorum immortalium vi ac potestate disputant
50 et iuventuti tradunt.

---

[1] system. [2] commit to memory.

16. Natio est omnium Gallorum admodum dedita religionibus, atque ob eam causam, qui sunt affecti gravioribus morbis quique in proeliis periculisque versantur, aut pro victimis homines immolant aut se immolaturos vovent administrisque ad ea sacrificia Druidibus utuntur, quod, pro vitā hominis nisi hominis vita 55 reddatur, non posse deorum immortalium numen placari arbitrantur, publiceque eiusdem generis habent instituta sacrificia. Alii immani magnitudine simulacra habent, quorum contexta viminibus membra vivis hominibus complent; quibus succensis circumventi flammā exanimantur homines.   Supplicia eorum, 60 qui in furto aut in latrocinio aut aliqua noxā sint comprehensi, gratiora dis immortalibus esse arbitrantur; sed cum eius generis copia defecit, etiam ad innocentium supplicia descendunt.

17. Deum maxime Mercurium colunt.   Huius sunt plurima simulacra, hunc omnium inventorum artium ferunt, hunc viarum 65 atque itinerum ducem, hunc ad quaestus pecuniae mercaturasque habere vim maximam arbitrantur.   Post hunc Apollinem et Martem et Iovem et Minervam.   De his eandem fere, quam reliquae gentes, habent opinionem : Apollinem morbos depellere, Minervam operum atque artificiorum initia tradere, Iovem im- 70 periuн caelestium tenere, Martem bella regere.   Huic, cum proelio dimicare constituerunt, ea, quae bello ceperint, plerumque devovent; cum superaverunt, animalia capta immolant reliquasque res in unum locum conferunt.   Multis in civitatibus harum rerum exstructos tumulos locis consecratis conspicari licet; neque 75 saepe accidit, ut neglectā quispiam religione aut capta apud se occultare aut posita tollere auderet, gravissimumque ei rei supplicium cum cruciatu constitutum est.

18. Galli se omnes ab Dite [1] patre prognatos praedicant idque ab Druidibus proditum dicunt.   Ob eam causam spatia omnis 80 temporis non numero dierum, sed noctium finiunt; dies natales

---

[1] Pluto.

et mensium et annorum initia sic observant, ut noctem dies sub-
sequatur.　In reliquis vitae institutis hoc fere ab reliquis differ-
unt, quod suos liberos, nisi cum adoleverunt, ut munus militiae
85　sustinere possint, palam ad se adire non patiuntur filiumque
puerili aetate in publico in conspectu patris assistere turpe ducunt.

19.　Viri, quantas pecunias ab uxoribus dotis [1] nomine accepe-
runt, tantas ex suis bonis aestimatione factā cum dotibus com-
municant.　Huius omnis pecuniae coniunctim ratio habetur

DYING GAUL.
(*Capitoline Museum. Rome.*)

90　fructusque [2] servantur; uter eorum vitā superavit, ad eum pars
utriusque cum fructibus superiorum temporum pervenit.　Viri in
uxores, sicuti in liberos, vitae necisque habent potestatem; et
cum paterfamiliae illustriore loco natus decessit, eius propinqui
conveniunt et, de morte si res in suspicionem venit, de uxoribus
95　in servilem modum quaestionem [3] habent et, si compertum est,
igni atque omnibus tormentis excruciatas interficiunt.　Funera
sunt pro cultu Gallorum magnifica et sumptuosa; omniaque, quae
vivis cordi fuisse [4] arbitrantur, in ignem inferunt, etiam animalia.

---

[1] dowry.　[2] interest.　[3] investigation, trial.　[4] dear to.

ac paulo supra hanc memoriam servi et clientes, quos ab iis dilectos
esse constabat, iustis funeribus confectis una cremabantur.   100

20. Quae civitates commodius suam rem publicam administrare
existimantur, habent legibus sanctum, si quis quid de re publicā
a finitimis rumore aut famā acceperit, uti ad magistratum deferat
neve cum quo alio communicet, quod saepe homines temerarios
atque imperitos falsis rumoribus terreri et ad facinus impelli et de 105
summis rebus consilium capere cognitum est.   Magistratus, quae
visa sunt, occultant, quaeque esse ex usu iudicaverunt, multi-
tudini produnt.   De re publicā nisi per concilium loqui non conceditur.

The Hercynian Forest.   (*B. G.* vi. 25-28.)

25. Huius Hercyniae silvae, quae supra demonstrata est,
latitudo novem dierum iter expedito[1] patet; non enim aliter
finiri potest, neque mensuras itinerum noverunt.   Oritur ab
Helvetiorum et Nemetum et Rauricorum finibus rectāque flumi-
nis Danuvii regione pertinet ad fines Dacorum et Anartium;   5
hinc se flectit sinistrorsus diversis ab flumine regionibus multa-
rumque gentium fines propter magnitudinem attingit: neque
quisquam est huius Germaniae, qui se aut adisse ad initium eius
silvae dicat, cum dierum iter LX processerit, aut, quo ex loco
oriatur, acceperit, multaque in ea genera ferarum nasci constat, 10
quae reliquis in locis visa non sint; ex quibus quae maxime
differant ab ceteris et memoriae prodenda videantur, haec sunt.

26. Est bos cervi figurā, cuius a mediā fronte inter aures unum
cornu exsistit excelsius magisque directum his, quae nobis nota
sunt, cornibus; ab eius summo sicut palmae ramique late diffun- 15
duntur.   Eadem est feminae marisque natura, eadem forma
magnitudoque cornuum.

27. Sunt item, quae appellantur alces.[2]   Harum est consimilis
capris figura et varietas pellium, sed magnitudine paulo ante-

---

[1] active.   [2] elks.

20 cedunt mutilaeque [1] sunt cornibus et crura sine nodis articulisque
habent, neque quietis causā procumbunt neque, si quo afflictae
casu conciderunt, erigere sese aut sublevare possunt. His sunt
arbores pro cubilibus [2]: ad eas se applicant atque ita paulum modo
reclinatae quietem capiunt. Quarum ex vestigiis cum est animad-
25 versum a venatoribus, quo se recipere consuerint, omnes eo loco
aut ab radicibus subruunt aut accidunt arbores tantum, ut summa
species earum stantium relinquatur. Huc cum se consuetudine
reclinaverunt, infirmas arbores pondere affligunt atque una ipsae
concidunt.

30 28. Tertium est genus eorum, qui uri [3] appellantur. Ii sunt
magnitudine paulo infra elephantos, specie et colore et figurā
tauri. Magna vis eorum est et magna velocitas, neque homini
neque ferae, quam conspexerunt, parcunt. Hos studiose foveis [4]
captos interficiunt. Hoc se labore durant adulescentes atque hoc
35 genere venationis exercent, et qui plurimos ex his interfecerunt,
relatis in publicum cornibus, quae sint testimonio, magnam ferunt
laudem. Sed assuescere ad homines et mansuefieri ne parvuli
quidem excepti possunt. Amplitudo cornuum et figura et species
multum a nostrorum boum cornibus differt. Haec studiose con-
40 quisita ab labris [5] argento circumcludunt atque in amplissimis
epulis pro poculis utuntur.

---

[1] without horns.   [2] resting place.   [3] bisons.   [4] pitfalls.   [5] rims.

IX. PUBLILIUS SYRUS.

Publilius Syrus, who was probably a native of Antioch, flourished in Rome toward the second half of the first century B.C. He was a very successful writer for the stage, contributing pieces (mimes, *mimi*) that were remarkable for their epigrammatic sayings, which were collected and published after his death under the title of *Sententiae* (moral maxims). About seven hundred of these have been preserved and have been separately edited by O. Friedrich (Berlin, 1880). They are in various kinds of verse (iambic and trochaic) and consist of a single line each.

Saws and Maxims.

1. Aut amat aut odit mulier, nihil est tertium.

2. Amici vitia si feras, facias tua.[1]

3. Absentem laedit, cum ebrio qui litigat.[2]

4. Amans quod suspicatur, vigilans somniat.

5. Bis gratum est, quo dato opus est ultro si offeras.

6. Beneficium accipere libertatem est vendere.

7. Bona nemini hora est, ut non alicui sit mala.

8. Bonus animus laesus gravius multo irascitur.

9. Beneficium dando accepit qui digno dedit.

10. Crudelem medicum intemperans[3] aeger[4] facit.

11. Cum inimico nemo in gratiam tuto redit.

12. Comes facundus in via pro vehiculo est.

13. Discipulus est prioris posterior dies.

14. Deliberandum est saepe, statuendum est semel.

15. Ducis in consilio posita est virtus militum.

---

[1] your own.   [2] wrangles.   [3] disobedient.   [4] patient.

16. Deliberando saepe perit occasio.

17. Deos ridere credo cum felix vocer.

18. Fortunam citius reperias quam retineas.

19. Formosa facies muta commendatio est.

20. Fraus est accipere quod non potest reddere.

21. Feminae naturam regere desperare[1] est otium.

22. Fortuna vitrea est: tum cum splendet frangitur.

23. Gravis animi poena est quem post[2] facti paenitet.

24. Heu quam est timendus qui mori tutum putat!

25. Heredis fletus sub personā[3] risus est.

26. Improbe Neptunum accusat qui iterum naufragium facit.

27. Mala secum agit aeger, medicum qui heredem facit.

28. Malum est consilium quod mutari non potest.

29. Non turpis est cicatrix quam virtus parit.

30. Non pote non sapere qui se stultum intellegit.

31. Pars benefici est, quod petitur si belle neges.

32. Stultum facit Fortuna quem vult perdere.

33. Thesaurum in sepulcro ponit, qui senem heredem facit.

34. Unus dies poenam adfert quam multi citant.

35. Voluptas e difficili data dulcissima est.

36. Ubi peccat aetas maior, male discit minor.

---

[1] give up all hope of. [2] afterward (adverb). [3] mask.

The Roman Forum, Restoration. (*Von Falke.*)

X. MARCUS TULLIUS CICERO.

CICERO.
Capitoline Museum, Rome.

Marcus Tullius Cicero was born Jan. 3, 106 B.C., at Arpinum. His family was of equestrian rank, although not belonging to the nobility. He was educated at the best schools of Rome, and, after assuming the toga virilis, devoted himself to the study of rhetoric, philosophy, and law, under the greatest teachers of the day. During the Social War he served for a short time (89 B.C.), retiring then to private pursuits. His reputation was established by his speech in defense of Sex. Roscius (81 B.C.), in whose trial he came into opposition to Sulla. In 79 B.C. he undertook a two years' journey to Greece and Asia, in which he embraced every opportunity of continuing his rhetorical and philosophical studies. Returning to Rome, he filled the office of quaestor at Lilybaeum (75 B.C.), and increased his renown by the exercise of his oratorical talent, notably by his speech at the trial of C. Verres, former praetor in Sicily. In 69 B.C. he became aedile, and as praetor (66 B.C.), in his oration *Pro Lege Manilia*, aided in securing the command in the Mithridatic War for Pompey, to whose interests he had attached himself closely. He attained the consulship in 63 B.C., and rendered important service in the detection and suppression of Catiline's conspiracy, but incurred great hostility because of the illegal execution of the conspirators. Forced into exile by the Triumvirate (58 B.C.), he was recalled the succeeding year, but found himself shut out from all public activity. During this period of enforced leisure he produced the treatises *De Oratore* and *De Republica* (55 and 54 B.C.). During the years 51 and 50 he served as proconsul in Cilicia, administering the office with great energy and unselfishness. Returning at the time of the rupture between Caesar and Pompey, he espoused the cause of the latter, but after the battle of Pharsalus withdrew his support, and obtained pardon from Caesar and permission to return to Rome. During the interval previous to the death of Caesar most of his great literary works were composed. After Caesar's

assassination, which he greeted with great joy, he once more entered public life
in the struggle against Antony ; but when, after the defeat of the latter, Octavi-
anus turned his arms against the Senate, and the Second Triumvirate was
formed, Cicero became one of the first victims of the proscriptions which
followed.   He was overtaken, while fleeing, near his estate at Formiae, and
murdered (Dec. 7, 43 B.C.).   Cicero's immense literary activity, his participa-
tion in the public affairs of an important period, and his supreme command of
oratory, produced a body of rhetorical Latin which for literary perfection and
historical value takes first rank among Latin prose writings.   The style of the
orations is of sustained dignity, showing absolute command of the niceties of
language, but permeated throughout by the unconquerable vanity and egotism
of the author, and frequently weakened by the very perfection of the rhetoric.
The titles of nearly eighty orations are given, of which only thirty-six have
come down to us complete, while about twenty are extant in more or less
fragmentary form.   Almost all of these orations represent some important
juncture in Roman affairs, and are invaluable aids to the historical study of the
period.

Cicero's philosophical writings embrace thirty titles, of which the best known
are the treatises *De Oratore*. *De Officiis*, and *De Natura Deorum*, each in three
books ; *De Senectute* (*Cato Maior*) ; *De Amicitia* (*Laelius*) ; *Tusculanae Dis-
putationes*, in five books ; *Academica*, in four books ; *De Finibus*, in five books ;
and *De Legibus*, in six books.

Of his correspondence we have upwards of eight hundred letters, extending
over a space of twenty-six years.   Of his other writings, poetical, historical, and
miscellaneous, only fragments and rare traces remain.

The standard text of the whole of Cicero is that of C. F. W. Müller (Leipzig,
1878 foll.).   A fine edition of his correspondence, with notes, is that by Tyrrell
and Purser (Dublin and London), still in course of publication.   The most
vivid and striking life of Cicero is that by Anthony Trollope (1880) ; the most
recent, that by Davidson (1894).   Reference may also be made to Church's
Roman Life in the Days of Cicero (1883); Boissier's *Cicéron et ses Amis* (last
ed. 1888); and Fausset's adaptation from Munk, under the English title of
The Student's Cicero (1890).

The Praises of Literature.   (*Pro Archia*. vi.)

Ego vero fateor me his studiis esse deditum : ceteros pudeat,
si qui ita se litteris abdiderunt, ut nihil possint ex iis neque ad
communem afferre fructum neque in aspectum lucemque proferre;
me autem quid pudeat, qui tot annos ita vivo, iudices, ut a

nullius unquam me tempore aut commodo[1] aut otium meum 5
abstraxerit aut voluptas avocarit aut denique somnus retardarit?

Quare quis tandem me reprehendat aut quis mihi iure suc-
censeat,[2] si quantum ceteris ad suas res obeundas, quantum ad
festos dies ludorum celebrandos, quantum ad alias voluptates et
ad ipsam requiem animi et corporis conceditur temporum, quan- 10
tum alii tribuunt tempestivis[3] conviviis, quantum denique
alveolo,[4] quantum pilae,[5] tantum mihi egomet ad haec studia
recolenda sumpsero? Atque hoc eo mihi concedendum est magis,
quod ex his studiis haec quoque crescit oratio et facultas, quae,
quantacumque in me est, nunquam amicorum periculis defuit. 15
Quae si cui levior videtur, illa quidem certe, quae summa sunt,
ex quo fonte hauriam sentio. Nam nisi multorum praeceptis
multisque litteris mihi ab adolescentiā suasissem, nihil esse in
vitā magno opere expetendum nisi laudem atque honestatem, in
eā autem persequendā omnes cruciatus corporis, omnia pericula 20
mortis atque exsilii parvi esse ducenda, nunquam me pro salute
vestrā in tot ac tantas dimicationes atque in hos profligatorum
hominum cotidianos impetus obiecissem. Sed pleni omnes
sunt libri, plenae sapientium voces, plena exemplorum vetustas:
quae iacerent in tenebris omnia, nisi litterarum lumen accederet. 25
Quam multas nobis imagines[6] non solum ad intuendum, verum
etiam ad imitandum fortissimorum virorum expressas scriptores
et Graeci et Latini reliquerunt; quas ego mihi semper in admini-
strandā re publicā proponens animum et mentem meam ipsā
cogitatione hominum excellentium conformabam. 30

Quaeret quispiam: 'Quid? illi ipsi summi viri, quorum virtutes
litteris proditae sunt, istāne doctrinā, quam tu effers laudibus,
eruditi fuerunt?' Difficile est hoc de omnibus confirmare, sed
tamen est certum, quod respondeam. Ego multos homines
excellenti animo ac virtute fuisse sine doctrinā, et naturae ipsius 35

---

[1] needs. [2] be offended. [3] early. [4] dice. [5] ball. [6] portraits.

habitu prope divino per se ipsos et moderatos et graves exstitisse fateor; etiam illud adiungo, saepius ad laudem atque virtutem naturam sine doctrinā quam sine naturā valuisse doctrinam. Atque[1] idem ego hoc contendo, cum ad naturam eximiam atque
40 illustrem accesserit ratio quaedam conformatioque doctrinae, tum illud nescio quid praeclarum ac singulare solere exsistere: ex hoc esse hunc numero, quem patres nostri viderunt, divinum hominem Africanum;[2] ex hoc C. Laelium, L. Furium, moderatissimos homines et continentissimos; ex hoc fortissimum virum
45 et illis temporibus doctissimum, M. Catonem illum senem: qui profecto, si nihil ad percipiendam colendamque virtutem litteris adiuvarentur, numquam se ad earum studium contulissent.

Quod si non hic tantus fructus ostenderetur et si ex his studiis delectatio sola peteretur, tamen, ut opinor, hanc animi adversi-
50 onem humanissimum ac liberalissimum iudicaretis. Nam ceterae neque temporum sunt neque aetatum omnium neque locorum: haec studia adulescentiam alunt, senectutem oblectant, secundas res ornant, adversis perfugium ac solacium praebent, delectant domi, non impediunt foris, pernoctant nobiscum, peregrinantur, rusti-
55 cantur.

A Good Old Age. (*De Senectute*, xviii.)

Sed in omni oratione mementote eam me senectutem laudare quae fundamentis adulescentiae constituta sit. Ex quo efficitur id quod ego magno quondam cum assensu omnium dixi, "miseram esse senectutem quae se oratione[3] defenderet." Non cani, non
5 rugae[4] repente auctoritatem arripere possunt; sed honeste acta superior aetas fructus capit auctoritatis extremos. Haec enim ipsa sunt honorabilia quae videntur levia atque communia, salutari, appeti, decedi, assurgi, deduci, reduci, consuli; quae et apud nos et in aliis civitatibus, ut quaeque optime morata, ita
10 diligentissime observantur. Lysandrum Lacedaemonium, cuius

---

1 also. 2 Scipio the younger. 3 argument. 4 wrinkles.

modo mentionem feci, dicere aiunt solitum Lacedaemonem esse
honestissimum domicilium senectutis: nusquam enim tantum
tribuitur aetati, nusquam est senectus honoratior. Quin etiam
memoriae proditum est, cum Athenis ludis quidam in theatrum
grandis natu venisset, in magno consessu locum nusquam ei datum 15
a suis civibus; cum autem ad Lacedaemonios accessisset, qui
legati[1] cum essent certo in loco consederant, consurrexisse
omnes et senem illum sessum recepisse. Quibus cum a cuncto
consessu plausus esset multiplex datus, dixisse ex iis quendam,
"Athenienses scire quae recta essent, sed facere nolle." Multa in 20
nostro collegio praeclara, sed hoc de quo agimus in primis, quod,
ut quisque aetate antecedit, ita sententiae principatum tenet;
neque solum honore antecedentibus[2] sed iis etiam qui cum
imperio[3] sunt maiores natu augures anteponuntur. Quae sunt
igitur voluptates corporis cum auctoritatis praemiis comparandae? 25
Quibus qui splendide usi sunt, ii mihi videntur fabulam[4] aetatis
peregisse, nec tamquam inexercitati histriones in extremo actu
corruisse.[5] At sunt morosi et anxii et iracundi et difficiles senes.
Si quaerimus, etiam avari: sed haec morum[6] vitia sunt, non
senectutis. Ac morositas tamen et ea vitia quae dixi habent 30
aliquid excusationis, non illius quidem iustae sed quae probari
posse videatur: contemni se putant, despici, illudi: praeterea in
fragili corpore odiosa omnis offensio est. Quae tamen omnia
dulciora fiunt et moribus bonis et artibus; idque cum in vitā tum
in scenā intelligi potest ex iis fratribus qui in *Adelphis* sunt. 35
Quanta in altero duritas, in altero comitas! Sic se res habet; ut
enim non omne vinum, sic non omnis aetas vetustate coacescit.[7]
Severitatem in senectute probo, sed eam sicut alia modicam; acer-
bitatem nullo modo. Avaritia vero senilis quid sibi velit non
intellego. Potest enim quidquam esse absurdius quam quo minus 40
viae restat eo plus viatici quaerere?

---

[1] ambassadors.　[2] superior.　[3] military authority.　[4] drama.　[5] to have broken down.
[6] character.　[7] grows sour.

A Letter from Exile. (*Ad Fam.* xiv. 4.)

TULLIUS TERENTIAE ET TULLIOLAE ET CICERONI SUIS S. P. D.[1]

Ego minus saepe do ad vos litteras, quam possum, propterea quod cum omnia mihi tempora sunt misera, tum vero, cum aut scribo ad vos, aut vestras lego, conficior lacrimis sic, ut ferre non possim. Quod utinam minus vitae cupidi fuissemus! certe nihil
5 aut non multum in vitā mali vidissemus. Quodsi nos ad aliquam alicuius commodi aliquando reciperandi spem fortuna reservavit, minus est erratum a nobis; sin haec mala fixa sunt, ego vero te quam primum, mea vita, cupio videre et in tuo complexu emori, quoniam neque dii, quos tu castissime coluisti, neque
10 homines quibus ego semper servivi, nobis gratiam rettulerunt. Nos Brundisii apud M. Laenium Flaccum dies XIII. fuimus, virum optimum, qui periculum fortunarum et capitis sui prae meā salute neglexit, neque legis improbissimae poenā deductus est, quo minus hospitii et amicitiae ius officiumque praestaret.
15 Huic utinam aliquando gratiam referre possimus! habebimus quidem semper. Brundisio profecti sumus prid. Kalendas Maias: per Macedoniam Cyzicum petebamus. O me perditum! O afflictum! quid nunc rogem te ut venias, mulierem aegram, et corpore et animo confectam? Non rogem? Sine te igitur sim? Opinor,
20 sic agam : si est spes nostri reditus, eam confirmes et rem adiuves; sin, ut ego metuo, transactum est,[2] quoquo modo potes ad me fac venias. Unum hoc scito : si te habebo, non mihi videbor plane perisse. Sed quid Tulliolā meā fiet? Iam id vos videte; mihi deest consilium. Sed certe, quoquo modo se res habebit, illius
25 misellae[3] et matrimonio et famae serviendum est. Quid? Cicero meus quid aget? Iste vero sit in sinu semper et complexu meo. Non queo plura iam scribere : impedit maeror. Tu quid egeris nescio : utrum aliquid teneas, an, quod metuo, plane sis spoliata.

---

[1] *salutem plurimum dicit.* [2] all is up. [3] poor girl.

Pisonem, ut scribis, spero fore semper nostrum. De familiā
liberatā, nihil est, quod te moveat. Primum, tuis ita promissum 30
est, te facturam esse, ut quisque esset meritus. Est autem in
officio adhuc Orpheus; praeterea magno opere nemo. Ceterorum
servorum ea causa est, ut, si res a nobis abisset, liberti nostri
essent, si obtinere potuissent; sin ad nos pertineret, servirent,
praeterquam oppido[1] pauci. Sed haec minora sunt. Tu quod 35
me hortaris, ut animo sim magno et spem habeam reciperandae
salutis, id velim sit eius modi, ut recte sperare possimus. Nunc,
miser quando tuas iam litteras accipiam? quis ad me perferet?
quas ego exspectâssem Brundisii, si esset licitum per nautas, qui
tempestatem praetermittere noluerunt. Quod reliquum est, sus- 40
tenta te, mea Terentia, ut potes, honestissime. Viximus; flo-
ruimus; non vitium nostrum sed virtus nostra nos afflixit.
Peccatum est nullum, nisi quod non una animam cum orna-
mentis amisimus. Sed si hoc fuit liberis nostris gratius, nos
vivere, cetera, quamquam ferenda non sunt, feramus. Atque 45
ego, qui te confirmo, ipse me non possum. Clodium Philhe-
taerum, quod valetudine oculorum impediebatur, hominem fide-
lem, remisi. Salustius officio vincit omnes. Pescennius est
perbenevolus nobis; quem semper spero tui fore observantem.
Sicca dixerat se mecum fore, sed Brundisio discessit. Cura, 50
quoad potes, ut valeas, et sic existimes, me vehementius tuā
miseriā quam meā commoveri. Mea Terentia, fidissima atque
optima uxor, et mea carissima filiola, et spes reliqua nostra,
Cicero, valete.

Pridie Kalendas Maias, Brundisio. 55

---

[1] exceedingly.

XI. PUBLIUS VERGILIUS MARO.

Publius Vergilius Maro was born 70 B.C. at Andes near Mantua, and died at Brundusium, 19 B.C. Little is known with certainty of his personal history, and no information is afforded by his own writings. His education was begun at Cremona and continued at Milan and Naples, where he devoted himself espe-

VERGIL.   HORACE.   VARIUS AND MAECENAS.
(*From the Painting by Jalabert.*)

cially to the study of Greek poetry and philosophy. To this period is assigned the composition of some of his minor poems. He then returned to his farm, and busied himself in study and writing. His first important work was a series of ten pastoral poems, to which he gave the name of *Eclogues*, and which at once established his fame and popularity. This work is said to have been undertaken at the suggestion of Asinius Pollio, then military governor of the region. After the defeat of the republican army at Philippi, a division of lands was made to reward the soldiery, and Vergil's farm was confiscated among the rest. On the advice of Pollio he went to Rome, and secured from Augustus the restoration of his estate, which, however, seems not to have been effected, as he is described as chased by the holder of the lands and forced to swim the Mincius to save his life. Shortly after this he removed to Rome, where his reputation brought him great respect among the highest circles. At the age of thirty-three he took up his residence at Nola, near Naples, where he spent a great portion of his time. At the request of Maecenas, it is said, he now undertook the composition of the *Georgics*, four books on husbandry, with the view of bringing back a love of rural pursuits. These poems are considered the most elaborate and highly polished of his works. In both *Eclogues* and *Georgics* the influence of Vergil's study of the Greek poets is evident, the *Eclogues* being an adaptation of Theocritus, and the *Georgics* an imitation of Hesiod. After the establishment of the Empire, Vergil, at the request of Augustus, began his greatest work, the *Aeneid*. This great epic was commenced in the year in which he completed the *Georgics*, and occupied him until his death. The poem uses the material and follows the arrangement of the *Iliad* and *Odyssey*, but unlike Homer's epic the *Aeneid* shows the highest perfection of literary art. It is the most elaborated production of a highly artificial age, and is dominated by one purpose, — the exaltation of Rome and the Julian gens. On the completion of the poem in its present form, Vergil went to Greece with the intention of spending some years in a final revision of his great work; but soon after his arrival there he was prevailed upon by Augustus to accompany him to Italy, where he died soon after reaching Brundusium. He is said to have ordered the *Aeneid* to be burned, being unwilling to have it published in its unfinished condition, but it was preserved by the request of Augustus and submitted to the judgment of his friends Tucca and Varius, who made it public. Vergil was buried, by his own desire, at Posilippo near Naples, where what purports to be his tomb is still shown.

In person he was tall, dark, and slender, of delicate health, and of a very shy and retiring disposition. It is related that he often entered shops or turned aside in the streets to avoid public recognition. There is no authentic portrait of Vergil known to be in existence. In the Middle Ages, popular tradition made Vergil a famous magician, and many marvelous stories were told of him, regarding which reference may be made to Tunison's *Master Vergil* (Cincinnati, 1889).

A standard text of the whole of Vergil is that of Ribbeck (Leipzig, 1867). There is an excellent commentary in English by Conington, revised by Nettleship, with admirable introductions (4th ed. London, 1881-83). Professor Conington also published a good prose translation (3d ed. London, 1882), and there is one by Lonsdale and Lee (12th ed. London, 1890). Good verse translations of the *Aeneid* are those of Conington (6th ed. London, 1881); W. Morris (London, 1876) ; and Thornhill (Dublin, 1886). There is an excellent literary study of Vergil in Sellar's *Roman Poets of the Augustan Age* (2d ed. Oxford, 1883) ; and of the *Aeneid* in Nettleship's *Lectures and Essays* (Oxford, 1885). Harper and Miller's edition of the *Aeneid* (Books I.-VI.) and *Bucolics* (New York, 1892) has excellent literary and historical notes.

Mine Hostess.   (*Copa.*)

Copa Surisca, caput Graiā redimita mitellā,[1]
    Crispum[2] sub crotalo[3] docta movere latus,
Ebria fumosā saltat lasciva tabernā,
    Ad cubitum[4] raucos excutiens calamos.
5   Quid iuvat aestivo defessum pulvere abesse?
    Quam potius bibulo[5] decubuisse toro!

FRESCO.   (*Pompeii.*)

Sunt cupae[6] et calices, cyathi, rosa, tibia, chordae,[7]
    Et trichila[8] umbriferis frigida arundinibus;
En et, Maenalio quae garrit dulce sub antro,
10   Rustica pastoris fistula[9] in ore sonat.
Est et vappa,[10] cado[11] nuper defusa picato,[12]
    Et strepitans rauco murmure rivus aquae.
Sunt etiam croceo violae de flore corollae,
    Sertaque purpureā lutea[13] mixta rosā,

---

[1] hood. [2] lithe. [3] castanet. [4] elbow. [5] jovial. [6] casks. [7] stringed instrument. [8] summer house. [9] shepherd's pipe. [10] cheap wine. [11] jar. [12] pitched. [13] golden.

Et quae virgineo libata Acheloïs ab amne 15
  Lilia vimineis attulit in calathis.
Sunt et caseoli,[1] quos iuncea fiscina · siccat;
  Sunt autumnali cerea pruna[3] die,
Castaneaeque[4] nuces et suave rubentia mala;
  Est hic munda Ceres, est Amor, est Bromius.[5] 20
Sunt et mora[6] cruenta, et lentis uva racemis,[7]
  Et pendet iunco caeruleus cucumis.[8]
Est tuguri[9] custos, armatus falce saligna,
  Sed non et vasto est inguine terribilis.
Huc, Alabita, veni: lassus iam sudat asellus; 25
  Parce illi: Vestae delicium est asinus.
Nunc cantu crebro rumpunt arbusta cicadae;
  Nunc viridis gelida saepe[10] lacerta latet.
Si sapis, aestivo recubans te prolue[11] vitro,
  Seu vis crystallo ferre novos calices. 30
Eia age pampinea[12] fessus requiesce sub umbra,
  Et gravidum roseo necte caput strophio,[13]
Formosus tenerae decerpens ora puellae.
  Ah pereat, cui sunt prisca supercilia!
Quid cineri ingrato servas bene olentia serta? 35
  Anne coronato vis lapide ossa tegi?
Pone merum et talos![14] Pereat, qui crastina[15] curat!
  Mors aurem vellens "Vivite" ait "venio."

Laocoön. (*Aen.* ii. 201-227.)

Laocoön, ductus Neptuno sorte sacerdos,
Sollemnes taurum ingentem mactabat ad aras.
Ecce autem gemini a Tenedo tranquilla per alta —

[1] cheeses. [3] rush-basket. [3] plums. [4] chestnuts. [5] Bacchus. [6] mulberries. [7] clusters. [8] cucumber. [9] cottage. [10] hedge. [11] moisten. [12] of the vine. [13] garland. [14] dice. [15] the morrow.

Horresco referens immensis orbibus angues

5   Incumbunt pelago, pariterque ad litora tendunt:

Pectora quorum inter fluctus arrecta iubaeque [1]

Sanguineae superant undas, pars cetera pontum

Pone [2] legit sinuatque immensa volumine terga.

Fit sonitus spumante salo. Iamque arva tenebant,

10   Ardentesque oculos suffecti [3] sanguine et igni,

Sibila [4] lambebant linguis vibrantibus ora.

Diffugimus visu exsangues. Illi agmine certo

Laocoönta petunt, et primum parva duorum

Corpora natorum serpens amplexus uterque

15   Implicat, et miseros morsu depascitur artus;

Post ipsum auxilio subeuntem ac tela ferentem

Corripiunt, spirisque ligant ingentibus, et iam

Bis medium amplexi, bis collo squamea [5] circum

Terga dati, superant capite et cervicibus altis.

20   Ille simul manibus tendit divellere nodos,

Perfusus sanie [6] vittas [7] atroque veneno,

Clamores simul horrendos ad sidera tollit:

Quales mugitus, [8] fugit cum saucius aram

Taurus et incertam excussit cervice securim. [9]

25   At gemini lapsu delubra ad summa dracones

Effugiunt, saevaeque petunt Tritonidis arcem,

Sub pedibusque deae clipeique sub orbe teguntur.

Tum vero tremefacta novus per pectora cunctis

Insinuat pavor; et scelus expendisse merentem

30   Laocoönta ferunt, sacrum qui cuspide robur

Laeserit et tergo sceleratam intorserit hastam.

Ducendum ad sedes simulacrum, orandaque divae

Numina conclamant.

---

[1] crest.   [2] behind.   [3] suffused.   [4] hissing.   [5] scaly.   [6] gore.   [7] fillets.   [8] roar.   [9] axe

DEATH OF LAOCOÖN. (Vatican Museum.)

Illi agmine certo
Laocoonta petunt II: 212.

The Harpies. (*Aen.* iii. 219-244.)

Huc ubi delati[1] portus intravimus, ecce
Laeta boum passim campis armenta[2] videmus
Caprigenumque pecus, nullo custode, per herbas.
Irruimus ferro, et divos ipsumque vocamus
In partem praedamque[3] Iovem: tum litore curvo   5
Exstruimusque toros, dapibusque[4] epulamur[5] opimis.[6]
At subitae horrifico lapsu de montibus adsunt
Harpyiae et magnis quatiunt[7] clangoribus[8] alas,

HARPY.
(*From an Etruscan vase*)

Diripiuntque dapes, contactuque omnia foedant
Immundo; tum vox taetrum dira inter odorem.   10
Rursum in secessu longo sub rupe cavatā,
Arboribus clausi circum atque horrentibus umbris,
Instruimus mensas, arisque reponimus ignem;
Rursum ex diverso caeli caecisque latebris
Turba sonans praedam pedibus circumvolat uncis,[9]   15
Polluit[10] ore dapes. Sociis tunc arma capessant,[11]
Edico, et dirā bellum cum gente gerendum.
Haud secus ac iussi faciunt, tectosque per herbam

---

[1] carried. [2] herds. [3] hendiadys. [4] banquet. [5] feast. [6] rich. [7] flap. [8] whirring. [9] hooked.
[10] pollute. [11] seize.

Disponunt enses et scuta latentia condunt.

20 Ergo ubi delapsae sonitum per curva dedere
Litora, dat signum speculâ[1] Misenus ab altâ
Aere cavo. Invadunt socii et nova[2] proelia tentant
Obscenas pelagi ferro foedare[3] volucres.
Sed neque vim plumis ullam nec vulnera tergo
25 Accipiunt, celerique fugâ sub sidera lapsae
Semiesam[4] praedam et vestigia foeda relinquunt.

The Cyclops. (Aen. iii. 591–683.)

Respicimus. Dira illuvies[5] immissaque[6] barba,
Consertum[7] tegumen[8] spinis[9]; at cetera Graius
Et quondam patriis ad Troiam missus in armis.
Isque ubi Dardanios habitus et Troia vidit
5 Arma procul, paulum adspectu conterritus haesit,
Continuitque gradum; mox sese ad littora praeceps
Cum fletu precibusque tulit: "Per sidera testor,
Per superos atque hoc coeli spirabile lumen,[10]
Tollite me, Teucri! quascumque abducite terras:
10 Hoc sat erit. Scio me Danaïs e classibus unum,
Et bello Iliacos fateor petiisse Penates.
Pro quo, si sceleris tanta est iniuria nostri,
Spargite[11] me in fluctus vastoque immergite ponto:
Si pereo, hominum manibus periisse iuvabit."
15 Dixerat, et genua amplexus genibusque volutans[12]
Haerebat. Qui sit, fari, quo sanguine cretus,
Hortamur; quae deinde agitet fortuna fateri.
Ipse pater dextram Anchises, haud multa moratus,
Dat iuveni, atque animum praesenti pignore firmat.
20 Ille haec, depositâ tandem formidine, fatur:

---

[1] look-out. [2] strange. [3] cut to pieces. [4] half-eaten. [5] filth. [6] straggling. [7] pinned. [8] garments. [9] thorn. [10] air we breathe. [11] tear in pieces and scatter. [12] groveling.

"Sum patriā ex Ithacā, comes infelicis Ulixi,
Nomen Achemenides, Troiam, genitore Adamasto
Paupere — mansissetque utinam fortuna! —, profectus.
Hic me, dum trepidi crudelia limina linquunt,
Immemores socii vasto Cyclopis in antro   25
Deseruere.   Domus sanie dapibusque cruentis,
Intus opaca, ingens.   Ipse arduus, altaque pulsat
Sidera — di, talem terris avertite pestem! —,
Nec visu facilis nec dictu affabilis ulli.
Visceribus miserorum et sanguine vescitur[1] atro.   30

BLINDING OF POLYPHEMUS.
(*Etruscan painting.*)

Vidi egomet, duo de numero cum corpora nostro
Prensa manu magnā medio resupinus in antro
Frangeret ad saxum, sanieque exspersa[2] natarent
Limina; vidi, atro cum membra fluentia tabo[3]
Manderet,[4] et tepidi tremerent sub dentibus artus.   35
Haud impune quidem; nec talia passus Ulixes,
Oblitusve sui est Ithacus discrimine tanto.
Nam simul, expletus dapibus vinoque sepultus,
Cervicem inflexam posuit, iacuitque per antrum
Immensus, saniem eructans[5] et frusta[6] cruento   40
Per somnum commixta mero; nos, magna precati
Numina sortitique vices,[7] una undique circum

[1] feeds. [2] bespattered. [3] gore. [4] crunched. [5] belching forth. [6] morsels of flesh. [7] choosing places by lot.

Fundimur, et telo lumen terebramus [1] acuto,
Ingens, quod torvā [2] solum sub fronte latebat,
45   Argolici clipei aut Phoebeae lampadis instar, [3]
Et tandem laeti sociorum ulciscimur umbras.
Sed fugite, o miseri, fugite, atque ab litore funem
Rumpite!
Nam, qualis quantusque cavo Polyphemus in antro
50   Lanigeras claudit pecudes atque ubera pressat,
Centum alii curva haec habitant ad litora vulgo
Infandi Cyclopes et altis montibus errant.
Tertia iam Lunae se cornua lumine complent,
Cum vitam in silvis inter deserta ferarum
55   Lustra [4] domosque traho, vastosque ab rupe Cyclopas
Prospicio, sonitumque pedum vocemque tremisco.
Victum infelicem, [5] bacas [6] lapidosaque corna,
Dant rami, et vulsis pascunt radicibus herbae.
Omnia collustrans, hanc primum ad litora classem
60   Conspexi venientem; huic me, quaecumque fuisset,
Addixi: [7] satis est gentem effugisse nefandam.
Vos animam hanc potius quocumque absumite leto.”
Vix ea fatus erat, summo cum monte videmus
Ipsum inter pecudes vastā se mole moventem
65   Pastorem Polyphemum et litora nota petentem,
Monstrum horrendum, informe, ingens, cui lumen ademptum.
Trunca manu pinus regit [8] et vestigia firmat;
Lanigerae comitantur oves — ea sola voluptas
Solamenque mali.
70   Postquam altos tetigit fluctus et aequora venit,
Luminis effossi [9] fluidum lavit inde cruorem,
Dentibus infrendens [10] gemitu, graditurque per aequor,
Iam medium, necdum fluctus latera ardua tinxit. [11]

---

[1] bore out.   [2] savage, shaggy.   [3] like.   [4] lairs.   [5] miserable.   [6] berries.   [7] surrendered.
[8] guides.   [9] dug out.   [10] gnashing.   [11] wet.

Nos procul inde fugam trepidi celerare, recepto
Supplice sic merito, tacitique incidere funem;   75
Verrimus [1] et proni certantibus aequora remis.
Sensit, et ad sonitum vocis vestigia torsit;
Verum ubi nulla datur dextrā adfectare potestas,
Nec potis [2] Ionios fluctus aequare sequendo,
Clamorem immensum tollit, quo pontus et omnes   80
Contremuere undae, penitusque exterrita tellus
Italiae, curvisque immugiit Aetna cavernis.
At genus e silvis Cyclopum et montibus altis
Excitum ruit ad portus et litora complent;
Cernimus adstantes nequiquam lumine torvo   85
Aetnaeos fratres, caelo capita alta ferentes,
Concilium horrendum; quales cum vertice celso
Aëriae quercus, aut coniferae cyparissi
Constiterunt, silva alta Iovis, lucusve Dianae.
Praecipites metus acer agit quocumque rudentes [3]   90
Excutere, [4] et ventis intendere vela secundis.

The Descent into Hell. (*Aen.* vi. 268 foll.)

Ibant obscuri solā sub nocte per umbram,
Perque domos Ditis vacuas et inania regna:
Quale per incertam lunam sub luce malignā
Est iter in silvis, ubi caelum condidit umbrā
Iuppiter, et rebus nox abstulit atra colorem.   5
Vestibulum ante ipsum primisque in faucibus Orci
Luctus et ultrices [5] posuere cubilia Curae;
Pallentesque habitant Morbi, tristisque Senectus,
Et Metus, et malesuada Fames, ac turpis Egestas,
Terribiles visu formae, Letumque, Labosque;   10
Tum consanguineus Leti Sopor, et mala mentis

---

[1] sweep over.   [2] sc. *erat.*   [3] rigging, cordage.   [4] shake out.   [5] avenging.

Gaudia, mortiferumque adverso in limine Bellum,
Ferreique Eumenidum thalami,[1] et Discordia demens,
Vipereum crinem vittis innexa cruentis.

15   In medio ramos annosaque[2] bracchia pandit
Ulmus opaca, ingens, quam sedem Somnia[3] volgo
Vana tenere ferunt, foliisque sub omnibus haerent.
Multaque praeterea variarum monstra ferarum,
Centauri in foribus stabulant Scyllaeque biformes

20 Et centumgeminus Briareus ac belua Lernae,
Horrendum stridens, flammisque armata Chimaera,
Gorgones Harpyiaeque et forma tricorporis umbrae.
Corripit hic subitā trepidus formidine ferrum
Aeneas, strictamque aciem[4] venientibus offert,

25 Et, ni docta comes tenuis sine corpore vitas
Admoneat volitare cavā sub imagine formae,
Inruat, et frustra ferro diverberet umbras.

     Hinc via, Tartarei quae fert Acherontis ad undas.
Turbidus hic caeno vastāque voragine gurges[5]

30 Aestuat atque omnem Cocyto eructat arenam.
Portitor[6] has horrendus aquas et flumina servat
Terribili squalore Charon, cui plurima mento[7]
Canities[8] inculta iacet, stant lumina[9] flammā,
Sordidus ex humeris nodo dependet amictus.[10]

35 Ipse ratem conto[11] subigit, velisque ministrat,
Et ferruginea[12] subvectat corpora cymbā,
Iam senior, sed cruda[13] deo viridisque senectus.
Huc omnis turba ad ripas effusa ruebat,
Matres atque viri, defunctaque corpora vitā

40 Magnanimûm heroum, pueri innuptaeque puellae,
Impositique rogis iuvenes ante ora parentum:
Quam multa in silvis autumni frigore primo

[1] chambers. [2] aged. [3] dreams. [4] blade. [5] whirlpool. [6] ferryman. [7] chin. [8] grisly beard.
[9] eyes. [10] garment. [11] pole. [12] rust-colored. [13] robust.

Lapsa cadunt folia, aut ad terram gurgite ab alto
Quam multae glomerantur aves, ubi frigidus annus
Trans pontum fugat et terris inmittit apricis.[1]   45
Stabant orantes primi transmittere cursum,
Tendebantque manus ripae ulterioris amore.
Navita sed tristis nunc hos nunc accipit illos,
Ast alios longe submotos arcet arena.
Aeneas miratus enim motusque tumultu   50
"Dic," ait, "O virgo, quid volt concursus ad amnem?
Quidve petunt animae? vel quo discrimine ripas
Hae linquunt, illae remis vada livida verrunt?"
Olli[2] sic breviter fata est longaeva sacerdos:
"Anchisa generate, deûm certissima proles,   55
Cocyti stagna alta vides Stygiamque paludem;
Di cuius iurare timent et fallere numen,
Haec omnis, quam cernis, inops inhumataque[3] turba est;
Portitor ille Charon; hi, quos vehit unda, sepulti.
Nec ripas datur horrendas et rauca fluenta   60
Transportare prius, quam sedibus ossa quiêrunt.
Centum errant annos volitantque haec litora circum;
Tum demum admissi stagna exoptata revisunt."
Constitit Anchisa satus[4] et vestigia pressit,
Multa putans, sortemque animo miseratus iniquam.   65
Cernit ibi maestos et mortis honore carentis
Leucaspim et Lyciae ductorem classis Oronten,
Quos simul, a Troia ventosa per aequora vectos,
Obruit Auster, aqua involvens navemque virosque.

    *   *   *   *   *   *   *   *   *

    Ergo iter inceptum peragunt fluvioque propinquunt.   70
Navita quos iam inde ut Stygia prospexit ab unda
Per tacitum nemus ire pedemque advertere ripae.

---

[1] sunny. [2] = illi. [3] unburied. [4] natus.

❊ ❊ ❊ ❊ ❊ ❊ ❊ ❊ ❊

Caeruleam advertit puppim, ripaeque propinquat.
Inde alias animas, quae per iuga longa sedebant,
75 Deturbat, laxatque foros; simul accipit alveo
Ingentem Aenean. Gemuit sub pondere cymba
Sutilis,[1] et multam accepit rimosa[2] paludem.
Tandem trans fluvium incolumis vatemque virumque
Informi limo[3] glaucaque exponit in ulva.[4]
80 Cerberus haec ingens latratu regna trifauci[5]
Personat,[6] adverso recubans inmanis in antro.
Cui vates, horrere videns iam colla colubris,[7]
Melle soporatam et medicatis frugibus offam[8]
Obiicit. Ille fame rabida tria guttura pandens
85 Corripit objectam, atque inmania terga resolvit
Fusus humi, totoque ingens extenditur antro.
Occupat Aeneas aditum custode sepulto,
Evaditque celer ripam inremeabilis undae.
Continuo auditae voces vagitus[9] et ingens
90 Infantumque animae flentes in limine primo,
Quos dulcis vitae exsortes[10] et ab ubere raptos
Abstulit atra dies et funere mersit acerbo.
Hos iuxta falso damnati crimine mortis.
Nec vero hae sine sorte datae, sine iudice, sedes:
95 Quaesitor Minos urnam movet; ille silentum
Conciliumque vocat vitasque et crimina discit.
Proxuma deinde tenent maesti loca, qui sibi letum
Insontes peperere manu, lucemque perosi[11]
Proicere animas. Quam vellent aethere in alto
100 Nunc et pauperiem et duros perferre labores!
Fas obstat, tristique palus inamabilis unda
Alligat, et noviens Styx interfusa coercet.

[1] patched up. [2] full of chinks. [3] mire. [4] sedge. [5] from his three throats. [6] makes resound. [7] serpents. [8] cake. [9] wailing. [10] deprive of. [11] loathing.

Nec procul hinc partem fusi monstrantur in omnem
Lugentes Campi; sic illos nomine dicunt.
Hic, quos durus amor crudeli tabe [1] peredit,   105
Secreti celant calles [2] et myrtea circum
Silva tegit; curae non ipsā in morte relinquunt.

*   *   *   *   *   *   *   *   *

     Respicit Aeneas subito, et sub rupe sinistrā
Moenia lata videt, triplici circumdata muro,
Quae rapidus flammis ambit torrentibus amnis,   110
Tartareus Phlegethon, torquetque sonantia saxa.
Porta adversa, ingens, solidoque adamante columnae,
Vis ut nulla virûm, non ipsi exscindere bello
Caelicolae [3] valeant; stat ferrea turris ad auras,
Tisiphoneque sedens, pallā succincta cruentā,   115
Vestibulum exsomnis servat noctesque diesque.
Hinc exaudiri gemitus, et saeva sonare
Verbera; tum stridor [4] ferri, tractaeque catenae.
Constitit Aeneas, strepituque exterritus haesit.
"Quae scelerum facies? O virgo, effare; quibusve   120
Urguentur poenis? quis tantus plangor ad auras?"
Tum vates sic orsa loqui: "Dux inclute Teucrûm,
Nulli fas casto sceleratum [5] insistere limen;
Sed me cum lucis Hecate praefecit Avernis,
Ipsa deûm poenas docuit, perque omnia duxit.   125
Gnosius haec Rhadamanthus habet durissima regna,
Castigatque auditque dolos, subigitque fateri,
Quae quis apud superos, furto laetatus inani,
Distulit in seram [6] commissa piacula [7] mortem.
Continuo sontis [8] ultrix accincta flagello   130
Tisiphone quatit insultans, torvosque [9] sinistrā
Intentans angues vocat agmina saeva sororum.

---

[1] wasting disease. [2] defiles (noun). [3] the celestials. [4] clanking. [5] accursed. [6] late. [7] expiations. [8] guilty. [9] savage.

Tum demum horrisono stridentes cardine sacrae
Panduntur portae. Cernis, custodia qualis

135   Vestibulo sedeat? facies quae limina servet?
Quinquaginta atris inmanis hiatibus[1] Hydra
Saevior intus habet sedem. Tum Tartarus ipse
Bis patet in praeceps[2] tantum tenditque sub umbras,
Quantus ad aetherium caeli suspectus[3] Olympum.

140   Hic genus antiquum Terrae, Titania pubes,
Fulmine deiecti fundo volvuntur in imo.
Hic et Aloïdas geminos immania vidi
Corpora, qui manibus magnum rescindere coelum
Adgressi, superisque Iovem detrudere regnis.

145   Vidi et crudeles dantem[4] Salmonea poenas,
Dum flammas Iovis et sonitus imitatur Olympi.
Quattuor hic invectus equis et lampada quassans
Per Graiûm populos mediaeque per Elidis urbem
Ibat ovans, divomque sibi poscebat honorem,

150   Demens! qui nimbos et non imitabile fulmen
Aere et cornipedum[5] pulsu simularet equorum.
At pater omnipotens densa inter nubila telum
Contorsit, non ille faces nec fumea taedis[6]
Lumina, praecipitemque inmani turbine adegit.

155   Nec non et[7] Tityon, Terrae omniparentis alumnum,
Cernere erat,[8] per tota novem cui iugera[9] corpus
Porrigitur, rostroque[10] inmanis voltur obunco[11]
Inmortale iecur tondens[12] fecundaque poenis
Viscera rimaturque[13] epulis habitatque sub alto

160   Pectore, nec fibris[14] requies datur ulla renatis.
Quid memorem Lapithas, Ixiona Pirithoumque?
Quos super atra silex[15] iam iam lapsura cadentique
Imminet adsimilis; lucent genialibus altis

---

[1] yawning jaws.   [2] depth.   [3] height.   [4] suffering.   [5] horny-hoofed.   [6] pitch.   [7] and also.
[8] = *poterat.*   [9] acres.   [10] beak.   [11] hooked.   [12] tearing.   [13] explores.   [14] entrails.   [15] flint.

Aurea fulcra[1] toris,[2] epulaeque ante ora paratae
Regifico luxu; Furiarum maxuma iuxta 165
Accubat, et manibus prohibet contingere mensas,
Exsurgitque facem attollens, atque intonat ore.
Hic, quibus invisi fratres, dum vita manebat,
Pulsatusve parens, et fraus innexa clienti,
Aut qui divitiis soli incubuere repertis, 170
Nec partem posuere suis, quae maxuma turba est,
Quique ob adulterium caesi, quique arma secuti
Impia nec veriti dominorum fallere dextras,
Inclusi poenam exspectant. Ne quaere doceri,
Quam poenam, aut quae forma viros fortunave mersit. 175
Saxum ingens volvunt alii, radiisque[3] rotarum
Districti[4] pendent; sedet, aeternumque[5] sedebit,
Infelix Theseus; Phlegyasque miserrimus omnes
Admonet et magnā testatur voce per umbras:
'Discite institiam moniti, et non temnere divos.' 180
Vendidit hic auro patriam, dominumque potentem
Inposuit; fixit leges pretio atque refixit;
Hic thalamum invasit natae vetitosque[6] hymenaeos;
Ausi[7] omnes immane nefas, ausoque potiti.
Non, mihi si linguae centum sint oraque centum, 185
Ferrea vox, omnes scelerum comprendere formas,
Omnia poenarum percurrere nomina possim!"

---

[1] posts. [2] couches. [3] spokes. [4] stretched. [5] (adverb). [6] forbidden. [7] having dared.

XII. GAIUS CILNIUS MAECENAS.

Gaius Cilnius Maecenas, a famous Roman statesman and patron of literary men, was born about 70 B.C., and died in the year 8 B.C. In public life, he was long the trusted adviser and friend of Augustus Caesar, but is now best known by his munificence to the great writers of his day, especially Vergil, whose property he saved from confiscation, and Horace, to whom he gave a competence, and who in return has immortalized his name. His house was also the rendezvous of Tibullus, Propertius, Varius, Tucca, and many other men of genius. As a man, he was in many ways peculiar, — nervous, a hypochondriac, affectedly effeminate, an epicure, and almost absurd in his whimsical luxury; but all this appears to have been largely superficial and did not conceal his genuine ability, generosity, and capacity for loyal friendship. He wrote on various topics, but only a few fragments of his work remain in quotation, and have been collected by Bährens in his *Fragmenta Poetarum Romanorum* (Leipzig, 1886). See Milman's *Life of Horace* (1853).

A Lover of Life.   (Quoted by Seneca, *Epist.* 101.)

> Debilem facito manu,
> Debilem pede, coxã[1];
> Tuber[2] adstrue gibberum,
> Lubricos quate dentes;
> Vita dum superest, bene est.[3]
> Hanc mihi, vel acutã
> Si sedeam cruce, sustine.

To Horace.   (Quoted by Suetonius, *Vit. Hor.*)

> Ni te visceribus meis, Horati,
> Plus iam diligo, tu tuum sodalem[4]
> Hinnulo[5] videas strigosiorem.[6]

---

[1] hip.   [2] hump.   [3] it's all right.   [4] friend.   [5] mule.   [6] more scraggy.

XIII. QUINTUS HORATIUS FLACCUS.

HORACE.
(*From gem in British Museum.*)

Quintus Horatius Flaccus was born 65 B.C. at Venusia in the Apennines, and died 8 B.C. Most of the known details of his life are gathered from his own writings. From them we learn that his father was a freedman, who had probably obtained his freedom before the birth of Horace. At an early age Horace was placed in school at Rome, and later was sent to Athens to finish his education. While he was studying there he was made tribune in the army of Brutus, with whom he went to Asia Minor, sharing the defeat at Philippi (42 B.C.). Receiving, with others, permission to return to Italy, he settled in Rome, suffering, however, the loss of his patrimony, which induced him to court notice by writing verses. He became acquainted with Vergil and Varius, who introduced him to his future patron, Maecenas. The latter was not at first desirous of receiving the tribune of Brutus into his circle, and it was not until nearly a year after the introduction that he sent for Horace. Thereafter he was the closest friend of the poet, who became intimate at his house with many influential men. Through him, probably, Horace was introduced to Augustus. From Maecenas also he received as a present a small estate in the Sabine country, near Tibur, where he passed a part of each year in retirement. His life was not eventful. Poor health forced him to seek frequent change of air at his farm, at Praeneste, and at his favorite Baiae. The latter part of his life was spent in the study of moral philosophy. Maecenas and Horace died in the same year and were buried near one another in the farthest part of the Esquiline.

The works of Horace consist of four books of *Odes*; the *Carmen Saeculare*, an ode written at the request of Augustus for the Ludi Seculares; one book of *Epodes*; the *Satires* and *Epistles*, each in two books, and the *Ars Poetica*.

The most convenient edition of the entire works of Horace with notes in English is that of Wickham in two volumes (London, 1892). Excellent notes on the *Satires* are those of Palmer (London, 1885), and on the *Epistles* those of Wilkins (London, 1884). There are lives of Horace by Dean Milman (London, 1853), and by Hovenden (London, 1876). For general literary criticism see W. Y. Sellar's *Roman Poets of the Augustan Age*, pt. ii. *Horace* (1892). There are verse translations of the *Odes* by Conington (1870) and by Gladstone (1894); of the *Satires* and *Epistles* together by Conington (1869); of the whole

of Horace by Sir Theodore Martin (1881). There is a prose rendering of the
whole by Lonsdale and Lee (1877). A good lexicon to Horace (German) is that
of Koch (1879).

The Flirt.　(*Carm.* i. 5.)

Quis multā gracilis te puer in rosā
Perfusus liquidis urget odoribus
　　Grato, Pyrrha, sub antro?
　　Cui flavam religas comam
5　Simplex munditiis?[1]　Heu quoties fidem
Mutatosque deos flebit et aspera
　　Nigris aequora ventis
　　Emirabitur insolens[2]
Qui nunc te fruitur credulus aureā;
10　Qui semper vacuam,[3] semper amabilem
　　Sperat nescius aurae
　　Fallacis.　Miseri quibus
Intentata nites![4]　Me tabulā sacer
Votivā paries[5] indicat uvida
15　Suspendisse potenti
　　Vestimenta maris deo.

Live while we Live.　(*Carm.* i. 11.)

Tu ne quaesieris, scire nefas, quem mihi, quem tibi
Finem di dederint, Leuconoë, nec Babylonios
Tentāris[6] numeros.[7]　Ut[8] melius quidquid erit pati,
Seu plures hiemes seu tribuit Iuppiter ultimam,
5　Quae nunc oppositis debilitat[9] pumicibus[10] mare
Tyrrhenum.　Sapias, vina liques[11] et spatio brevi
Spem longam reseces.[12]　Dum loquimur fugerit invida
Aetas: carpe diem quam minimum credula postero.

---

[1] elegance. [2] inexperienced. [3] fancy-free. [4] seem fair. [5] temple wall. [6] consult. [7] horoscopes. [8] how much. [9] breaks the strength. [10] corroded rocks. [11] strain off. [12] cut down.

Integer Vitae.   (*Carm.* i. 22.)

Integer vitae scelerisque purus
Non eget Mauris iaculis neque arcu
Nec venenatis gravidā sagittis,
    Fusce, pharetrā,
Sive per Syrtes iter aestuosas [1]   5
Sive facturus per inhospitalem
Caucasum vel quae loca fabulosus
    Lambit [2] Hydaspes.
Namque me silvā lupus in Sabinā,
Dum meam canto Lalagen et ultra   10
Terminum [3] curis vagor expeditis,
    Fugit inermem,
Quale portentum neque militaris
Daunias latis alit aesculetis, [4]
Nec Iubae tellus [5] generat leonum   15
    Arida nutrix.
Pone me pigris ubi nulla campis
Arbor aestivā recreatur aurā,
Quod latus mundi nebulae malusque
    Iuppiter [6] urget;   20
Pone sub curru nimium propinqui
Solis in terrā domibus [7] negatā:
Dulce ridentem Lalagen amabo,
    Dulce loquentem.

Chloë, the Bud.   (*Carm.* i. 23.)

Vitas hinnuleo [8] me similis, Chloë,
Quaerenti pavidam montibus aviis [9]

---

[1] boiling.   [2] laves.   [3] limits.   [4] oak forests.   [5] i.e., Mauritania.   [6] sky, climate.   [7] i.e., as a residence.   [8] fawn.   [9] pathless.

      Matrem non sine vano
      Aurarum et siluae metu.
5   Nam seu mobilibus veris[1] inhorruit[2]
      Adventus foliis seu virides rubum[3]
      Dimovere lacertae,[4]
      Et corde et genibus tremit.
      Atqui non ego te tigris ut aspera
10   Gaetulusve leo frangere persequor:
      Tandem desine[5] matrem
      Tempestiva sequi viro.

    Fons Bandusiae.   (*Carm.* iii. 13.)

      O fons Bandusiae, splendidior vitro,[6]
      Dulci digne mero[7] non sine floribus,
      Cras donaberis haedo[8]
      Cui frons turgida[9] cornibus
5   Primis et venerem et proelia destinat
      Frustra: nam gelidos inficiet[10] tibi
      Rubro sanguine rivos
      Lascivi suboles gregis.
      Te flagrantis atrox hora Caniculae[11]
10   Nescit tangere, tu frigus amabile
      Fessis vomere[12] tauris
      Praebes et pecori vago.
      Fies nobilium tu quoque fontium,
      Me dicente cavis impositam ilicem
15   Saxis, unde loquaces
      Lymphae[13] desiliunt tuae.

---

[1] spring. [2] has rustled. [3] bramble. [4] lizards. [5] cease. [6] crystal. [7] wine. [8] kid
[9] swelling. [10] tinge. [11] dog-star. [12] plow. [13] waters.

A Voyage on a Canal Boat. (*Sat.* i. 5.)

Egressum magnā me excepit Aricia Romā
Hospitio[1] modico; rhetor comes Heliodorus,
Graecorum longe doctissimus; inde Forum Appi,
Differtum[2] nautis cauponibus[3] atque malignis.

APPIAN WAY — RESTORATION.
(*Von Falke.*)

Hoc iter ignavi divisimus, altius ac[4] nos   5
Praecinctis[5] unum; minus est gravis Appia tardis.[6]
Hic ego propter aquam, quod erat deterrima, ventri
Indico bellum,[7] cenantes haud animo aequo[8]
Exspectans comites.   Iam nox inducere terris
Umbras et caelo diffundere signa parabat;   10

---

[1] inn.   [2] crowded.   [3] innkeepers.   [4] *ac* = *quam.*   [5] more active.   [6] the leisurely.   [7] lay an embargo on.   [8] impatiently.

Tum perui[1] nautis, pueris convicia[2] nautae
Ingerere. Huc appelle![3] Trecentos inseris:[4] ohe
Iam satis est! Dum aes[5] exigitur,[6] dum mula ligatur,
Tota abit hora. Mali culices[7] ranaeque[8] palustres
15   Avertunt somnos, absentem ut cantat amicam
Multā prolutus vappā[9] nauta atque viator
Certatim. Tandem fessus dormire viator
Incipit, ac missae pastum[10] retinacula[11] mulae
Nauta piger saxo religat stertitque[12] supinus.
20   Iamque dies aderat, nil cum procedere lintrem
Sentimus, donec cerebrosus[13] prosilit unus
Ac mulae nautaeque caput lumbosque saligno
Fuste[14] dolat[15]: quartā vix demum exponimur[16] horā.
Ora manusque tuā lavimus, Feronia, lymphā.
25   Millia tum pransi[17] tria repimus[18] atque subimus
Impositum saxis late candentibus[19] Anxur.

The Night Hags.   (*Sat.* i. 8.)

Olim truncus eram ficulnus,[20] inutile lignum,
Cum faber incertus scamnum[21] faceretne Priapum,
Maluit esse deum. Deus inde ego furum aviumque
Maxima formido;[22] nam fures dextra coërcet
5   Ast importunas volucres in vertice[23] arundo[24]
Terret fixa vetatque novis considere in hortis.
Huc prius angustis ciecta cadavera cellis[25]
Conservus vili portanda locabat[26] in arcā.[27]
Hoc miserae plebi stabat commune sepulcrum,
10   Pantolabo scurrae[28] Nomentanoque nepoti:[29]

---

[1] slaves. [2] curses. [3] sc. *lintrem*, boat. [4] take on. [5] fare. [6] collected. [7] gnats. [8] frogs.
[9] soaked with poor wine. [10] to graze. [11] tow-rope. [12] snores. [13] hot-tempered. [14] willow
club. [15] belabors. [16] put ashore. [17] having lunched. [18] crawl. [19] gleaming. [20] fig. [21] bench.
[22] terror. [23] head. [24] crown of reeds. [25] quarters. [26] bargained. [27] coffin. [28] buffoon.
[29] spendthrift.

Mille pedes in fronte,[1] trecentos cippus[2] in agrum[3]
Hic dabat heredes monumentum ne sequeretur.[4]
Nunc licet Esquiliis habitare salubribus atque
Aggere[5] in aprico[6] spatiari,[7] quo modo tristes
Albis informem spectabant ossibus agrum;   15
Cum mihi non tantum furesque feraeque suëtae
Hunc vexare locum curae sunt atque labori,
Quantum carminibus[8] quae versant[9] atque venenis
Humanos animos. Has nullo perdere possum
Nec prohibere modo, simul ac vaga luna decorum   20
Protulit os, quin ossa legant herbasque nocentes.
Vidi egomet nigrā succinctam[10] vadere pallā[11]
Canidiam pedibus nudis passoque[12] capillo,
Cum Saganā maiore ululantem:[13] pallor utrasque
Fecerat horrendas adspectu. Scalpere[14] terram   25
Unguibus et pullam[15] divellere mordicus[16] agnam
Coeperunt; cruor in fossam confusus ut inde
Manes elicerent, animas[17] responsa daturas.
Lanea[18] et effigies erat, altera cerea:[19] maior
Lanea, quae poenis compesceret[20] inferiorem;   30
Cerea suppliciter stabat servilibus ut quae
Iam peritura modis. Hecaten vocat altera, saevam
Altera Tisiphonen; serpentes atque videres
Infernas errare canes,[21] lunamque rubentem[22]
Ne foret his testis post magna latere sepulcra.   35
Singula quid memorem? quo pacto alterna loquentes
Umbrae cum Saganā resonarent triste et acutum,
Utque lupi barbam variae cum dente colubrae
Abdiderint furtim terris, et imagine cereā

---

[1] in breadth. [2] pillar. [3] i.e., back from the road. [4] descend to. [5] terrace. [6] sunny.
[7] stroll. [8] charms. [9] bewitch. [10] tucked up. [11] gown. [12] dishevelled. [13] howling.
[14] dig up. [15] black. [16] with the teeth. [17] specters. [18] of wool. [19] of wax. [20] restrain.
[21] hellhounds. [22] blushing.

40 Largior arserit ignis, et ut non testis inultus
Horruerim voces Furiarum et facta duarum.
Canidiae dentes, altum Saganae caliendrum.[1]
Excidere atque herbas atque incantata lacertis
Vincula[2] cum magno risuque iocoque videres.

The Poet and the Bore. (Sat. i. 9.)

Ibam forte Viā Sacrā, sicut meus est mos,
Nescio quid meditans nugarum,[3] totus in illis:
Accurrit quidam notus mihi nomine tantum.
Arreptāque manu, "Quid agis, dulcissime rerum?"[4]

5 "Suaviter ut nunc est," inquam, "et cupio omnia quae vis."
Cum assectaretur:[5] "Num quid vis?" occupo.[6] At ille,
"Nôris nos," inquit; "docti sumus." Hic ego, "Pluris[7]
Hoc," inquam, "mihi eris." Misere discedere quaerens,
Ire[8] modo ocius, interdum consistere, in aurem

10 Dicere nescio quid puero, cum sudor ad imos
Manaret talos.[9] O te, Bolane, cerebri[10]
Felicem! aiebam tacitus; cum quidlibet ille
Garriret,[11] vicos, urbem laudaret. Ut illi
Nil respondebam, "Misere cupis," inquit, "abire;

15 Iamdudum video; sed nil agis; usque tenebo;
Prosequar: hinc quo nunc iter est tibi?" "Nil opus est te
Circumagi; quendam volo visere non tibi notum,
Trans Tiberim longe cubat[12] is prope Caesaris hortos."
"Nil habeo quod agam et non sum piger; usque sequar te."

20 Demitto auriculas ut iniquae[13] mentis asellus,
Cum gravius dorso subiit onus. Incipit ille:
"Si bene me novi non Viscum pluris amicum,
Non Varium facies; nam quis me scribere plures

---

[1] chignon. [2] charms. [3] trifles. [4] how are you, my dear fellow? [5] went on. [6] break in.
[7] gen. of value. [8] historical inf. [9] ankles. [10] hot temper. [11] chatter. [12] lies sick. [13] surly.

Aut citius possit versus? quis membra movere
Mollius?[1] Invideat quod et[2] Hermogenes ego canto."   25
Interpellandi locus hic erat: "Est tibi mater,
Cognati, quis te salvo est opus?" — "Haud mihi quisquam.
Omnes composui."[3] — Felices! nunc ego resto.
Confice; namque instat fatum mihi triste Sabella
Quod puero cecinit divinā motā anus[4] urnā: 30

MOUTH OF CLOACA MAXIMA AND SO-CALLED
TEMPLE OF VESTA.

"Hunc neque dira venena nec hosticus auferet[5] ensis
Nec laterum dolor[6] aut tussis[7] nec tarda podagra.[8]
Garrulus hunc quando consumet cunque; loquaces
Si sapiat vitet simul atque adolverit aetas."
Ventum erat ad Vestae[9] quartā iam parte diei   35
Praeteritā, et casu tunc respondere vadato[10]
Debebat, quod ni fecisset perdere litem.[11]

---

[1] gracefully. [2] even. [3] laid to rest. [4] old witch. [5] carry off. [6] pleurisy. [7] consumption.
[8] gout. [9] sc. *templum.* [10] answer in court. [11] case.

"Si me amas," inquit, "paulum hic ades."[1]   "Inteream si
Aut valeo stare aut novi civilia iura;
40   Et propero quo scis."   "Dubius sum quid faciam," inquit,
"Tene relinquam an rem."   "Me sodes."[2]   "Non faciam" ille;
Et praecedere coepit.   Ego ut contendere durum est
Cum victore sequor.   "Maecenas quomodo tecum?"[3]
Hinc repetit; "paucorum hominum et mentis bene sanae;
45   Nemo dexterius fortunâ est usus.   Haberes
Magnum adiutorem posset qui ferre secundas,[4]
Hunc hominem velles si tradere,[5] dispeream ni
Summôsses[6] omnes."   "Non isto vivimus illic
Quo tu rere[7] modo; domus hac nec purior ulla est
50   Nec magis his aliena malis; nil mi officit[8] umquam
Ditior hic aut est quia doctior; est locus uni
Cuique unus."   "Magnum narras, vix credibile!"   "Atqui
Sic habet."   "Accendis, quare cupiam magis illi
Proximus esse."   "Velis tantummodo: quae tua virtus,
55   Expugnabis; et est qui vinci possit, eoque
Difficiles aditus primos habet."   "Haud mihi deero:
Muneribus servos corrumpam; non hodie si
Exclusus fuero desistam; tempora[9] quaeram,
Occuram in triviis, deducam.[10]   Nil sine magno
60   Vita labore dedit mortalibus."   Haec dum agit, ecce
Fuscus Aristius occurrit, mihi carus et illum
Qui pulchre nôsset.   Consistimus.   Unde venis? et
Quo tendis? rogat et respondet.   Vellere[11] coepi
Et prensare manu lentissima[12] bracchia, nutans,
65   Distorquens oculos, ut me eriperet.   Male salsus[13]
Ridens dissimulare: meum iecur[14] urere bilis.
"Certe nescio quid secreto velle loqui te

---

[1] help (as advocate).   [2] *si audes* = I beg.   [3] how does Maecenas stand with you?   [4] sc. *partes.*
[5] introduce.   [6] supplant.   [7] think.   [8] trouble.   [9] opportunities.   [10] accompany.   [11] twitch.
[12] unresponsive.   [13] malicious wag.   [14] liver.

Aiebas mecum." "Memini bene, sed meliore
Tempore dicam; hodie tricesima sabbata: vin [1] tu
Curtis Iudaeis oppedere [2]?" "Nulla mihi," inquam,   70
" Religio [3] est." "At mi; sum paulo infirmior, unus
Multorum; ignosces [4]; alias [5] loquar." Huncine solem
Tam nigrum surrexe [6] mihi! Fugit improbus ac me
Sub cultro [7] linquit. Casu venit obvius illi
Adversarius et: "Quo, [8] tu turpissime?" magnā   75
Inclamat voce, et " Licet antestari [9] ?" Ego vero
Oppono auriculam. Rapit in ius [10]; clamor utrinque,
Undique concursus. Sic me servavit Apollo.

An Invitation to Dinner. (*Epist.* i. 5.)

Si potes Archiacis [11] conviva recumbere lectis [12]
Nec modicā cenare times olus omne patellā [13]
Supremo [14] te sole [14] domi, Torquate, manebo.
Vina bibes iterum Tauro [15] diffusa palustres [16]
Inter Minturnas Sinuessanumque Petrinum.   5
Si melius quid habes arcesse [17] vel imperium fer.
Iamdudum splendet focus et tibi munda supellex.
Mitte leves spes et certamina divitiarum
Et Moschi causam: cras nato Caesare festus
Dat veniam somnumque dies; impune licebit   10
Aestivam sermone benigno tendere noctem.
Quo mihi fortunam si non conceditur uti?
Parcus ob heredis curam nimiumque severus
Assidet [18] insano: potare et spargere flores
Incipiam, patiarque vel inconsultus [19] haberi.   15
Quid non ebrietas designat? Operta [20] recludit,

---

[1] = *visne*. [2] offend. [3] scruple. [4] pardon. [5] another time. [6] = *surrexisse*. [7] knife.
[8] sc. *tendis*. [9] will you be witness. [10] court. [11] made by Archias, = plain. [12] couch.
[13] dish. [14] at sunset. [15] sc. *consule*. [16] marsh. [17] order. [18] = is next door to. [19] foolish.
[20] secrets.

Spes iubet esse ratas,[1] ad proelia trudit[2] inertem;
Sollicitis animis onus eximit, addocet artes.
Fecundi calices quem non fecere disertum?[3]
20   Contractā quem non in paupertate solutum?
Haec ego procurare et idoneus imperor et non
Invitus, ne turpe toral,[4] ne sordida mappa[5]
Corruget[6] nares, ne non et cantharus[7] et lanx[8]
Ostendat tibi te, ne fidos inter amicos
25   Sit qui dicta foras eliminet,[9] ut coëat par
Iungaturque pari.   Butram tibi Septiciumque,
Et nisi cena prior potiorque[10] puella Sabinum
Detinet, assumam; locus est et pluribus umbris[11];
Sed nimis arta[12] premunt olidae[13] convivia caprae.
30   Tu quotus[14] esse velis rescribe, et rebus omissis
Atria servantem postico[15] falle clientem.

A True Philosopher.   (*Sat.* i. 6. 110-131.)

Hoc[16] ego commodius[17] quam tu, praeclare senator,
Millibus atque aliis[16] vivo.   Quācunque libido[18] est,
Incedo solus; percontor quanti olus ac far[19];
Fallacem Circum vespertinumque pererro
5   Saepe Forum; adsisto[20] divinis[21]; inde domum me
Ad porri[22] et ciceris[23] refero laganique[24] catinum[25];
Cena ministratur pueris tribus, et lapis albus[26]
Pocula cum cyatho[27] duo sustinet; adstat echinus[28]
Vilis, cum paterā[29] guttus,[30] Campana supellex.[31]
10   Deinde eo dormitum, non sollicitus mihi quod cras
Surgendum sit mane, obeundus Marsya, qui se

[1] accomplished.   [2] pushes on.   [3] eloquent.   [4] covering.   [5] napkin.   [6] wrinkle.   [7] bowl.
[8] dish.   [9] repeat, divulge.   [10] very attractive.   [11] attendant friends.   [12] crowded.   [13] = rank
odors.   [14] how large a party.   [15] back door.   [16] abl. of spec.   [17] more comfortably.   [18] fancy.
[19] ask the price of vegetables and meal.   [20] stand beside.   [21] fortune tellers.   [22] onion.   [23] chick
pea.   [24] pancake.   [25] dish.   [26] shelf.   [27] ladle.   [28] saltcellar.   [29] bowl.   [30] cruet.   [31] pottery.

Vultum ferre negat Noviorum posse minoris.
Ad quartam[1] iaceo; post hanc vagor; aut ego, lecto
Aut scripto quod me tacitum iuvet, ungor olivo,
Non quo fraudatis[2] immundus[3] Natta lucernis.[4]   15
Ast ubi me fessum sol acrior ire lavatum
Admonuit, fugio Campum lusumque trigonem.[5]
Pransus non avide, quantum interpellet inani
Ventre diem durare,[6] domesticus[7] otior. Haec est
Vita solutorum miserā ambitione gravique;   20
His me consolor victurum suavius ac si
Quaestor avus pater atque meus patruusque fuisset.

Some Famous Passages.

O fortes, peioraque passi
Mecum saepe viri, nunc vino pellite curas!
Cras ingens iterabimus aequor.   (*Carm.* i. 7 30.)

O matre pulchrā filia pulchrior!   (i. 16. 1.)

Frui paratis et valido mihi,
Latoë, dones et, precor, integrā
    Cum mente nec turpem senectam
    Degere nec citharā carentem.   (i. 31. 17.)

At vulgus infidum et meretrix retro
Periura cedit, diffugiunt cadis
    Cum faece siccatis amici
    Ferre iugum pariter dolosi.   (i. 35. 25.)

Nunc est bibendum, nunc pede libero
Pulsanda tellus, nunc Saliaribus
    Ornare pulvinar deorum
    Tempus erat dapibus, sodales.   (i. 37. 1.)

---

[1] sc. *horam.*   [2] robbed.   [3] filthy.   [4] lamps.   [5] game of ball.   [6] from going.   [7] at home.

Aequam memento rebus in arduis
Servare mentem, non secus in bonis
  Ab insolenti temperatam
    Laetitiā, moriture Delli.   (ii. 3. 1.)

Ille terrarum mihi praeter omnes
Angulus ridet.   (ii. 6. 13.)

Auream quisquis mediocritatem
Diligit tutus caret obsoleti
Sordibus tecti, caret invidendā
    Sobrius aulā.   (ii. 10. 5.)

        Neque semper arcum
    Tendit Apollo.   (ii. 10. 19.)

Eheu fugaces, Postume, Postume,
Labuntur anni. nec pietas moram
  Rugis et instanti senectae
    Afferet indomitaeque morti.   (ii. 14. 1.)

Linquenda tellus et domus et placens
Uxor, neque harum quas colis arborum
  Te praeter invisas cupressos
    Ulla brevem dominum sequetur.   (ii. 14. 21.)

Odi profanum vulgus et arceo.   (iii. 1. 1.)

Dulce et decorum est pro patriā mori.   (iii. 2. 13.)

Iustum et tenacem propositi virum
Non civium ardor prava iubentium
  Non vultus instantis tyranni
    Mente quatit solidā.   (iii. 3. 1.)

Damnosa quid non imminuit dies ?   (iii. 6. 45.)

Quid leges sine moribus
Vanae proficiunt ?   (iii. 24. 35.)

Ille potens sui
Laetusque deget, cui licet in diem
Dixisse "Vixi." (iii. 29. 41.)

Exegi monumentum aere perennius
* * * * * * *
Non omnis moriar, multaque pars mei
Vitabit Libitinam. (iii. 30. 1.)

Fortes creantur fortibus et bonis. (iv. 4. 29.)

Nos ubi decidimus
Quo pius Aeneas, quo dives Tullus et Ancus,
Pulvis et umbra sumus. (iv. 7. 15.)

Vixere fortes ante Agamemnona
Multi; sed omnes illacrimabiles
   Urgentur ignotique longā
   Nocte, carent quia vate sacro. (iv. 9. 25.)

Beatus ille qui procul negotiis
   Ut prisca gens mortalium
Paterna rura bobus exercet suis
   Solutus omni fenore. (Epod. 2. 1.)

Tanti quantum habeas sis. (Sat. i. 1. 62.)

   Quid rides? mutato nomine de te
Fabula narratur. (Sat. i. 1. 69.)

            ab ovo
Usque ad mala. (Sat. i. 3. 6.)

   Disiecti membra poetae. (Sat. i. 4. 62.)

Hic niger est; hunc tu, Romane, caveto. (Sat. i. 4. 85.)

   Credat Iudaeus Apella. (Sat. i. 5. 100.)

Saepe stilum vertas iterum quae digna legi sint
Scripturus. (*Sat.* i. 10. 72)

Ieiunus raro stomachus vulgaria temnit. (*Sat.* ii. 2. 38.)

O noctes cenaeque deûm ! (*Sat.* ii. 6. 65.)

condicio dulcis sine pulvere palmae. (*Epist.* i. 1. 51.)

Isne tibi melius suadet qui rem[1] facias, rem,
Si possis, recte, si non, quocunque modo rem? (*Epist.* i. 1. 65.)

Quidquid delirant reges plectuntur Achivi. (*Epist.* i. 2. 14.)

Nos numerus[2] sumus et fruges consumere nati. (*Epist.* i. 2. 27.)

sapere aude.
Dimidium facti qui coepit habet. (*Epist.* i. 2. 40.)

Sincerum est nisi vas quodcunque infundis acescit.
Sperne voluptates, nocet empta dolore voluptas. (*Epist.* i. 2. 54.)

Nil admirari prope res est una, Numici,
Solaque quae possit facere et servare beatum. (*Epist.* i. 6. 1.)

Quae nocuere sequor, fugio quae profore credam. (*Epist.* i. 8. 11.)

Illic vivere vellem
Oblitusque meorum obliviscendus et illis. (*Epist.* i. 11. 8.)

Caelum, non animum, mutant qui trans mare currunt. (*Epist.* i. 11. 27.)

Non cuivis homini contingit adire Corinthum. (*Epist.* i. 17. 36.)

Nam tua res agitur paries cum proximus ardet. (*Epist.* i. 18. 84.)

Hinc illae lacrimae. (*Epist.* i. 19. 41.)

---

[1] money. [2] mere ciphers.

Ridentur mala qui componunt carmina; verum
Gaudent scribentes et se venerantur.   (*Epist*. ii. 2. 107.)

Grammatici certant et adhuc sub iudice lis est.   (*A. P*. 78.)

sesquipedalia verba.   (*A. P*. 97.)

Difficile est proprie communia dicere.   (*A. P*. 128.)

Nec deus intersit nisi dignus vindice nodus.   (*A. P*. 191.)

Indignor quandoque bonus dormitat[1] Homerus.   (*A. P*. 359.)

Tu nihil invitā dices faciesve Minervā.   (*A. P*. 385.)

Nescit vox missa reverti.   (*A. P*. 390.)

---

[1] nods.

XIV. PUBLIUS OVIDIUS NASO.

Publius Ovidius Naso was born 43 B.C. at Sulmo, about ninety miles from [R]ome, and died 18 A.D. In order to give his sons the benefit of residence in [th]e capital, their father removed to Rome, where Ovid received the usual train-[in]g in rhetoric and oratory. His early aspirations toward a literary career were [st]rongly discouraged by his father, but, coming into possession of a moderate [fo]rtune at the death of his elder brother, he was enabled to pursue his natural [be]nt, and rapidly became a favorite in the circle of court poets. He was three [ti]mes married and twice divorced. For many years he enjoyed great prosper-[it]y, but when about fifty years old incurred the sudden displeasure of the [e]mperor, and was banished to Tomi, on the Black Sea. The cause of his [ban]ishment is not known. He refers to it in his poems, but does not explain [w]hat his offense was. He was unable to mollify the anger of Augustus, and [di]ed in the place of his exile.

The most important work of Ovid is the *Metamorphoses*, which professes [to] give in order the stories of Greek and Roman mythology, beginning with [th]e creation. There is very little continuity, and the style is rambling and [dis]cursive, the narrative running through some twelve thousand verses. The [ve]rses are smooth and easy, but lacking in elaborate finish. The poem is of [gr]eat value as the best known collection of ancient fables, set down by an [ex]cellent story-teller. In the *Fasti*, of which six books are extant, Ovid [at]tempts a poetical version of the Roman Calendar, describing the various fes-[ti]vals of the year, the customs and ancient rites of the people. The *Heroides* [a]re a set of letters from various legendary characters ; the *Amores*, a collection [o]f miscellaneous short poems in three books ; the *Tristia*, five books of poems [w]ritten during Ovid's banishment, full of personal biography and deep feeling. [H]is other works are his *Epistulæ ex Ponto*, addressed to various persons [an]d similar to the *Tristia* in character ; the *Ars Amatoria* and *Remedium [A]moris ;* and the *Ibis*, an invective against a false friend.

The standard text of the whole of Ovid is that of A. Riese (2d ed. Leipzig, [1]889). There is a good edition of the *Fasti* with English notes by Paley [(]London, 1888) ; of the *Heroides*, by Shuckburgh (London, 1879) ; of the [A]mores and *Ars Amatoria*, by J. H. Williams (London, 1884) ; of the *Meta-[m]orphoses* (selections), by Simmons (London, 1887) ; of the *Tristia*, by S. G. [O]wen (London, 1890) ; of the *Epistulæ ex Ponto* (Bk. I.), by Keene (London, [1]887). The *Ibis* is edited with Latin notes by R. Ellis (Oxford, 1881). There [is] a lexicon to the *Metamorphoses* by Eichert (9th ed. Hanover, 1886) ; a life [(]in French) by Nageotte (Dijon, 1872) ; and a general introduction by Church [in] *Ancient Classics for English Readers* (1876).

The Rape of the Sabines.　(Ars Am. i. 101.)

Primus sollicitos[1] fecisti, Romule, ludos,
　Cum iuvit viduos[2] rapta Sabina viros.
Tunc neque marmoreo pendebant vela[3] theatro,
　Nec fuerant liquido pulpita[4] rubra croco.[5]
Illic, quas tulerant nemorosa Palatia, frondes　　　　5
　Simpliciter positae, scena sine arte fuit.
In gradibus sedit populus de cespite[6] factis,
　Quālibet hirsutas[7] fronde[8] tegente comas.
Respiciunt, oculisque notat sibi quisque puellam,
　Quam velit: et tacito pectore multa movent.　　　10
Dumque, rudem praebente modum tibicine Tusco,
　Ludius[9] aequatam ter pede pulsat humum;
In medio plausu (plausus tunc arte carebat,)
　Rex populo praedae signa petenda dedit.
Protinus exsiliunt, animum clamore fatentes,[10]　　　15
　Virginibus cupidas iniciuntque manus.
Ut fugiunt aquilas, timidissima turba, columbae,
　Utque fugit visos agna novella[11] lupos;
Sic illae timuere viros sine lege ruentes.
　Constitit in nullā qui fuit ante color.　　　20
Nam timor unus erat; facies non una timoris.
　Pars laniat[12] crines: pars sine mente sedet:
Altera maesta silet; frustra vocat altera matrem:
　Haec queritur; stupet haec: haec fugit, illa manet.
Ducuntur raptae, genialis[13] praeda, puellae,　　　25
　Et potuit multas ipse decere pudor.
Si qua repugnabat nimium, comitemque negabat,
　Sublatam cupido vir tulit ipse sinu:
Atque ita, "Quid teneros lacrimis corrumpis ocellos?

---

[1] anxious.　[2] unmarried.　[3] awnings.　[4] stage.　[5] saffron.　[6] turf.　[7] shaggy.　[8] chaplet.
[9] actor.　[10] showing.　[11] young.　[12] tear.　[13] charming.

30   Quod matri pater est, hoc tibi," dixit. "ero."
     Romule, militibus scisti dare commoda[1] solus.
     Haec mihi si dederis commoda, miles ero.

A Popular Holiday.   (*Fasti*, iii. 523–542.)

     Idibus est Annae festum geniale[2] Perennae.
        Haud procul a ripis, advena[3] Thybri, tuis
     Plebs venit ac virides passim disiecta per herbas
        Potat, et accumbit cum pare[4] quisque suā.
5   Sub Iove[5] pars durat, pauci tentoria[6] ponunt,
        Sunt quibus e ramis frondea[7] facta casa[8] est;
     Pars, ubi pro rigidis calamos statuere columnis,
        Desuper extentas imposuere togas.
     Sole tamen vinoque calent, annosque precantur,
10   Quot sumant cyathos, ad numerumque bibunt.
     Invenies illic, qui Nestoris ebibat annos,
        Quae sit per calices facta Sibylla suos.
     Illic et cantant quidquid didicere theatris,
        Et iactant faciles ad sua verba manus;
15   Et ducunt posito duras cratere choreas,[9]
        Cultaque diffusis saltat amica comis.
     Cum redeunt, titubant[10] et sunt spectacula vulgi,
        Et fortunatos obvia turba vocat.
     Occurri nuper: visa est mihi digna relatu
20   Pompa[11]: senem potum[12] pota trahebat anus.

Atalanta's Race.   (*Met*. x. 560–680.)

     "Forsitan audieris aliquam certamine cursus
     Veloces superasse viros. Non fabula rumor

---

1 reward, pay.   2 merry.   3 stranger.   4 mate.   5 open sky.   6 tents.   7 leafy.   8 hut
9 dances.   10 reel.   11 procession.   12 drunk.

ATALANTA'S RACE.
(*From the painting by Poynter.*)

Ille fuit; superabat enim; nec dicere posses,
Laude pedum, formaene bono praestantior esset.
Scitanti[1] deus[2] huic de coniuge 'Coniuge,' dixit,   5
· Nil opus est, Atalanta, tibi: fuge coniugis usum.
Nec tamen effugies, teque ipsā viva carebis.'[3]
Territa sorte dei per opacas innuba silvas
Vivit. et instantem turbam violenta procorum[4]
Condicione fugat, nec 'Sum potiunda, nisi,' inquit,   10
'Victa prius cursu; pedibus contendite mecum:
Praemia veloci coniunx thalamique dabuntur;
Mors pretium tardis.   Ea lex certaminis esto.'
Illa quidem immitis: sed tanta potentia formae est,
Venit ad hanc legem temeraria turba procorum.   15
    Sederat Hippomenes cursus spectator iniqui,
Et 'Petitur cuiquam per tanta pericula coniunx?'
Dixerat, ac nimios iuvenum damnârat amores.
Ut faciem et posito corpus velamine[5] vidit.
Quale meum,[6] vel quale tuum,[7] si femina fias,   20
Obstipuit, tollensque manus · Ignoscite,' dixit,
'Quos modo culpavi.   Nondum mihi praemia nota,
Quae peteretis. erant.'   Laudando concipit ignes,

Et, ne quis iuvenum currat velocius, optat

25   Invidiāque timet. 'Sed cur certaminis huius

Intemptata mihi fortuna relinquitur?' inquit

'Audentes deus ipse iuvat.' Dum talia secum

Exigit Hippomenes, passu volat alite[1] virgo.

Quae quamquam Scythicā non secius[2] ire sagittā

30   Aonio[3] visa est inveni, tamen ille decorem

Miratur magis. Et cursus facit ille decorem.

Aura refert ablata citis talaria[4] plantis[5]:

Tergaque iactantur crines per eburnea,[6] quaeque

Poplitibus[7] suberant picto genualia[8] limbo[9]:

35   Inque puellari[10] corpus candore ruborem

Traxerat, haud aliter, quam cum super atria[11] velum

Candida purpureum simulatas inficit umbras.

Dum notat haec hospes, decursa novissima meta[12] est,

Et tegitur festā victrix Atalanta coronā.

40   Dant gemitum victi, penduntque[13] ex foedere poenas:

Non tamen eventu iuvenis deterritus horum

Constitit in medio, vultuque in virgine fixo

'Quid facilem titulum superando quaeris inertes?

Mecum confer!' ait 'seu me fortuna potentem

45   Fecerit, a tanto non indignabere vinci.

Namque mihi genitor Megareus Onchestius: illi

Est Neptunus avus: pronepos[14] ego regis aquarum.

Nec virtus citra genus est. Seu vincar, habebis

Hippomene victo magnum et memorabile nomen.'

50   Talia dicentem mollī Schoeneïa[15] vultu

Aspicit, et dubitat, superari an vincere malit.

Atque ita 'quis deus hunc formosis' inquit 'iniquus

Perdere vult, caraeque iubet discrimine vitae

---

[1] winged.   [2] otherwise.   [3] Boeotian.   [4] wings.   [5] feet.   [6] ivory.   [7] knee.   [8] leggings.   [9] fringe.   [10] maiden.   [11] court.   [12] goal.   [13] pay.   [14] great-grandson.   [15] daughter of Schoeneus.

Coniugium petere hoc? non sum, me iudice, tanti.
Nec formā tangor,—poteram tamen hac quoque tangi— 55
Sed quod adhuc puer est. Non me movet ipse, sed aetas.
Quid, quod inest virtus et mens interrita leti?
Quid, quod ab aequoreā numeratur origine quartus?
Quid, quod amat, tantique putat conubia nostra;
Ut pereat, si me fors illi dura negaret? 60
Dum licet, hospes, abi, thalamosque relinque cruentos.
Coniugium crudele meum est. Tibi nubere nulla
Nolet; et optari potes a sapiente puellā.
Cur tamen est mihi cura tui, tot iam ante peremptis?
Viderit![1] intereat, quoniam tot caede procorum 65
Admonitus non est, agiturque in taedia[2] vitae.
Occidet hic igitur, voluit quia vivere mecum,
Indignamque necem pretium patietur amoris?
Non erit invidiae victoria nostra ferendae.
Sed non culpa mea est. Utinam desistere velles! 70
Aut, quoniam es demens, utinam velocior esses!
At quam virgineus puerili vultus in ore est!
Ah, miser Hippomene, nollem tibi visa fuissem!
Vivere dignus eras. Quod si felicior essem,
Nec mihi coniugium fata importuna negarent, 75
Unus eras, cum quo sociare[3] cubilia vellem.'
    Dixerat: utque rudis[4] primoque Cupidine tacta,
Quid facit, ignorans, amat et non sentit amorem.
Iam solitos poscunt cursus populusque paterque:
Cum me sollicitā proles Neptunia voce 80
Invocat Hippomenes, 'Cytherea' que 'comprecor, ausis
Adsit' ait 'nostris et quos dedit, adiuvet ignes.'
Detulit aura preces ad me non invida blandas;
Motaque sum, fateor. Nec opis mora longa dabatur.

---

[1] hortatory subj.   [2] weariness.   [3] share.   [4] inexperienced.

85   Est ager, indigenae Tamasenum nomine dicunt,
    Telluris Cypriae pars optima, quam mihi prisci
    Sacravere senes, templisque accedere dotem [1]
    Hanc iussere meis. Medio nitet arbor in arvo,
    Fulva comam, fulvo ramis crepitantibus auro.
90   Hinc tria forte meâ veniens decerpta [2] ferebam
    Aurea poma manu: nullique videnda nisi ipsi
    Hippomenen adii, docuique, quis usus in illis.
    Signa tubae dederant, cum carcere [3] pronus [4] uterque
    Emicat, et summam celeri pede libat [5] harenam.
95   Posse putes illos sicco freta radere [6] passu,
    Et segetis canae [7] stantes percurrere aristas. [8]
    Adiciunt animos [9] iuveni clamorque favorque,
    Verbaque dicentum 'Nunc, nunc incumbere tempus,
    Hippomene, propera! nunc viribus utere totis.
100   Pelle moram, vinces:' dubium, Megareïus heros
    Gaudeat, an virgo magis his Schoeneïa dictis.
    O quotiens, cum iam posset transire, morata est,
    Spectatosque diu vultus invita reliquit!
    Aridus e lasso veniebat anhelitus ore,
105   Metaque erat longe. Tum denique de tribus unum
    Fetibus arboreis proles Neptunia misit.
    Obstipuit virgo, nitidique cupidine pomi
    Declinat cursus, aurumque volubile tollit:
    Praeterit Hippomenes: resonant spectacula [10] plausu.
110   Illa moram celeri cessataque [11] tempora cursu
    Corrigit, atque iterum iuvenem post terga relinquit.
    Et rursus pomi iactu remorata secundi,
    Consequitur transitque virum. Pars ultima cursus
    Restabat. 'Nunc' inquit 'ades, dea muneris auctor!'
115   Inque latus campi, quo tardius illa rediret,

---

[1] endowment. [2] plucked. [3] barrier. [4] bending forward. [5] skims. [6] graze. [7] white, yellow.
[8] grain. [9] courage. [10] field. [11] lost.

Iecit ab obliquo nitidum iuvenaliter[1] aurum.
An peteret, virgo visa est dubitare: coegi
Tollere, et adieci sublato pondera malo,[2]
Impediique oneris pariter gravitate moraque.
Neve meus sermo cursu sit tardior ipso,   120
Praeterita est virgo: duxit sua praemia victor."

The Poet's Banishment from Rome.   (*Tristia*, i. 3.)

Cum subit illius tristissima noctis imago,
   Quā mihi supremum tempus in urbe fuit,
Cum repeto noctem, quā tot mihi cara reliqui,
   Labitur ex oculis nunc quoque gutta[3] meis.
Iam prope lux aderat, quā me discedere Caesar   5
   Finibus extremae iusserat Ausoniae.
Nec spatium fuerat, nec mens satis apta parandi:
   Torpuerant longā pectora nostra morā.
Non mihi servorum, comitis non cura legendi,
   Non aptae profugo[4] vestis opisve fuit.   10
Non aliter stupui, quam qui Iovis ignibus ictus
   Vivit, et est vitae nescius ipse suae.
Ut tamen hanc animi nubem dolor ipse removit,
   Et tandem sensus convaluere mei,
Alloquor extremum maestos abiturus amicos,   15
   Qui modo de multis unus et alter[5] erant.
Uxor amans flentem flens acrius ipsa tenebat,
   Imbre[6] per indignas usque cadente genas.[7]
Nata procul Libycis aberat diversa[8] sub oris,
   Nec poterat fati certior esse mei.   20
Quocumque aspiceres, luctus gemitusque sonabant,
   Formaque non taciti funeris intus erat.

---

[1] with youthful strength. [2] apple. [3] tear. [4] exile. [5] one or two. [6] flood of tears. [7] cheeks.
[8] in an opposite direction (to Scythia).

Femina virque meo, pueri quoque, funere maerent:
    Inque domo lacrimas angulus omnis habet.

25 Si licet exemplis in parvo grandibus uti,
    Haec facies Troiae, cum caperetur, erat.

Iamque quiescebant voces hominumque canumque,
    Lunaque nocturnos alta regebat equos.

Hanc ego suspiciens, et ab hac Capitolia cernens,
30   Quae nostro frustra iuncta fuere lari,[1]

"Numina vicinis habitantia sedibus," inquam
    "Iamque oculis numquam templa videnda meis,

Dique relinquendi, quos urbs habet alta Quirini,
    Este salutati tempus in omne mihi!

35 Et quamquam sero clipeum post vulnera sumo,
    Attamen hanc odiis exonerate fugam,

Caelestique viro,[2] quis me deceperit error,
    Dicite, pro culpā ne scelus esse putet!

Ut quod vos scitis, poenae quoque sentiat auctor,
40   Placato possum non miser esse deo."

Hac prece adoravi superos ego, pluribus uxor,
    Singultu[3] medios impediente sonos.

Illa etiam ante lares passis adstrata capillis
    Contigit extinctos ore tremente focos,

45 Multaque in adversos effudit verba Penates
    Pro deplorato non valitura viro.

Iamque morae spatium nox praecipitata negabat,
    Versaque ab axe suo Parrhasis[4] arctos erat.

Quid facerem? blando patriae retinebar amore:
50   Utima sed iussae nox erat illa fugae.

Ah, quotiens certam me sum mentitus habere
    Horam, propositae quae foret apta[5] viae.

Ter limen tetigi, ter sum revocatus, et ipse

---

[1] home.   [2] i.e., Augustus.   [3] sob.   [4] Arcadian.   [5] lucky.

Indulgens animo pes mihi tardus erat.
Saepe 'vale' dicto rursus sum multa locutus,   55
  Et quasi discedens oscula summa dedi.
Saepe eadem mandata dedi, meque ipse fefelli,
  Respiciens oculis pignora[1] cara meis.
Denique, "Quid propero? Scythia est, quo mittimur," inquam,
  "Roma relinquenda est. Utraque iusta mora est.   60
Uxor in aeternum vivo mihi viva negatur,
  Et domus et fidae dulcia membra domus,
Quosque ego fraterno dilexi more sodales,
  O mihi Theseā pectora iuncta fide!
Dum licet, amplectar. Nunquam fortasse licebit   65
  Amplius. In lucro[2] est quae datur hora mihi."
Nec mora, sermonis verba imperfecta relinquo,
  Complectens animo proxima quaeque meo.
Dum loquor et flemus, caelo nitidissimus alto,
  Stella gravis nobis, Lucifer ortus erat.   70
Dividor haud aliter, quam si mea membra relinquam,
  Et pars abrumpi corpore visa suo est.
Sic doluit Metus tunc, cum in contraria versos
  Ultores habuit proditionis equos.
Tum vero exoritur clamor gemitusque meorum,   75
  Et feriunt maestae pectora nuda manus.
Tum vero coniunx, umeris abeuntis inhaerens,
  Miscuit haec lacrimis tristia dicta suis:
"Non potes avelli. Simul, ah, simul ibimus," inquit:
  "Te sequar et coniunx exulis exul ero.   80
Et mihi facta via est. Et me capit ultima tellus:
  Accedam profugae sarcina[3] parva rati.
Te iubet a patriā discedere Caesaris ira,
  Me pietas; pietas haec mihi Caesar erit."

---

[1] pledges.   [2] counted as gain.   [3] burden.

85   Talia temptabat, sicut temptaverat ante,
           Vixque dedit[1] victas utilitate[2] manus.
         Egredior, sive illud erat sine funere ferri,[3]
           Squalidus inmissis hirta[4] per ora comis.
         Illa dolore amens tenebris narratur obortis[5]
90   Semianimis mediā procubuisse domo,
         Utque resurrexit foedatis pulvere turpi
           Crinibus et gelidā membra levavit humo,
         Se modo, desertos modo complorâsse Penates,
           Nomen et erepti saepe vocasse viri,
95   Nec gemuisse minus, quam si nataeque meumque
           Vidisset structos corpus habere rogos,[6]
         Et voluisse mori, moriendo ponere sensus,
           Respectuque tamen non periisse mei.
         Vivat! et absentem — quoniam sic fata tulerunt —
100   Vivat ut auxilio sublevet usque suo.

---

[1] submit.   [2] = what was best.   [3] carry out (of a corpse)   [4] rough.   [5] rising.   [6] funeral bier.

XV. TITUS LIVIUS.

Titus Livius was born at Patavium (Padua) 59 B.C., and died at the same place 17 A.D. He passed most of his life at Rome in literary work. His great history of Rome from the coming of Aeneas to the death of Drusus, 9 B.C., was contained in one hundred and forty-two books, of which only thirty-five have been preserved. He was a raconteur rather than a historian, and collated from various and often conflicting authorities the accounts of the events which he described in vivid and animated language. No attempt is made in his work to sift historical evidence or to present the results of original research. He has therefore been called "the Roman Herodotus."

A standard text is that of Weissenborn in 6 vols. (Leipzig, 1878). There is a fair translation by Spillane and others in the Bohn Library; and an excellent one of the part relating to the Second Punic War (Bks. XXI.-XXV.) by Church and Brodribb (London, 1883). For criticism of Livy as a writer and historian see the monograph in French by H. A. Taine, *Essai sur Tite Live* (Paris, 1860); and for his language and style the *Étude sur la Langue et Grammaire de Tite Live* by Riemann (Paris, 1879).

The Founding of Rome. (i. 6, 3.)

BRONZE WOLF STATUE.
(*Rome.*)

Romulum Remumque cupido cepit in his locis, ubi expositi ubique educati erant, urbis condendae. Et supererat multitudo Albanorum Latinorumque; ad id pastores quoque accesserant, qui omnes facile spem facerent 10 parvam Albam, parvum Lavinium prae eā urbe quae conderetur, fore. Intervenit deinde his cogitationibus avitum malum, regni cupido, atque inde foe-

15 dum[1] certamen coortum a satis miti principio. Quoniam gemini essent, nec aetatis verecundia[2] discrimen facere posset, ut dii, quorum tutelae[3] ea loca essent, auguriis legerent, qui nomen novae urbi daret, qui conditam imperio regeret, Palatium Romulus, Remus Aventinum ad inaugurandum templa capiunt.

20 Priori Remo augurium venisse fertur sex vultures, iamque nuntiato augurio cum duplex numerus Romulo sese ostendisset, utrumque regem sua multitudo[4] consalutaverat. Tempore[5] illi praecepto, at hi numero avium regnum trahebant. Inde cum altercatione congressi certamine irarum ad caedem vertuntur.

25 Ibi in turbā ictus Remus cecidit. Vulgatior fama est ludibrio[6] fratris Remum novos transiluisse muros; inde ab irato Romulo, cum verbis quoque increpitans adiecisset "Sic deinde quicumque alius transiliet moenia mea!" interfectum. Ita solus potitus imperio Romulus; condita urbs conditoris nomine appellata.

HUT-URN FROM ALBA LONGA.
(*British Museum.*)

30 Palatium primum, in quo ipse erat educatus, muniit. Sacra diis aliis Albano ritu, Graeco Herculi, ut ab Evandro instituta erant, facit.[7] Herculem in ea loca Geryone interempto boves mirā specie abegisse memorant, ac prope Tiberim fluvium, quā prae

35 se armentum agens nando traiecerat, loco herbido,[8] ut quiete et pabulo laeto reficeret boves, et ipsum fessum viā procubuisse.

Ibi cum eum cibo vinoque gravatum sopor oppressisset, pastor 40 accola[9] eius loci nomine Cacus, ferox viribus, captus pulchritudine boum cum avertere[10] eam praedam vellet, quia, si agendo armentum in speluncam compulisset, ipsa vestigia quaerentem dominum eo deductura erant, aversos boves, eximium quemque pulchritudine, caudis in speluncam traxit. Hercules ad primam 45 auroram somno excitus cum gregem perlustrāsset oculis et par-

---

[1] unseemly. [2] respect. [3] protection (gen.). [4] followers. [5] = on account of priority. [6] sport. [7] perform. [8] grassy. [9] inhabitant. [10] drive off.

tem abesse numero sensisset, pergit ad proximam speluncam, si
forte eo vestigia ferrent. Quae ubi omnia foras versa vidit nec
in partem aliam ferre, confusus atque incertus animi ex loco
infesto[1] agere porro[2] armentum occepit.[3]   Inde cum actae
boves quaedam ad desiderium, ut fit,[4] relictarum mugissent, red-   50
dita inclusarum ex speluncā boum vox Herculem convertit.
Quem cum vadentem ad speluncam Cacus vi prohibere conatus
esset, ictus clavā fidem pastorum nequiquam invocans morte
occubuit.

Horatius at the Bridge.   (ii. 10.)

   Cum hostes adessent, pro se quisque[5] in urbem ex agris demi-
grant, urbem ipsam saepiunt praesidiis. Alia muris, alia Tiberi
obiecto videbantur tuta. Pons sublicius[6] iter paene hostibus
dedit, ni unus vir fuisset Horatius Cocles: id munimentum illo
die fortuna urbis Romanae habuit. Qui positus forte in statione[7]   5
pontis, cum captum repentino impetu Ianiculum atque inde
citatos decurrere hostes vidisset, trepidamque turbam suorum
arma ordinesque relinquere, reprehensans singulos, obsistens
obtestansque[8] deûm et hominum fidem testabatur, nequiquam
deserto praesidio eos fugere; si transitum[9] pontem a tergo   10
reliquissent, iam plus hostium in Palatio Capitolioque quam in
Ianiculo fore. Itaque monere praedicere, ut pontem ferro igni,
quācumque vi possint, interrumpant: se impetum[10] hostium,
quantum corpore uno posset obsisti, excepturum. Vadit inde in
primum aditum pontis, insignisque inter conspecta cedentium   15
pugnae terga obversis comminus ad ineundum proelium armis
ipso miraculo audaciae obstupefecit hostis. Duos tamen cum eo
pudor tenuit, Sp. Lartium ac T. Herminium, ambos claros genere
factisque. Cum his primam periculi procellam et quod tumul-
tuosissimum pugnae erat parumper[11] sustinuit. Deinde eos   20

---

[1] uncanny. [2] further. [3] began. [4] as is apt to happen. [5] with one accord. [6] of piles. [7] on
guard. [8] call to witness. [9] as a passage. [10] onset. [11] for a while.

quoque ipsos exiguā parte pontis relictā, revocantibus qui
rescindebant, cedere in tutum coegit. Circumferens inde truces
minaciter oculos ad proceres Etruscorum nunc singulos provocare,
nunc increpare omnes, servitia regum superborum, suae libertatis
25 inmemores alienam oppugnatum venire. Cunctati aliquamdiu
sunt, dum alius alium, ut proelium incipiant, circumspectant.
Pudor deinde commovit aciem, et clamore sublato undique in
unum hostem tela coniciunt. Quae cum in obiecto cuncta scuto
haesissent, neque ille minus obstinatus ingenti[1] pontem obtineret
30 gradu,[2] iam impetu conabantur detrudere virum, cum simul fragor
rupti pontis simul clamor Romanorum, alacritate perfecti operis
sublatus, pavore subito impetum sustinuit. Tum Cocles "Tiberine pater" inquit, "te sancte precor, haec arma et hunc militem
propitio flumine accipias!" ita sic[3] armatus in Tiberim desiluit,
35 multisque incidentibus telis incolumis ad suos tranavit, rem
ausus plus famae habituram ad posteros quam fidei. Grata erga
tantam virtutem civitas fuit: statua in Comitio posita, agri quantum uno die circumaravit datum. Privata[4] quoque inter pub-
licos honores studia eminebant: nam in magnā inopia pro
40 domesticis copiis unusquisque ei aliquid fraudans se ipse victu
suo contulit.

The Deed of Mucius Scaevola. (ii. 12.)

C. Mucius, adulescens nobilis, cui indignum videbatur populum
Romanum servientem, cum sub regibus esset, nullo bello nec ab
hostibus ullis obsessum esse, liberum eundem populum ab iisdem
Etruscis obsideri, quorum saepe exercitus fuderit,—magno au-
5 dacique aliquo facinore[5] eam indignitatem vindicandam ratus,[6]
primo suā sponte penetrare in hostium castra constituit; dein
metuens, ne, si consulum iniussu et ignaris omnibus iret, forte
deprehensus a custodibus Romanis retraheretur ut transfuga,[7]

---

[1] firm. [2] position. [3] as he was. [4] of individuals. [5] deed. [6] thinking. [7] deserter.

fortunā tum urbis crimen adfirmante, senatum adit. "Transire
Tiberim" inquit, "patres, et intrare, si possim, castra hostium 10
volo, non praedo[1] nec populationum in vicem ultor: maius, si di
iuvant, in animo est facinus." Adprobant patres. Abdito intra
vestem ferro proficiscitur. Ubi eo venit, in confertissimā turbā
prope regium tribunal constitit. Ibi cum stipendium militibus
forte daretur, et scriba[2] cum rege sedens pari fere ornatu multa 15
ageret, eum milites volgo adirent, timens sciscitari,[3] uter Porsena
esset, ne ignorando regem semet ipse aperiret quis esset, quo
temere traxit[4] fortuna facinus, scribam pro rege obtruncat.
Vadentem inde, quā per trepidam turbam cruento mucrone sibi
ipse fecerat viam, cum concursu ad clamorem facto conprehensum 20
regii satellites retraxissent, ante tribunal regis destitutus[5] tum
quoque inter tantas fortunae minas metuendus magis quam
metuens, "Romanus sum" inquit "civis, C. Mucium vocant.
Hostis hostem occidere volui, nec ad mortem minus animi est
quam fuit ad caedem: et facere et pati fortia Romanum est. 25
Nec unus in te ego hos animos gessi; longus post me ordo est
idem petentium decus.[6] Proinde in hoc discrimen, si iuvat,
accingere,[7] ut in singulas horas capite dimices[8] tuo, ferrum
hostemque in vestibulo habeas regiae. Hoc tibi iuventus Romana
indicimus bellum. Nullam aciem, nullum proelium timueris; 30
uni tibi et cum singulis res erit." Cum rex simul[9] irā infensus
periculoque conterritus circumdari ignis minitabundus iuberet,
nisi expromeret propere, quas insidiarum sibi minas per ambages[10]
iaceret, "En tibi" inquit, "ut sentias, quam vile corpus sit iis,
qui magnam gloriam vident," dextramque accenso ad sacrificium 35
foculo inicit. Quam cum velut alienato ab sensu torreret animo,
prope attonitus miraculo rex cum ab sede suā prosiluisset,
amoverique ab altaribus iuvenem iussisset, "In vero abi," inquit,

---

[1] as a plunderer. [2] secretary. [3] inquire. [4] happened to draw. [5] set down alone. [6] distinction. [7] prepare for. [8] *ut ... dimices*, apposition with *discrimen*. [9] forthwith. [10] mysterious words.

"in te magis quam in me hostilia ausus.   Iuberem macte virtute[1]
40 esse, si pro meâ patriâ ista virtus staret: nunc iure[2] belli liberum
te intactum inviolatumque hinc dimitto."   Tunc Mucius quasi
remunerans   meritum,   "Quandoquidem," inquit,   "est apud te
virtuti honos, ut beneficio tuleris a me, quod minis nequisti:
trecenti coniuravimus principes iuventutis Romanae, ut in te hac
45 viâ grassaremur.[3]   Mea prima sors fuit; ceteri, utcumque ceci-
derit primi, quoad te opportunum fortuna dederit, suo quisque
tempore aderunt."

---

[1] go on and prosper.   [2] abl. of separation.   [3] attack.

XVI. GAIUS PETRONIUS [ARBITER].

Gaius Petronius [Arbiter], a writer concerning whose personality there has been much discussion, is probably to be identified with the Gaius Petronius who was for some time the *maître de plaisirs* of Nero, — the Beau Brummel of Imperial Rome in the first century A.D. A man of great natural ability and unusual cultivation, he preferred a life of elegant dissipation to any serious pursuit. In 66 A.D., he was accused to the emperor of complicity in a plot, and at once committed suicide by opening his veins in a bath (Tacitus, *Annales*, xvi. 17). He wrote the work entitled *Satira* or *Satiricon* from which the following extracts are taken, — the best surviving example of the ancient world of manners. It depicts with absolute fidelity the daily life of the author's time, in narrating the adventures of two friends, Encolpius and Ascyltus, in one of the small cities of Campania. All classes of society are drawn with unusual power and merciless realism, from the standpoint of the man of the world. Its dialogue gives many specimens of the Latin of common life. Only a portion, however, of the work has survived, and the gaps in the existing portions are frequent.

The standard edition of the text is by Bücheler (Berlin, 1862; smaller edition, 1882). There is an edition of a portion of the work (the *Cena Trimalchionis*) with notes and a German translation by Friedländer (Leipzig, 1891); an edition in English (announced) by Waters (1895); an English translation of the whole by Kelly (London, 1854), and a good French translation by De Guerle (Paris, 1862).

A Parvenu's Dinner Party.   (ch. 31 foll.)

Tandem ergo discubuimus[1] pueris Alexandrinis aquam in manus nivatam infundentibus aliisque insequentibus ad pedes ac paronychia[2] cum ingenti subtilitate tollentibus. Ac ne in hoc quidem tam molesto tacebant officio, sed obiter cantabant. Ego experiri volui, an tota familia cantaret, itaque potionem poposci.   5
Paratissimus puer non minus me acido cantico excepit, et quisquis aliquid rogatus erat ut daret. Pantomimi chorum, non patris familiae[3] triclinium crederes. Allata est tamen gustatio[4] valde lauta; nam iam omnes discubuerant praeter ipsum Trimalchionem, cui locus novo more primus servabatur. Ceterum inter pro- 10

---

[1] took our places.   [2] agnails.   [3] a private gentleman.   [4] first course.

mulsidaria[1] asellus erat Corinthius cum bisaccio[2] positus, qui habebat olivas in alterā parte albas, in alterā nigras. Tegebant[3] asellum duae lances, in quarum marginibus nomen Trimalchionis inscriptum erat et argenti pondus. Ponticuli etiam ferruminati
15 sustinebant glires[4] melle ac papavere[5] sparsos. Fuerunt et tomacula super craticulam[6] argenteam ferventia posita, et infra craticulam Syriaca pruna cum granis Punici mali.[7]

In his eramus lautitiis, cum ipse Trimalchio ad symphoniam allatus est positusque inter cervicalia[8] munitissima[9] expressit

THE CAROUSAL.
(*From the painting by Alma Tadema.*)

20 imprudentibus risum. Pallio enim coccineo adrasum[10] excluserat caput circaque oneratas veste cervices laticlaviam immiserat mappam[11] fimbriis[12] hinc atque illinc pendentibus. Habebat etiam in minimo digito sinistrae manus anulum grandem subauratum,[13] extremo vero articulo digiti sequentis minorem, ut mihi vide-
25 batur, totum aureum, sed plane ferreis veluti stellis ferrumina-tum. Et ne has tantum ostenderet divitias, dextrum nudavit lacertum armillā aureā cultum et eboreo[14] circulo laminā[15] splen-dente conexo. Ut deinde pinnā[16] argenteā dentes perfodit,

---

[1] dainties. [2] double pack. [3] flanked. [4] dormice. [5] poppy. [6] gridiron. [7] pomegranate. [8] cushions. [9] well-stuffed. [10] shaven. [11] napkin. [12] fringed edges. [13] gilded. [14] ivory. [15] clasp. [16] toothpick.

"Amici," inquit "nondum mihi suave erat in triclinium venire, sed ne diutius absentivos morae vobis essem, omnem voluptatem mihi negavi. Permittetis tamen finiri lusum." Sequebatur puer cum tabulā terebinthinā[1] et crystallinis tesseris,[2] notavique rem omnium delicatissimam. Pro calculis enim albis ac nigris aureos argenteosque habebat denarios. Interim dum ille omnium textorum dicta inter lusum consumit, gustantibus adhuc nobis repositorium[3] allatum est cum corbe,[4] in quo gallina erat lignea patentibus in orbem alis, quales esse solent quae incubant ova. Accessere continuo duo servi et symphoniā strepente scrutari paleam[5] coeperunt erutaque subinde pavonina ova divisere convivis. Convertit ad hanc scaenam Trimalchio vultum et "Amici," ait "pavonis ova gallinae iussi supponi. Et mehercules timeo ne iam concepti[6] sint; temptemus tamen, si adhuc sorbilia[7] sunt." Accipimus nos coclearia non minus selibras pendentia ovaque ex farinā[8] pingui figurata pertundimus. Ego quidem paene proieci partem meam, nam videbatur mihi iam in pullum coisse. Deinde ut audivi veterem convivam: "Hic nescio quid boni debet esse," persecutus putamen[9] manu pinguissimam ficedulam[10] inveni piperato vitello[11] circumdatam.

Advenerunt ministri ac toralia[12] praeposuerunt toris, in quibus retia erant picta subsessoresque cum venabulis et totus venationis apparatus. Necdum sciebamus, quo mitteremus suspiciones nostras, cum extra triclinium clamor sublatus est ingens, et ecce canes Laconici etiam circa mensam discurrere coeperunt. Secutum est hos repositorium, in quo positus erat primae magnitudinis aper, et quidem pilleatus,[13] e cuius dentibus sportellae[14] dependebant duae palmulis textae, altera caryotis[15] altera thebaicis[16] repleta. Circa autem minores porcelli ex coptoplacentis[17] facti, quasi uberibus imminerent, scrofam[18] esse positam significabant.

---

[1] pine. [2] checkers. [3] tray. [4] basket. [5] straw. [6] ready to be hatched. [7] worth sucking. [8] paste. [9] shell. [10] reed-bird. [11] yolk. [12] coverings. [13] with a cap on. [14] little baskets. [15] dates. [16] figs. [17] cake. [18] sow.

Et hi quidem apophoreti[1] fuerunt. Ceterum ad scindendum aprum
60 accessit barbatus ingens, fasciis[2] cruralibus alligatus et aliculā[3]
subornatus polymitā[4] strictoque venatorio cultro latus apri
vehementer percussit, ex cuius plagā turdi[5] evolaverunt. Parati
aucupes[6] cum harundinibus fuerunt et eos circa triclinium voli-
tantes momento exceperunt. Inde cum suum cuique iussisset
65 referri, Trimalchio adiecit: "Etiam videte, quam porcus ille
silvaticus lotam comederit glandem." Statim pueri ad sportellas
accesserunt, quae pendebant e dentibus, thebaicasque et caryotas
ad numerum[7] divisere cenantibus.

Repositorium cum sue ingenti mensam occupavit. Mirari nos
70 celeritatem coepimus et iurare, ne gallum quidem gallinaceum
tam cito percoqui[8] potuisse, tanto quidem magis, quod longe
maior nobis porcus videbatur esse, quam paulo ante aper fuerat.
Deinde magis magisque Trimalchio intuens eum, "Quid? Quid?"
inquit "porcus hic non est exinteratus?[9] Non mehercules est.
75 Voca, voca cocum in medio." Cum constitisset ad mensam cocus
tristis et diceret se oblitum esse exinterare, "Quid? oblitus?"
Trimalchio exclamat "Putes illum piper et cuminum[10] non
coniecisse. Despolia."[11] Non fit mora, despoliatur cocus atque
inter duos tortores[12] maestus consistit. Deprecari tamen omnes
80 coeperunt et dicere: "Solet fieri; rogamus, mittas; postea si
fecerit, nemo nostrûm pro illo rogabit." Ego, crudelissimae
severitatis,[13] non potui me tenere, sed inclinatus ad aurem Aga-
memnonis "Plane" inquam "hic debet servus esse nequissimus;
aliquis obliviscatur porcum exinterare? Non mehercules illi
85 ignoscerem, si piscem praeterisset." At non Trimalchio, qui
relaxato in hilaritatem vulto "Ergo" inquit "quia tam malae
memoriae es, palam nobis illum exintera." Receptā cocus tunicā
cultrum arripuit porcique ventrem hinc atque illinc timidā manu

[1] souvenirs. [2] drawers. [3] light cloak. [4] richly wrought. [5] thrushes. [6] bird catchers.
[7] to music. [8] well-cooked. [9] dressed. [10] seasoning. [11] strip him. [12] overseers. [13] genitive
of characteristic.

secuit. Nec mora, ex plagis ponderis inclinatione crescentibus
tomacula cum botulis [1] effusa sunt. 90

Plausum post hoc automatum [2] familia dedit et "Gaio feliciter!" [3] conclamavit.

Nec diu mirari licuit tam elegantes strophas [4]; nam repente
lacunaria [5] sonare coeperunt totumque triclinium intremuit. Con-
sternatus ego exsurrexi et timui, ne per tectum petauristarius [6] 95
aliquis descenderet. Nec minus reliqui convivae mirantes erexere
vultus, expectantes quid novi de coelo nuntiaretur. Ecce autem
diductis lacunaribus subito circulus ingens, de cupā [7] videlicet
grandi excussus demittitur, cuius per totum orbem coronae aureae
cum alabastris unguenti pendebant. Haec apophoreta [8] iubemur 100
sumere.

Iam illic repositorium cum placentis aliquot erat positum,
quod medium Priapus a pistore factus tenebat, gremioque satis

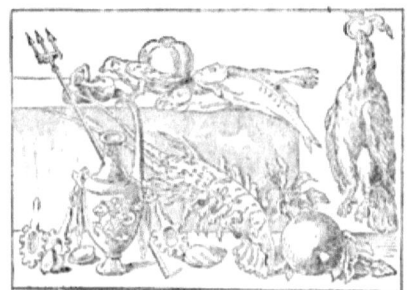

ROMAN LARDER.
(*Herculaneum.*)

amplo omnis generis poma et
uvas sustinebat more vulga- 105
to. Avidius ad pompam [9]
manus porreximus, et repente
nova ludorum missio hilaritatem hic refecit. Omnes
enim placentae [10] omniaque 110
poma etiam minimā vexa-
tione contacta coeperunt ef-
fundere crocum [11] et usque ad
os molestus umor accidere. Rati ergo sacrum esse fericulum
tam religioso apparatu [12] perfusum, consurreximus altius et 115
"Augusto, patri patriae, feliciter," diximus. Quibusdam tamen
etiam post hanc venerationem poma rapientibus et ipsi mappas
implevimus, ego praecipue, qui nullo satis amplo munere puta-

---

[1] mincemeat. [2] spontaneous. [3] good luck to Gaius ! [4] devices. [5] ceiling. [6] acrobat.
[7] dome. [8] souvenirs. [9] magnificent display. [10] cakes. [11] saffron water (perfume). [12] preparation.

bam me onerare Gitonis sinum. Inter haec tres pueri candidas
120 succincti tunicas intraverunt, quorum duo Lares bullatos[1] super
mensam posuerunt, unus pateram[2] vini circumferens "Dii propitii" clamabat.

The Werewolf. (ch. 62.)

MILIARIUM.

Forte dominus Capuam exierat ad scruta[3] scita
expedienda. Nactus ego occasionem persuadeo hospitem nostrum, ut mecum ad quintum miliarium[4] veniat.
Erat autem miles, fortis tanquam Orcus. Apocula-
5 mus[5] nos circa gallicinia[6]; luna lucebat tanquam
meridie. Venimus intra monumenta: homo meus
coepit ad stelas[7] facere,[8] sedeo ego cantabundus et
stelas numero. Deinde ut respexi ad comitem, ille
exuit se et omnia vestimenta secundum viam posuit.
10 Mihi anima in naso esse; stabam tanquam mortuus.
At ille circumivit vestimenta sua et subito lupus factus est.
Nolite me iocari putare; ut mentiar, nullius patrimonium tanti
facio. Sed, quod coeperam dicere, postquam lupus factus est,
ululare coepit et in silvas fugit. Ego primitus[9] nesciebam ubi
15 essem, deinde accessi, ut vestimenta eius tollerem: illa autem
lapidea facta sunt. Qui mori timore nisi ego? Gladium tamen
strinxi et in totā viā umbras[10] cecidi,[11] donec ad villam amicae
meae pervenirem. Ut larva[12] intravi, paene animam ebullivi,[13]
sudor mihi per bifurcum[14] volabat, oculi mortui, vix unquam
20 refectus sum. Melissa mea mirari coepit. quod tam sero ambu-
larem, et "Si ante" inquit "venisses, saltem nobis adiutâsses;
lupus enim villam intravit et omnia pecora perculit, tanquam
lanius[15] sanguinem illis misit. Nec tamen derisit. etiam si
fugit; servus enim noster lanceā collum eius traiecit." Haec ut

---

[1] wearing amulets. [2] bowl. [3] wares. [4] milestone. [5] start off. [6] cock-crow. [7] tombstones. [8] sc. se; "betake himself." [9] at first. [10] ghosts. [11] hacked at. [12] pale as a ghost. [13] kicked the bucket. [14] crotch. [15] butcher.

audivi, operire oculos amplius non potui, sed luce clarā Gai 25
nostri domum fugi tanquam copo[1] compilatus, et postquam veni
in illum locum, in quo lapidea vestimenta erant facta, nihil
inveni nisi sanguinem.   Ut vero domum veni, iacebat miles
meus in lecto tanquam bovis, et collum illius medicus curabat.
Intellexi illum versipellem[2] esse, nec postea cum illo panem 30
gustare potui, non si me occidisses.   Viderint alii quid de hoc
exopinissent[3]; ego si mentior, genios vestros iratos habeam.

---

[1] peddler.   [2] "turn-skin," i.e. werewolf.   [3] think (present subjunctive).

XVII. GAIUS PLINIUS SECUNDUS MAIOR.

Gaius Plinius Secundus Maior, a famous encyclopaedic writer, usually spoken of as "Pliny the Elder" to distinguish him from his nephew, was born in the north of Italy (probably at Novum Comum) in 23 A.D. After seeing service in the German campaign of which he wrote an account now lost, he studied law; but gave up active practice to devote himself to study and the composition of literature. As a student his industry was extraordinary. He rose at two o'clock in the morning and read all day, having a slave read aloud to him at meal-time and while he was in his bath; and of all that was read he took copious notes, so that on his death he left to his nephew one hundred and sixty volumes of memoranda. From these materials he wrote, among other works, the monumental *Historia Naturalis* in thirty-seven books, -- a great storehouse of encyclopaedic knowledge that has been of inestimable value to archaeologists and historians. It deals with astronomy, geography, botany, mineralogy, meteorology, medicine, zoölogy, inventions and institutions, and the fine arts, — besides touching on many other topics of great interest. In his preface he says that in its compilation he drew upon some two thousand books; and he has, besides, incorporated many facts observed by himself. Pliny died in the eruption of Vesuvius, 79 A.D.

The standard edition of the Latin text is that of Detlefsen in 6 vols. (Berlin, 1882). There is an English translation with an index, by Bostock and Riley, in the Bohn Series (London, 1859); and one in French by Littré (Paris, 1848–50).

The Jewels of Lollia Paulina.   (ix. 58.)

Lolliam Paulinam quae fuit Gai principis matrona,[1] ne serio[2] quidem aut sollemni caerimoniarum aliquo apparatu sed mediocrium etiam sponsalium cenā, vidi smaragdis[3] margaritisque[4] opertam, alterno textu fulgentibus toto capite, crinibus, spiris,[5]
5 auribus, collo, manibus,[6] digitisque: quae summa quadringenties IIS.[7] colligebat: ipsa confestim parata mancipationem[8] tabulis[9] probare. Nec dona prodigi principis fuerant, sed avitae opes, provinciarum scilicet spoliis partae. Hic est rapinarum exitus: hoc fuit quare M. Lollius infamatus regum muneribus in toto

---

[1] wife. [2] formal. [3] emeralds. [4] pearls. [5] braids. [6] arms. [7] 40,000,000 sesterces. [8] value.
[9] receipted bills.

126

Oriente, interdictā amicitiā a Gaio Caesare Augusti filio venenum 10
biberet ut neptis[1] eius quadringenties HS. operta spectaretur
ad lucernas.[2] Computet nunc aliquis ex alterā parte quantum
Curius aut Fabricius in triumphis tulerint; imaginetur illorum
fercula; et ex alterā parte Lolliam, unam imperii mulierculam
accubantem: non illos curru detractos quam in hoc vicisse 15
malit?

A Cure for the Hydrophobia. (XXIX. 32.)

In canis rabiosi morsu tuetur a pavore aquae capitis canini
cinis illitus[3] vulneri. Oportet autem comburi omnia eodem
modo, ut semel dicamus, in vase fictili novo, argillā[4] circumlito,
atque ita in furnum indito. Idem et in potione proficit. Quidam
ob id edendum dederunt. Aliqui et vermem e cadavere canino 5
adalligavere, . . . aut ipsius caudae pilos combustos insuere vulneri. Cor caninum habentem fugiunt canes. Non latrant[5] vero
linguā caninā in calceamento[6] subditā pollici,[7] aut caudam
mustelae[8] quae abscissa dimissa sit habentes. Est limus salivae
sub linguā rabiosi canis qui datus in potu fieri hydrophobus non 10
patitur. Multo tamen utilissime iecur eius qui in rabie momorderit datur, si possit fieri, crudum[9] mandendum[10]: si minus,
quoquo modo coctum aut ius coctis carnibus. Est vermiculus
in linguā canum qui vocatur a Graecis *lytta;* quo exempto
infantibus catulis nec rabidi fiunt nec fastidium sentiunt. . . . 15
Et cerebello gallinaceo occurritur; sed id devoratum anno tantum
eo prodest. Aiunt et cristam galli contritam efficaciter imponi
et anseris adipem[11] cum melle. Saliuntur et carnes eorum qui
rabidi fuerunt ad eadem remedia in cibo dandae. Quin et necan-
tur catuli statim in aquā ad sexum eius qui momorderit ut iecur 20
crudum devoretur ex iis.

---

[1] granddaughter. [2] by lamplight. [3] plastered over. [4] clay. [5] bark. [6] shoe. [7] great toe.
[8] weasel. [9] raw. [10] to be chewed. [11] goose-grease.

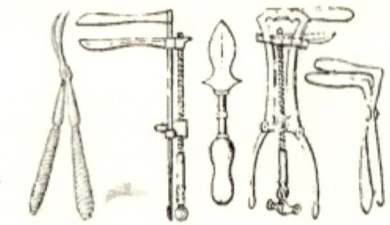

SURGICAL INSTRUMENTS FOUND AT
POMPEII.

Dissederuntque diu scholae:
et omnes eas damnavit Herophilus, in musicos pedes venarum
pulsu descripto per aetatum
gradus. Deserta deinde et[1] haec
secta est: quoniam necesse erat
in ea literas scire. Mutata et
quam postea Asclepiades (ut
retulimus) invenerat. Auditor eius Themison fuit, qui quae inter
initia scripsit, illo mox recedente a vitã, ad sua placita[2] mutavit.
Sed et[1] illa Antonius Musa eiusdem auctoritate Divi Augusti,
quem contrariã medicinã gravi periculo exemerat. Multos prae-
tereo medicos, celeberrimosque ex iis Cassios, Calpetanos, Arrun-
tios, Albutios, Rubrios. Ducena quinquagena HS[3] annuã
mercede iis fuere apud principes. Q. vero Stertinius imputavit
principibus, quod HS quingenis[4] annuis contentus esset: sex-
cena[5] enim sibi quaestu urbis fuisse numeratis domibus ostende-
bat. Par et fratri eius merces[6] a Claudio Caesare infusa est:
censusque, quamquam exhausti, operibus Neapoli exornatã, heredi
HS CCC[7] reliquere, quantum ad eam aetatem Arruntius solus.
Exortus deinde est Vectius Valens, adulterio Messalinae Claudii[8]
Caesaris nobilitatus.[9] pariterque eloquentiae assectator. Is eam
potentiam nactus,[10] novam instituit sectam. Eadem aetas Nero-
nis principatu ad Thessalum transilivit, delentem cuncta maiorum placita, et rabie quãdam in omnis aevi medicos perorantem:
quali prudentiã ingenioque. aestimari vel uno argumento abunde
potest, cum monumento suo (quod est Appiã Viã) IATRONICEN
se inscripserit. Nullius histrionum equarumque trigarii[11] comi-
tatior egressus in publico erat: cum Crinas Massiliensis arte

---

[1] = *etiam*. [2] according to his own whims. [3] 250,000 sesterces. [4] 500,000. [5] 600,000. [6] income. [7] 30,000,000. [8] sc. *mulieris*. [9] made notorious. [10] having acquired. [11] jockey.

geminatā[1] ut cautior religiosiorque, ad siderum motus ex 30
ephemeride mathematicā cibos dando, horasque observando,
auctoritate eum praecessit : nuperque centies HS reliquit, muris
patriae, moenibusque aliis paene non minori summā exstructis.
Hi regebant fata, cum repente civitatem Charmis ex eādem
Massilia invasit, damnatis non solum prioribus medicis, verum 35
et[2] balineis : frigidāque[3] etiam hibernis algoribus lavari persuasit. Mersit aegros in lacus. Videbamus senes consulares
usque in ostentationem[4] rigentes. Quā de re exstat etiam Annaei
Senecae stipulatio.[5] Nec dubium est, omnes istos famam novitate aliquā aucupantes[6] animā statim nostrā negotiari. Hinc 40
illae circa aegros miserae sententiarum concertationes, nullo
idem censente, ne videatur accessio[7] alterius. Hinc illa infelicis monumenti inscriptio, TURBĀ SE MEDICORUM PERISSE.
Mutatur ars quotidie, toties interpolis,[8] et ingeniorum Graeciae
flatu impellimur : palamque est, ut quisque inter istos loquendo 45
polleat, imperatorem ilico vitae nostrae necisque fieri : ceu[9] vero
non milia gentium sine medicis degant, nec tamen sine medicinā :
sicut populus Romanus ultra sexcentesimum annum, nec ipse in
accipiendis artibus lentus, medicinae vero etiam avidus, donec
expertam[10] damnavit. 50

Etenim percensere insignia priscorum in his moribus convenit.
Cassius Hemina ex antiquissimis auctor est primum e medicis
venisse Romam Peloponneso Archagatum Lysaniae filium, L.
Aemilio, L. Iulio consulibus anno urbis DXXXV., eique ius
Quiritium datum, et tabernam in compito Acilio emptam ob id 55
publice : "Vulnerarium" eum fuisse e re dictum : mireque gratum adventum eius initio : mox a saevitiā secandi urendique.
transisse nomen in "Carnificem,"[11] et in taedium artem omnes-
que medicos : quod clarissime intelligi potest ex M. Catone,

---

[1] pursuing a twofold trade.   [2] = etiam.   [3] sc. aquā.   [4] for show.   [5] statement.   [6] hunting
for reputation.   [7] yielding to another.   [8] revamped.   [9] just as if.   [10] after having tried it.
[11] executioner.

60 cuius auctoritati triumphus atque censura minimum conferunt[1];
tanto plus in ipso est. Quamobrem verba eius ipsa ponemus : —
    "Dicam de istis Graecis suo loco, Marce fili : quid Athenis
exquisitum habeam, et quod bonum sit illorum litteras inspicere,
non perdiscere, vincam.[2] Nequissimum et indocile genus illo-
65 rum ; et hoc puta vatem[3] dixisse : Quandocumque ista gens suas
litteras dabit, omnia corrumpet : tum etiam magis, si medicos
suos huc mittet. Iurârunt inter se barbaros necare omnes medi-
cinâ. Et hoc ipsum mercede faciunt, ut fides iis sit, et facile
disperdant. Nos quoque dictitant barbaros, et spurcius[4] nos,
70 quam alios Opicos, appellatione foedant.[5] Interdixi tibi de
medicis."
    Atque hic Cato DCV anno urbis nostrae obiit, LXXXV suo, ne
quis illi defuisse publice tempora aut privatim vitae spatia ad
experiendum arbitretur. Quid ergo ? damnatam ab eo rem uti-
75 lissimam credimus? Minime hercules! subiicit enim quâ medi-
cinâ, et se et coniugem usque ad longam senectam perduxerit,
iis ipsis scilicet, quae nunc nos tractamus ; profiteturque esse
commentarium sibi, quo medeatur filio, servis, familiaribus, quem
nos per genera usus sui digerimus. Non rem antiqui damnabant,
80 sed artem. Maxime vero quaestum esse immani pretio vitae
recusabant. Ideo templum Aesculapii, etiam cum reciperetur is
deus, extra urbem fecisse, iterumque in insulâ traduntur. Et
cum Graecos Italiâ pellerent, diu etiam post Catonem, excepisse[6]
medicos. Augebo providentiam illorum. Solam hanc artium
85 Graecarum nondum exercet Romana gravitas[7] in tanto fructu :
paucissimi Quiritium attigere, et ipsi statim ad Graecos transfugae : immo vero auctoritas aliter quam Graece eam tractanti-
bus, etiam apud imperitos expertesque linguae, non est. Ac
minus credunt, quae ad salutem suam pertinent, si intelligunt.
90 Itaque, hercule, in hac artium solâ evenit, ut cuicumque medicum

---

[1] ascribe.   [2] I shall set forth.   [3] a prophet.   [4] more outrageously.   [5] insult.   [6] expressly
mentioned.   [7] dignity.

se professo statim credatur, cum sit periculum in nullo menda-
cio maius.   Non tamen illud intuemur, adeo blanda est sperandi
pro se cuique dulcedo!   Nulla praeterea lex, quae puniat insci-
tiam [1]: capitale nullum exemplum vindictae.[2]   Discunt periculis
nostris, et experimenta per mortes agunt: medicoque tantum 95
hominem occidisse impunitas summa est!

---

[1] malpractice.   [2] punishment.

XVIII. MARCUS FABIUS QUINTILIANUS.

Marcus Fabius Quintilianus was a native of Spain, where he was born about
40 A.D. Educated at Rome, he long resided at the capital as a professional
teacher of rhetoric and oratory, receiving a regular salary from the imperial
treasury. Among his pupils were Pliny the Younger and the grandnephew of
the emperor Domitian. In the later years of his life he published a work, in
twelve books, on the complete training of an orator from childhood up, in which
he summarized his own practical experiences and observations as a teacher.
This treatise, which is entitled *Institutio Oratoria*, is written in a clear and
pleasant style, and exhibits both good taste and common sense. Its illustra-
tions drawn from Roman sources, its judgments upon the great works of ancient
literature, and its occasional anecdotes regarding historical personages, are all
of permanent interest and value. Quintilian died about 95 A.D.

The standard edition of the text of Quintilian is that of Carl Halm, revised
by Meister (Prague, 1886-87), and of Books X. and XII., with notes by Frieze
(New York, 1889). There is a fair translation by Watson, in the Bohn series;
and a lexicon by Bonnell, in Spalding's edition (1834).

On the Whipping of Boys in School. (i. 3.)

Caedi[1] vero discipulos, quamlibet et receptum sit et Chrysippus
non improbet, minime velim. Primum, quia deforme atque ser-
vile est et certe, quod convenit si aetatem mutes,[2] iniuria; deinde,
quod, si cui tam est mens illiberalis, ut obiurgatione non corriga-
5 tur, is etiam ad plagas ut pessima quaeque mancipia[3] durabitur;
postremo, quod ne opus erit quidem hac castigatione, si assiduus
studiorum exactor astiterit. Nunc fere negligentia paedagogorum
sic emendari videtur, ut pueri non facere, quae recta sunt, cogantur
sed, cum non fecerint, puniantur. Denique cum parvulum ver-
10 beribus coegeris, quid iuveni facias, cui nec adhiberi potest hic
metus et maiora discenda sunt? Adde, quod multa vapulantibus[4]
dictu deformia et mox verecundiae futura saepe dolore vel metu
acciderunt, qui pudor frangit animum et abiicit atque ipsius lucis

---

[1] to be beaten. [2] i.e., if you imagine the age to be changed. [3] slaves. [4] those who are beaten.

fugam et taedium dictat. Non morabor in parte hac ; nimium est
quod intelligitur.   Quare hoc dixisse satis est ; in aetatem infir- 15
mam et iniuriae obnoxiam nemini debet nimium licere.

Some Roman Jokes.   (vi. 3.)

Refutatio [1] cum sit in negando, redarguendo,[2] defendendo, ele-
vando[3]: ridicule negavit Manius Curius ; nam, cum eius accusator
in sipario[4] omnibus locis aut nudum eum in nervo[5] aut ab amicis re-
demptum ex aleā pinxisset: " Ergo ego," inquit. "numquam vici?"
Redarguimus interim aperte, ut Cicero Vibium Curium multum de   5
annis aetatis suae mentientem, "Tum ergo, cum una declamaba-
mus, non eras natus" ; interim et simulatā assensione, ut idem
Fabiā Dolabellae[6] dicente, triginta se annos habere, "Verum est,"
inquit ; " nam hoc illam viginti annis audio."   Belle interim
subiicitur pro eo, quod neges, aliud mordacius : ut Iunius Bassus,   10
querente Domitiā Passieni, quod incusans eius sordes calceos eam
veteres diceret vendere solere, " Non mehercules," inquit, " hoc umquam dixi ; sed dixi, emere te solere."   Defensionem imitatus est
eques Romanus, qui obiicienti Augusto, quod patrimonium come-
disset, " Meum," inquit, " putavi."   Elevandi ratio est duplex, ut   15
aut verecundiam quis aut iactantiam minuat : quemadmodum C.
Caesar Pomponio ostendenti vulnus ore exceptum in seditione
Sulpicianā, quod is se passum pro Caesare pugnantem gloriaba-
tur,[7] "Numquam fugiens respexeris," inquit : aut crimen obiectum,
ut Cicero obiurgantibus, quod sexagenarius Publiliam virginem   20
duxisset, "Cras mulier erit," inquit.   Hoc genus dicti consequens
vocant quidam, atque illi simile, quod Cicero Curionem semper
ab excusatione aetatis incipientem, " facilius cotidie prooemium [8]
habere," dixit ; quia ista naturā sequi et cohaerere videantur.
Sed elevandi genus est etiam causarum relatio, quā Cicero est   25

---

[1] retort.   [2] rebuttal.   [3] extenuation.   [4] on a curtain.   [5] in bonds.   [6] i.e., the wife of Dolabella.
[7] was boasting.   [8] exordium.

usus in Vatinium. Qui pedibus aeger, cum vellet videri commodioris valetudinis factus et diceret, se iam bina milia passuum ambulare, "Dies enim," inquit, "longiores sunt." Et Augustus nuntiantibus Tarraconensibus, palmam in arā eius enatam, "Apparet," inquit, "quam saepe accendatis.[1]" Transtulit[2] crimen Cassius Severus. Nam cum obiurgaretur a praetore, quod advocati eius L. Varo Epicureo, Caesaris amico, convicium fecissent, "Nescio," inquit, "qui conviciati sint, et puto Stoicos fuisse."

---

[1] make a fire on it. [2] shifted (to another).

XIX. MARCUS VALERIUS MARTIALIS.

Marcus Valerius Martialis was born at Bilbilis in Spain in the year 40 A.D., and died in the year 102. He went to Rome to pursue legal studies, but preferred, as he himself says, *casu vivere*, to get his living by flattering the emperors, especially Domitian, and the rich nobles. He returned to his native home so poor that the younger Pliny was obliged to give him money for the journey. His fame rests on fifteen books of epigrams, depicting all the follies and vices of his time, with spirit and cutting wit, but without any moral feeling.

The chief edition of the text is that of Friedländer (Leipzig, 1886). There are no adequate translations of the epigrams into English.

Thirteen Epigrams.

i. 9.

Bellus[1] homo et magnus vis idem, Cotta, videri:
　Sed qui bellus homo est, Cotta, pusillus[2] homo est.

i. 16.

Sunt bona, sunt quaedam mediocria, sunt mala plura
　Quae legis hic[3]: aliter non fit, Avite, liber.

i. 19.

Si memini, fuerant tibi quattuor, Aelia, dentes:
　Expulit una duos tussis[4] et una duos.
Iam secura[5] potes totis tussire diebus:
　Nil istic quod agat tertia tussis habet.

i. 32.

Non amo te, Sabidi, nec possum dicere quare:
　Hoc tantum possum dicere, non amo te.

---

[1] pretty. [2] petty. [3] i.e., in my book. [4] cough. [5] at your ease.

i. 47.

Nuper erat medicus, nunc est vispillo [1] Diaulus:
Quod vispillo facit, fecerat et medicus.

i. 56.

Continuis vexata madet vindemia nimbis:
Non potes, ut cupias, vendere, copo, [2] merum.

i. 72.

Nostris versibus esse te poetam,
Fidentine, putas cupisque credi?
Sic dentata [3] sibi videtur Aegle
Emptis ossibus Indicoque cornu; [4]

5   Sic quae nigrior est cadente moro, [5]
Cerussata [6] sibi placet Lycoris.
Hac et tu ratione qua poeta es,
Calvus [7] cum fueris, eris comatus.

i. 109.

Issa est purior osculo columbae,
Issa est blandior omnibus puellis,
Issa est carior Indicis lapillis, [8]
Issa est deliciae catella [9] Publi.

5   Hanc tu, si queritur, loqui putabis;
Sentit tristitiamque gaudiumque.
Collo nixa [10] cubat capitque somnos,
Ut suspiria nulla sentiantur;
Ignorat Venerem; nec invenimus

10   Dignum tam tenera virum [11] puella.
Hanc ne lux rapiat suprema totam,

---

[1] undertaker.   [2] barkeeper.   [3] possessed of teeth.   [4] ivory.   [5] mulberry.   [6] enameled.
[7] bald.   [8] precious stones.   [9] lapdog.   [10] resting.   [11] mate.

Pictā Publius exprimit tabellā,
In quā tam similem videbis Issam,
Ut sit tam similis sibi nec ipsa.
Issam denique pone [1] cum tabellā: 15
Aut utramque putabis esse veram,
Aut utramque putabis esse pictam.

ii. 12.

Esse quid hoc dicam, quod olent tua basia myrrham
  Quodque tibi est nunquam non alienus odor?
Hoc mihi suspectum est, quod oles bene, Postume, semper:
  Postume, non bene olet qui bene semper olet.

ii. 25.

Das nunquam, semper promittis. Galla, roganti.
  Si semper fallis, iam rogo, Galla, nega.

iii. 15.

Plus credit [2] nemo totā quam Cordus in urbe.
  "Cum sit tam pauper, quomodo?" Caecus amat. [3]

v. 43.

Thaïs habet nigros, niveos Laecania dentes.
  Quae ratio est? Emptos [4] haec habet, illa suos.

---

[1] compare.   [2] gives more credit.   [3] he is blindly in love.   [4] bought.

XX. DECIMUS IUNIUS IUVENALIS.

Decimus Iunius Iuvenalis was born about 47 A.D. at the Volscian town of Aquinum, and died about 130. He was either the son or protégé of a rich freedman, but raised himself to the rank of knight. His extant works consist of sixteen satires on the foibles and vices of society at Rome under Domitian, and were probably written at an advanced age. Juvenal is supposed to have been banished for satirizing the influence of the actor Paris at the imperial court, and hence died in exile. The Satires are highly rhetorical in their tone, so much so as to lessen their effect by producing an impression of insincerity. They abound in epigrammatic lines and phrases, many of which have become proverbial; while his studied antitheses and anticlimaxes with his occasional irreverent freedom of expression have led some editors to compare him with James Russell Lowell in the *Biglow Papers*, and to describe his rather grim wit as "the earliest known instance of American humor." A very full commentary is that of Mayor (London, 1886); a very convenient one, that of Lindsay (N. Y., 1890). A good verse translation is that of Gifford, and a good prose rendering that of J. D. Lewis. Dr. Samuel Johnson's paraphrase of Satires III. and X., under the respective titles of *London* and *The Vanity of Human Wishes*, are fine imitations in spirited and energetic verse, and contain lines that by their epigrammatic form have become almost as famous as any in the original.

City Life in Rome. (iii. 193-314.)

Nos urbem colimus tenui tibicine[1] fultam[2]
Magnā parte sui; nam sic labentibus obstat
Vilicus[3] et, veteris rimae[4] cum texit hiatum,
Securos pendente iubet dormire ruinā.
5 Vivendum est illic, ubi nulla incendia, nulli
Nocte metus. Iam poscit aquam, iam frivola[5] transfert
Ucalegon; tabulata[6] tibi iam tertia fumant;
Tu nescis; nam si gradibus trepidatur[7] ab imis,
Ultimus ardebit, quem tegula[8] sola tuetur
10 A pluviā, molles ubi reddunt ova columbae.

---

[1] prop. [2] : imported. [3] steward. [4] crack. [5] traps. [6] story. [7] alarm begins. [8] tile.

A CHARIOT RACE.
(*Painting by Gérôme.*)

Lectus erat Codro Proculā minor, urceoli[1] sex,
Ornamentum abaci,[2] nec non et parvulus infra
Cantharus[3] et recubans sub eodem marmore Chiron.
Iamque vetus Graecos servabat cista[4] libelios,
Et divina opici[5] rodebant carmina mures.[6]   15
Nil habuit Codrus; quis enim negat? et tamen illud
Perdidit infelix totum nihil: ultimus autem
Aerumnae[7] est cumulus, quod nudum et frusta rogantem
Nemo cibo, nemo hospitio tectoque iuvabit.
Si magna Asturici cecidit domus, horrida[8] mater,   20
Pullati[9] proceres,[10] differt vadimonia[11] praetor;
Tunc gemimus casus urbis, tunc odimus ignem.
Ardet adhuc, et iam accurrit qui marmora donet,
Conferat impensas[12]: hic nuda et candida signa,[13]
Hic aliquid praeclarum Euphranoris et Polycliti,   25
Haec Asianorum vetera ornamenta deorum,
Hic libros dabit et forulos[14] mediamque[15] Minervam,
Hic modium[16] argenti; meliora ac plura reponit
Persicus orborum[17] lautissimus et merito iam

[1] jugs. [2] sideboard. [3] goblet. [4] chest. [5] vandal. [6] mice. [7] distress. [8] dishevelled.
[9] in mourning. [10] nobles. [11] adjourns court. [12] expenses. [13] statues. [14] bookcases. [15] bust
of. [16] peck. [17] destitute.

30   Suspectus, tamquam ipse suas incenderit aedes.
        Si potes avelli circensibus,[1] optima Sorae
        Aut Fabrateriae domus aut Frusinone paratur,
        Quanti nunc tenebras unum conducis[2] in annum.
        Hortulus hic puteusque[3] brevis nec reste[4] movendus
35   In tenues plantas facili diffunditur haustu.
        Vive bidentis[5] amans, et culti vilicus horti,
        Unde epulum possis centum dare Pythagoreis.

REDA.
(*Von Falke.*)

        Est aliquid, quocumque loco, quocumque recessu,
        Unius sese dominum fecisse lacertae.[6]
40   Plurimus hic aeger moritur vigilando: sed illum
        Languorem peperit cibus imperfectus et haerens
        Ardenti stomacho. Nam quae meritoria[7] somnum
        Admittunt? Magnis opibus dormitur in urbe:
        Inde caput morbi. Redarum transitus arcto[8]
45   Vicorum in flexu, et stantis convicia mandrae,[9]
        Eripient somnum Druso vitulisque[10] marinis.
        Si vocat officium, turbā cedente vehetur

---

[1] public shows.   [2] hire.   [3] well.   [4] rope.   [5] hoe.   [6] lizard.   [7] lodgings.   [8] narrow.   [9] team. [10] seals.

Dives, et ingenti curret super ora Liburno,[1]
Atque obiter[2] leget aut scribet vel dormiet intus,
Namque facit somnum clausā lectica[3] fenestrā.   50
Ante tamen veniet; nobis properantibus obstat
Unda prior, magno populus premit agmine lumbos
Qui sequitur; ferit hic cubito,[4] ferit assere[5] duro
Alter; at hic tignum[6] capiti incutit, ille metretam.[7]
Pinguia crura luto,[8] plantā[9] mox undique magnā   55
Calcor,[10] et in digito[11] clavus[12] mihi militis haeret.

WINE CART.
(*Pompeian Fresco.*)

Nonne vides quanto celebretur sportula[13] fumo?
Centum convivae; sequitur sua quemque culina.[14]
Corbulo vix ferret tot vasa ingentia, tot res
Impositas capiti, quot recto vertice portat   30
Servulus infelix et cursu ventilat[15] ignem.
Scinduntur[16] tunicae sartae[17]: modo longa coruscat[18]
Sarraco[19] veniente abies,[20] atque altera pinum
Plaustra[21] vehunt; nutant alte populoque minantur:
Nam si procubuit qui saxa Ligustica portat   65
Axis, et eversum fudit super agmina montem,

[1] sc. slave.   [2] on the way.   [3] litter.   [4] elbow.   [5] pole.   [6] beam.   [7] cask.   [8] mud.   [9] foot.
[10] trod.   [11] toe.   [12] hobnail.   [13] hamper,—here, food distributed.   [14] kitchen.   [15] blows.   [16] tear.
[17] patched.   [18] sways.   [19] cart.   [20] fir-beam.   [21] wagons.

Quid superest de corporibus? quis membra, quis ossa
Invenit?   Obtritum vulgi perit omne cadaver
More animae.[1]   Domus [2] interea secura patellas
Iam lavat, et buccā [3] foculum excitat, et sonat unctis
Striglibus,[4] et pleno componit lintea [5] gutto.[6]
Haec inter pueros varie properantur: at ille
Iam sedet in ripā, taetrumque novicius[7] horret
Porthmea,[8] nec sperat coenosi [9] gurgitis alnum,[10]
Infelix, nec habet quem porrigat [11] ore trientem.[12]
   Respice nunc alia ac diversa pericula noctis:
Quod spatium tectis sublimibus, unde cerebrum
Testa [13] ferit, quoties rimosa et curta [14] fenestris
Vasa cadunt; quanto percussum pondere signent
Et laedant [15] silicem.[16]   Possis ignavus haberi
Et subiti casus improvidus, ad cenam si
Intestatus eas.   Adeo tot fata, quot illā
Nocte patent vigiles, te praetereunte, fenestrae.
Ergo optes, votumque feras miserabile tecum,
Ut sint contentae patulas [17] defundere pelves.[18]
   Ebrius ac petulans,[19] qui nullum forte cecidit,
Dat poenas,[20] noctem patitur lugentis amicum [21]
Pelidae,[22] cubat in faciem, mox deinde supinus.
Ergo non aliter poterit dormire?   Quibusdam
Somnum rixa facit: sed, quamvis improbus annis,
Atque mero fervens, cavet hunc, quem coccina laena [23]
Vitari iubet, et comitum longissimus ordo,
Multum praeterea flammarum et aënea lampas.
Me, quem luna solet deducere, vel breve lumen
Candelae, cuius dispenso et tempero filum,[24]

70

75

80

85

90

95

---

[1] like a breath.   [2] household.   [3] mouth.   [4] flesh-scrapers.   [5] linen.   [6] oil flask.   [7] newcomer.
[8] ferryman = Charon.   [9] foul.   [10] bark.   [11] offer.   [12] copper.   [13] potsherd.   [14] chipped.
[15] indent.   [16] flint pavement.   [17] broad.   [18] basins.   [19] quarrelsome.   [20] suffers torments.
[21] i.e., Patroclus.   [22] Achilles.   [23] scarlet cloak.   [24] wick.

Contemnit. Miserae cognosce prooemia[1] rixae,
Si rixa est, ubi tu pulsas, ego vapulo[2] tantum.
Stat contra starique iubet; parere necesse est:
Nam quid agas, cum te furiosus cogat et idem
Fortior? "Unde venis?" exclamat: "cuius aceto,[3]   100
Cuius conche[4] tumes[5]? quis tecum sectile porrum[6]
Sutor[7] et elixi vervecis[8] labra comedit?
Nil mihi respondes? Aut die, aut accipe calcem.[9]
Ede ubi consistas[10]; in quâ te quaero proseuchâ[11]?"
Dicere si temptes aliquid tacitusve recedas,   105
Tantumdem est: feriunt pariter, vadimonia[12] deinde
Irati faciunt; libertas pauperis haec est:
Pulsatus rogat et pugnis concisus[13] adorat,
Ut liceat paucis cum dentibus inde reverti.
Nec tamen haec tantum metuas; nam qui spoliet te   110
Non deerit, clausis domibus postquam omnis ubique
Fixa catenatae siluit compago[14] tabernae.
Interdum et ferro subitus grassator[15] agit rem:
Armato quoties tutae custode tenentur
Et Pomptina palus et Gallinaria pinus,   115
Sic inde huc omnes tamquam ad vivaria[16] currunt.
Quâ fornace[17] graves, quâ non incude[18] catenae?
Maximus in vinclis ferri modus,[19] ut timeas, ne
Vomer deficiat, ne marrae[20] et sarcula[21] desint.
Felices proavorum[22] atavos,[22] felicia dicas   120
Saecula, quae quondam sub regibus atque tribunis
Viderunt uno contentam carcere Romam.

---

[1] prelude. [2] get the beating. [3] sour wine. [4] beans. [5] puffed up. [6] chopped leek. [7] cobbler. [8] boiled sheepshead. [9] take a kick. [10] stand (as a beggar). [11] synagogue. [12] make you give bail. [13] cut up. [14] fastening. [15] footpad. [16] preserve. [17] forge. [18] anvil. [19] quantity. [20] mattocks. [21] hoes. [22] forefathers.

The Bluestocking.   (vi. 434-456.)

Illa tamen gravior, quae, cum discumbere[1] coepit,
Laudat Vergilium, periturae ignoscit Elissae,[2]
Committit vates[3] et comparat,[4] inde Maronem
Atque alia parte in trutina[5] suspendit Homerum.

5   Cedunt grammatici, vincuntur rhetores, omnis
Turba tacet; nec causidicus,[6] nec praeco[7] loquetur,
Altera nec mulier: verborum tanta cadit vis;
Tot pariter pelves[8] ac tintinnabula[9] dicas
Pulsari.   Iam nemo tubas, nemo aera[10] fatiget;

10   Una laboranti poterit succurrere lunae.
Imponit finem sapiens et rebus honestis;
Nam quae docta nimis cupit et facunda videri,
Crure tenus[11] medio tunicas succingere debet,
Caedere Silvano porcum, quadrante lavari.

15   Non habeat matrona, tibi quae iuncta recumbit,
Dicendi genus, aut curvum sermone rotato

---

[1] recline.   [2] Dido.   [3] bards.   [4] contrasts.   [5] balance.   [6] lawyer.   [7] herald.   [8] pans.
[9] bells.   [10] trumpet.   [11] as far as.

Torqueat enthymema [1] nec historias sciat omnes;
Sed quaedam ex libris et non intellegat.   Odi
Hanc ego, quae repetit volvitque Palaemonis artem,
Servatā semper lege et ratione loquendi,   20
Ignotosque mihi tenet antiquaria versus,
Nec curanda viris opicae castigat amicae
Verba: soloecismum [2] liceat fecisse marito.

Mens Sana in Corpore Sano.   (x. 346–366.)

"Nil ergo optabunt homines?"   Si consilium vis,
Permittes ipsis expendere [3] numinibus, quid
Conveniat nobis, rebusque sit utile nostris.
Nam pro iucundis aptissima quaeque dabunt di:
Carior est illis homo, quam sibi.   Nos, animorum   5
Impulsu et caecā magnāque cupidine ducti,
Coniugium petimus partumque [4] uxoris: at illis
Notum, qui pueri qualisque futura sit uxor.
Ut tamen et poscas aliquid, voveasque sacellis [5]
Exta, [6] et candiduli divina tomacula [7] porci: 10
Orandum est, ut sit mens sana in corpore sano;
Fortem posce animum, mortis terrore carentem,
Qui spatium vitae extremum inter munera ponat
Naturae, qui ferre queat quoscunque labores,
Nesciat irasci, cupiat nihil, et potiores   15
Herculis aerumnas credat saevosque labores
Et Venere et cenis et plumā [8] Sardanapali.
Monstro quod ipse tibi possis dare: semita [9] certe
Tranquillae per virtutem patet unica vitae.
Nullum numen habes, si sit prudentia: nos te,   20
Nos facimus, Fortuna, deam caeloque locamus.

---

[1] logical puzzle.   [2] blunder.   [3] decide.   [4] offspring.   [5] shrines.   [6] vitals.   [7] mincemeat.
[8] downy couch.   [9] path.

XXI. GAIUS PLINIUS CAECILIUS SECUNDUS (MINOR).

Gaius Plinius Caecilius Secundus (Minor) was born at Comum 61 A.D. Having lost his father at an early age, he was adopted by his uncle, the elder Pliny, whose name he assumed. From his earliest years he was devoted to literature, and his acquirements made him one of the most learned men of the age. When about seventeen years old he was at Misenum during the great eruption of Vesuvius, which destroyed Pompeii and in which his uncle lost his life. He filled various political offices under Domitian, and under Trajan served two years as propraetor of Pontus. This office, as his letters show, he administered with much activity and fidelity.

His private character and tastes appear in his own letters. He was a kindly and upright man, of cultivated mind, fond of simple country life, liberal, and public-spirited. He was twice married, but had no children. His letters are valuable as throwing light upon a great variety of topics, and present an agreeable picture of his own life and that of his friends and associates. They are written with much care, evidently with a view to publication, and in them the author constantly betrays an amiable desire for fame. Nothing is known as to the date or manner of his death.

His extant works are the *Panegyricus* (a eulogy on Trajan) and the ten books of his *Epistles*.

A standard text of Pliny is that of Keil (Leipzig, 1870). There is a good English translation of the letters by Lewis (London, 1879). There is a good edition of Bks. I. and II. by Cowan with English notes (London, 1889), and of Bk. III. by Mayor (London, 1880). Selected letters by Prichard and Bernard (Oxford, 1873).

The Eruption of Vesuvius. (*Epist.* vi. 20.)

C. PLINIUS TACITO SUO S.[1]

Ais te adductum litteris quas exigenti tibi [2] de morte avunculi mei scripsi cupere cognoscere quos ego Miseni [3] relictus (id enim ingressus abruperam) non solum metus verum etiam casus pertulerim. Quamquam animus meminisse horret, incipiam. Profecto
5 avunculo ipse reliquum tempus studiis (ideo enim remanseram)

---

[1] *salutem*, "greeting." [2] at your request. [3] locative.

impendi [1]: mox balineum,[2] cena, somnus inquietus et brevis.
Praecesserat per multos dies tremor terrae minus formidolosus
quia Campaniae solitus. Illā vero nocte ita invaluit[3] ut non
moveri omnia sed verti crederentur. Inrumpit cubiculum [4] meum
mater: surgebam invicem, si quiesceret, excitaturus. Residi- 10
mus in areā [5] domus, quae mare a tectis modico spatio dividebat.
Dubito constantiam vocare an inprudentiam debeam; agebam
enim duodevicensimum annum: posco librum Titi Livi et quasi

VESUVIUS AND REMAINS OF FORUM, POMPEII.

per otium lego atque etiam, ut coeperam, excerpo.[6] Ecce, amicus
avunculi, qui nuper ad eum ex Hispaniā venerat, ut me et matrem 15
sedentes, me vero etiam legentem videt, illius patientiam, securi-
tatem meam corripit[7]: nihilo segnius[8] ego intentus in librum.
Iam hora diei prima, et adhuc dubius et quasi languidus dies.
Iam quassatis circumiacentibus tectis, quamquam in aperto loco,
angusto tamen, magnus et certus ruinae metus. Tum demum 20
excedere oppido visum: sequitur vulgus attonitum, quodque in

---

[1] devoted. [2] bath. [3] became strong. [4] bedroom. [5] court. [6] make extracts. [7] reproves.
[8] less diligently.

pavore simile prudentiae, alienum consilium suo praefert in-
gentique agmine abeuntes premit et impellit. Egressi[1] tecta
consistimus. Multa ibi miranda, multas formidines patimur.
25 Nam vehicula quae produci iusseramus, quamquam in planissimo
campo, in contrarias partes agebantur ac ne lapidibus quidem
fulta in eodem vestigio quiescebant. Praeterea mare in se
resorberi[2] et tremore terrae quasi repelli videbamus. Certe
processerat litus multaque animalia maris siccis harenis detine-
30 bat. Ab altero latere nubes atra et horrenda ignei spiritus[3]
tortis vibratisque discursibus rupta in longas flammarum figuras
dehiscebat[4]: fulguribus[5] illae et similes et maiores erant. Tum
vero idem ille ex Hispaniā amicus acrius et instantius "Si frater"
inquit "tuus, tuus avunculus vivit, vult esse vos salvos: si
35 periit, superstites voluit: proinde quid cessatis evadere?" Re-
spondimus non commissuros[6] nos ut de salute illius incerti
nostrae consuleremus. Non moratus ultra proripit se effusoque
cursu periculo aufertur. Nec multo post illa nubes descendere
in terras, operire[7] maria: cinxerat Capreas et absconderat.[8]
40 Miseni quod procurrit abstulerat. Tum mater orare, hortari,
iubere quoquo modo fugerem; posse enim iuvenem, se et annis
et corpore gravem bene morituram, si mihi causa mortis non
fuisset. Ego contra, salvum me nisi una non futurum: dein
manum eius amplexus, addere gradum cogo. Paret aegre in-
45 cusatque se quod me moretur. Iam cinis, adhuc tamen rarus:
respicio; densa caligo[9] tergis imminebat, quae nos torrentis
modo infusa terrae sequebatur. "Deflectamus" inquam, "dum
videmus ne in viā strati[10] comitantium turbā in tenebris optera-
mur.[11]" Vix consideramus, et nox, non qualis inlunis aut nubila,
50 sed qualis in locis clausis lumine extincto. Audires ululatus[12]
feminarum, infantum quiritatus[13]; clamores virorum: alii parentes, alii liberos, alii coniuges vocibus requirebant, vocibus

---

[1] passing beyond. [2] sucked down. [3] flash. [4] parted. [5] sheet lightnings. [6] be guilty of.
[7] cover. [8] hide. [9] darkness. [10] throw down. [11] crushed. [12] shrieks. [13] cries.

noscitabant[1]: hi suum casum, illi suorum miserabantur: erant
qui metu mortis mortem precarentur: multi ad deos manus
tollere, plures nusquam iam deos ullos, aeternamque illam et 55
novissimam[2] noctem mundo interpretabantur. Nec defuerunt
qui fictis metitisque terroribus vera pericula augerent. Aderant
qui Miseni[3] illud ruisse, illud ardere falso, sed credentibus
nuntiabant. Paulum reluxit; quod non dies nobis sed adven-
tantis ignis indicium videbatur. Et ignis quidem longius[4] 60
substitit,[5] tenebrae rursus, cinis rursus multus et gravis. Hunc
identidem adsurgentes excutiebamus[6]: operti alioqui[7] adque
etiam oblisi[8] pondere essemus. Possem gloriari non gemitum

PLASTER CAST OF BODY.
(*Pompeii.*)

mihi, non vocem parum fortem in tantis periculis excidisse, nisi
me cum omnibus, omnia mecum perire misero, magno tamen 65
mortalitatis solacio credidissem. Tandem illa caligo tenuata
quasi in fumum nebulamve discessit: mox dies verus, sol etiam
effulsit, luridus tamen, qualis esse, cum deficit,[9] solet. Occursa-
bant trepidantibus adhuc oculis mutata omnia altoque cinere,
tamquam nive, obducta.[10] Regressi Misenum, curatis utcumque 70
corporibus, suspensam dubiamque noctem spe ac metu eximus.
Metus praevalebat: nam et tremor terrae perseverabat et plerique
lymphati[11] terrificis vaticinationibus et sua et aliena mala ludifi-
cabantur.[12] Nobis tamen ne tunc quidem, quamquam et expertis

---

[1] tried to recognize. [2] last. [3] locative. [4] at some distance. [5] stopped. [6] shook off. [7] otherwise. [8] crushed. [9] in an eclipse. [10] covered. [11] distracted. [12] made ridiculous.

75 periculum et exspectantibus, abeundi consilium, donec de avunculo nuntius. Haec nequaquam historiâ digna non scripturus leges et tibi, scilicet qui requisisti, imputabis, si digna ne epistulâ quidem videbuntur. Vale.

A Haunted House. (*Epist.* vii. 27.)

Erat Athenis spatiosa et capax domus, sed infamis et pestilens. Per silentium noctis sonus ferri, et si attenderes acrius, strepitus vinculorum longius primo, deinde e proximo reddebatur: mox apparebat idolon,[1] senex macie et squalore confectus, promissâ
5 barbâ, horrenti capillo: cruribus compedes,[2] manibus catenas gerebat quatiebatque. Inde inhabitantibus tristes diraeque noctes per metum vigilabantur: vigiliam morbus et crescente formidine mors sequebatur. Nam interdiu quoque, quamquam abscesserat imago, memoria imaginis oculis inerrabat, longiorque causis
10 timoris timor erat. Deserta inde et damnata solitudine domus totaque illi monstro relicta; proscribebatur[3] tamen, seu quis emere, seu quis conducere[4] ignarus tanti mali vellet. Venit Athenas philosophus Athenodorus, legit titulum,[5] auditoque pretio, quia suspecta vilitas,[6] percunctatus, omnia docetur ac
15 nihilo minus, immo tanto magis conducit. Ubi coepit advesperascere, iubet sterni[7] sibi primâ domus parte, poscit pugillares,[8] stilum,[9] lumen: suos omnes in interiora dimittit, ipse ad scribendum animum, oculos, manum intendit, ne vacua mens audita simulacra[10] et inanes sibi metus fingeret. Initio, quale ubique,
20 silentium noctis, dein concuti ferrum, vincula moveri: ille non tollere oculos, non remittere stilum, sed offirmare animum auribusque praetendere[11]: tum crebrescere fragor, adventare, et iam ut in limine, iam ut intra limen audiri: respicit, videt agnoscitque narratam sibi effigiem. Stabat innuebatque digito, similis

---

[1] ghost. [2] shackles. [3] advertised. [4] rent. [5] advertisement. [6] cheapness. [7] make arrangements (for sleeping). [8] writing tablets. [9] pen. [10] imaginary noises. [11] place as a screen.

vocanti: hic contra ut paulum exspectaret manu significat rur- 25
susque ceris [1] et stilo incumbit: illa scribentis capiti catenis
insonabat: respicit rursus idem quod prius innuentem, nec
moratus tollit lumen et sequitur. Ibat illa lento gradu, quasi
gravis vinculis: postquam deflexit in aream domus, repente

AULA OF GREEK HOUSE.
(*Von Falke.*)

dilapsa [2] deserit comitem: desertus herbas et folia concerpta 30
signum loco ponit. Postero die adit magistratus, monet ut
illum locum effodi iubeant. Inveniuntur ossa inserta catenis et
inplicita, quae corpus aevo terrāque putrefactum nuda et exesa [3]
reliquerat vinculis: collecta publice sepeliuntur. Domus postea
rite conditis [4] manibus caruit. 35

---

[1] tablets. [2] vanished. [3] consume. [4] duly laid to rest.

Sollemne[1] est mihi, domine,[2] omnia de quibus dubito ad te
referre. Quis enim potest melius vel cunctationem meam regere
vel ignorantiam extruere? Cognitionibus[3] de Christianis inter-
fui numquam: ideo nescio quid et quatenus aut puniri soleat aut
5 quaeri. Nec mediocriter haesitavi sitne aliquod discrimen aetatum an quamlibet[4] teneri[5] nihil a robustioribus differant, detur
paenitentiae venia[6] an ei qui omnino Christianus fuit desisse
non prosit, nomen ipsum, si flagitiis careat, an flagitia cohaerentia
nomini puniantur. Interim in iis qui ad me tamquam Christiani
10 deferebantur hunc sum secutus modum. Interrogavi ipsos an
essent Christiani. Confitentes iterum ac tertio interrogavi, supplicium minatus: perseverantes duci[7] iussi. Neque enim dubi-
tabam, qualecumque esset quod faterentur, pertinaciam certe et
inflexibilem obstinationem debere puniri. Fuerunt alii similis
15 amentiae quos, quia cives Romani erant, adnotavi in urbem
remittendos. Mox ipso tractatu, ut fieri solet, diffundente se
crimine plures species inciderunt. Propositus est libellus sine
auctore multorum nomina continens. Qui negabant esse se
Christianos aut fuisse, cum praeeunte me deos appellarent et
20 imagini tuae, quam propter hoc iusseram cum simulacris numinum
adferri, ture[8] ac vino supplicarent, praeterea male dicerent
Christo, quorum nihil posse cogi dicuntur qui sunt re verā Christiani, dimittendos esse putavi. Alii ab indice nominati esse se
Christianos dixerunt et mox negaverunt; fuisse quidem, sed
25 desisse, quidam ante plures annos, non nemo etiam ante viginti
quoque. Omnes et imaginem tuam deorumque simulacra ven-
erati sunt [ii] et Christo male dixerunt. Adfirmabant autem
hanc fuisse summam vel culpae suae vel erroris, quod essent
soliti stato die ante lucem convenire carmenque Christo quasi

---

[1] custom. [2] your Majesty. [3] examinations. [4] however. [5] tender, young. [6] pardon
[7] sc. *ad supplicium.* [8] incense.

deo dicere secum invicem, seque sacramento[1] non in scelus 30
aliquod obstringere, sed ne furta, ne latrocinia, ne adulteria
committerent, ne fidem fallerent, ne depositum appellati abne-
garent: quibus peractis morem sibi discedendi fuisse, rursusque
ad capiendum cibum, promiscuum tamen et innoxium; quod
ipsum facere desisse post edictum meum, quo secundum mandata 35

SUPPOSED CARICATURE OF THE
CRUCIFIXION.
(*Kircherian Museum, Rome.*)

tua hetaerias[2] esse vetueram. Quo
magis necessarium credidi ex duabus
ancillis,[3] quae ministrae[4] dicebantur,
quid esset veri et per tormenta quaerere. Nihil aliud inveni quam super- 40
stitionem pravam inmodicam.[5] Ideo
dilatā[6] cognitione ad consulendum te
decucurri. Visa est enim mihi res
digna consultatione, maxime propter
periclitantium[7] numerum. Multi 45
enim omnis aetatis, omnis ordinis,
utriusque sexus etiam, vocantur in
periculum et vocabuntur. Neque
civitates tantum sed vicos etiam

atque agros superstitionis istius contagio pervagata est; quae 50
videtur sisti[8] et corrigi posse. Certe satis constat prope iam
desolata templa coepisse celebrari et sacra sollemnia diu inter-
missa repeti pastumque venire[9] victimarum, cuius adhuc raris-
simus emptor inveniebatur. Ex quo facile est opinari quae
turba hominum emendari possit, si sit paenitentiae locus. 55

---

[1] pledge. [2] religious fraternities. [3] maid-servants. [4] deaconesses. [5] excessive. [6] put off.
[7] of those endangered. [8] stop. [9] from *veneo*.

XXII. GAIUS.

An accomplished teacher of Roman law, of whose personality nothing is known, but whose introductory treatise on the subject (*Institutiones*), in four books, was a favorite authority with Roman students, and is much quoted by modern writers on Roman jurisprudence. The first book relates to persons; the second and third, to property; and the fourth, to legal procedure. There is an edition of the text with an English translation in parallel columns, and notes on the subject-matter, by Poste (Oxford, 1875); other editions by Muirhead (Edinburgh, 1880), and Mears (London, 1882).

The Business Capacity of Women. (i. 190-193.)

Feminas vero perfectae[1] aetatis in tutelā esse, fere nulla pretiosa[2] ratio suasisse videtur: nam quae vulgo[3] creditur, quia levitate animi plerumque decipiuntur et aequum erat eas tutorum auctoritate regi, magis speciosa videtur quam vera; mulieres
5 enim, quae perfectae aetatis sunt, ipsae sibi negotia tractant, et in quibusdam causis, dicis gratiā,[4] tutor interponit auctoritatem suam; saepe etiam invitus auctor fieri a praetore cogitur. Unde cum tutore nullum ex tutelā iudicium mulieri datur: at ubi pupillorum[5] pupillarumve[5] negotia tutores tractant, eis post pubertatem
10 tem tutelae iudicio[6] rationem reddunt. Sane patronorum et parentum legitimae tutelae vim aliquam habere intelleguntur eo, quod hi neque ad testamentum faciendum, neque ad res mancipi alienandas, neque ad obligationes suscipiendas auctores[7] fieri coguntur, praeterquam si magna causa alienandarum rerum
15 mancipi[8] obligationisque suscipiendae interveniat. Eaque omnia ipsorum causā constituta sunt, ut quia ad eos intestatarum mortuarum hereditates pertinent, neque per testamentum excludantur ab hereditate, neque alienatis pretiosioribus rebus susceptoque aere alieno minus locuples ad eos hereditas perveniat.

---

[1] mature. [2] good. [3] popularly. [4] for form's sake. [5] male or female wards. [6] to the court. [7] principals. [8] mancipible = an adjective.

XXIII. WALL-INSCRIPTIONS

Many inscriptions have been found in Pompeii and Rome scratched upon the walls, doorposts, pillars, and tombs by all classes of idlers, — slaves, schoolboys, loungers, policemen, — and often giving information of much interest concerning the popular ways of living, thinking, and speaking. These inscriptions (*graffiti*) are sometimes made with a *stilus* or some other sharp instrument, and sometimes drawn with charcoal or chalk. The best collections of these are those of Bishop C. Wordsworth in his *Miscellanies* (London, 1879); Père Garrucci's *Graffiti de Pompéi* (Paris, 1856); and the fourth volume of the *Corpus Inscriptionum Latinarum*, edited by Zangemeister. See also Parton's *Caricature and Other Comic Art* (New York, 1878).

Graffito from the Palace of the Caesars, Rome.

LABORA ASE IIE QVOMODOEGO LABORAVI
EIPRODERIITIBI

Announcement of a Ball Game.

Amianthus, Epaphra. Tertius ludant cum Hedysio. Iucandus Nolanus petat.[1] Numerent[2] Citus et Iacus. Amianthus.

---

[1] pick up (the dropped ball). [2] score.

To a Ball Player.

Epaphra! pilicrepus[1] non es!

To a Blonde.

Candida me docuit nigras[2] odisse puellas.

By a Diner-out.

Ad quem non ceno, barbarus ille mihi est.

By Lovers.

(1) Nemo est bellus nisi qui amavit.
(2) Quisquis amat valeat: pereat qui parcit amare.
(3) Auge amat Arabienun.

A New Year's Wish.

Ianuarias nobis felices multos annos !

Graffito, Pompeii.

An Election Appeal.

Aulum Vettium Firmum aedilem oro vos faciatis,[3] dignum re publicā virum! Oro vos faciatis! Pilicrepi, facite!

---

[1] ball-player.   [2] brunettes.   [3] elect.

A Lover's Quarrel.

Virgula Tertio suo: indecens [1] es.

Letter to a Dead Man.

Pyrrhus C. Heio collegae S. — Moleste fero [2] quia audivi te mortuum: itaque vale.

Warning by a Stern Parent.

Quisquis amat veniat veneri [3] volo frangere costas [4]
Fustibus [5] et lumbos debilitare bene.
Sermo est ille mihi tenerum pertundere pectus
Quoi ego non possim caput illud frangere fuste.

---

[1] real mean.   [2] am very sorry.   [3] bent on love.   [4] ribs.   [5] clubs.

CARICATURE OF SOLDIER
(*Pompeii.*)

XXIV. CORNELIUS TACITUS.

Cornelius Tacitus, one of the greatest of the Roman historians, was born about 55 A.D., and died about 120 A.D. He is the last of the truly classic writers of Roman literature. He was trained in rhetoric and writing, and held a number of public offices under Vespasian and succeeding emperors, being praetor in the year 88. His works are a life of his father-in-law Agricola (*Vita Agricolae*); *Historiae*, a history of the Empire from 69 to 96 A.D., of which there remain only four complete books; *Annales*, a history of the Empire from the death of Augustus (14 A.D.) to the death of Nero (68 A.D.), in sixteen books, of which nearly five are lost; a description of Germany (*De Moribus et Populis Germaniae*) of great historical and ethnographic value; and a dialogue on Roman oratory (*Dialogus de Oratoribus*), of which some writers have refused to admit the Tacitean authorship.

Tacitus is a powerful and impressive writer, a remarkable analyzer of character, and fond of psychological investigation. His language is epigrammatic, highly rhetorical, and at times almost unduly condensed.

The best edition of the *Dialogus* is that of Gudeman (N. Y. 1894); a good one of the *Agricola* and *Germania*, that of Church and Brodribb (2d ed. London, 1889); of the *Historiae*, that of Spooner (London, 1891); and of the *Annales*, that of Furneaux (Oxford, 1884). A good English translation of Tacitus is that by Church and Brodribb.

A British Chieftain to his Warriors. (*Agricola*, xxx.-xxxii.)

"Quotiens causas belli et necessitatem nostram intueor, magnus mihi animus[1] est hodiernum diem consensumque[2] vestrum initium libertatis toti Britanniae fore. Nam et universi servitutis expertes, et nullae ultra terrae, ac ne mare quidem securum
5 imminente nobis classe Romanā. Ita proelium atque arma, quae fortibus honesta, eadem etiam ignavis tutissima sunt. Priores pugnae, quibus adversus Romanos variā fortunā certatum est, spem ac subsidium in nostris manibus habebant, quia nobilissimi totius Britanniae, iique in ipsis penetralibus[3] siti, nec servien-
10 tium littora aspicientes, oculos quoque a contactu dominationis

---

[1] confidence. [2] union. [3] sanctuaries.

inviolatos habebamus. Nos terrarum ac libertatis extremos
recessus ipse ac sinus famae in hunc diem defendit, atque omne
ignotum pro magnifico est. Sed nunc terminus Britanniae patet.
Nulla iam ultra gens, nihil nisi fluctus et saxa, et infestiores
Romani, quorum superbiam frustra per obsequium ac modestiam[1] 15
effugeris. Raptores orbis, postquam cuncta vastantibus[2] defuere
terrae, iam et mare scrutantur; si locuples hostis est, avari; si
pauper, ambitiosi, quos non Oriens, non Occidens satiaverit.
Soli omnium opes atque inopiam pari affectu[3] concupiscunt.
Auferre, trucidare, rapere falsis nominibus imperium, atque ubi 20
solitudinem[4] faciunt, pacem appellant.

"Liberos cuique ac propinquos suos natura carissimos esse
voluit. Hi per delectus[5] alibi servituri auferuntur; coniuges
sororesque, etiamsi hostilem libidinem effugiant, nomine amicorum atque hospitum polluuntur. Bona fortunaeque in tribu- 25
tum, ager atque annus in frumentum, corpora ipsa ac manus
silvis ac paludibus[6] emuniendis inter verbera ac contumelias
conteruntur. Nata servituti mancipia[7] semel veneunt,[8] atque
ultro a dominis aluntur; Britannia servitutem suam cotidie
emit, cotidie pascit.[9] Ac sicut in familia recentissimus quis- 30
que servorum etiam conservis ludibrio[10] est, sic in hoc orbis
terrarum vetere famulatu[11] novi nos et viles in excidium[12] peti-
mur. Neque enim arva nobis aut metalla[13] aut portus sunt,
quibus exercendis reservemur. Virtus porro ac ferocia subiec-
torum ingrata imperantibus; et longinquitas[14] ac secretum[15] 35
ipsum quo tutius, eo suspectius. Ita sublata spe veniae tandem
sumite animum, tam quibus salus quam quibus gloria carissima
est. Brigantes femina duce exurere coloniam, expugnare castra,
ac, nisi felicitas in socordiam vertisset, exuere iugum potuere;
nos integri et indomiti et libertatem non in poenitentiam laturi,[16] 40

---

[1] meekness. [2] sc. *sibi.* [3] longing. [4] a desert. [5] conscriptions. [6] marshes. [7] slaves.
[8] are sold. [9] maintains it. [10] dative. [11] slave-troop. [12] destruction. [13] mines. [14] distance.
[15] retirement. [16] sustain.

primo statim congressu[1] ostendamus, quos sibi Caledonia viros seposuerit.

"An eandem Romanis in bello virtutem quam in pace lasciviam adesse creditis? Nostris illi dissensionibus ac discordiis clari
45 vitia hostium in gloriam exercitus sui vertunt; quem contractum ex diversissimis gentibus ut secundae res tenent, ita adversae dissolvent, nisi Gallos et Germanos et (pudet dictu) Britannorum plerosque, licet dominationi alienae sanguinem commodent, diutius tamen hostes quam servos, fide et affectu teneri putatis.
50 Metus ac terror est, infirma vincla loco caritatis[2]; quae ubi removeris, qui timere desierint, odisse incipient. Omnia victoriae incitamenta pro nobis sunt; nullae Romanos coniuges accendunt; nulli parentes fugam exprobraturi sunt; aut nulla plerisque patria aut alia est. Paucos numero, trepidos ignorantiā, caelum
55 ipsum ac mare et silvas, ignota omnia, circumspectantes, clausos quodammodo ac vinctos dii nobis tradiderunt. Ne terreat vanus aspectus et auri fulgor atque argenti, quod neque tegit neque vulnerat. In ipsā hostium acie inveniemus nostras manus; agnoscent Britanni suam causam, recordabuntur Galli priorem
60 libertatem, deserent illos ceteri Germani, tamquam nuper Usipii relinquerunt. Nec quicquam ultra formidinis; vacua castella, senum coloniae, inter male parentes et iniuste imperantes aegra municipia et discordantia. Hic dux, hic exercitus; illic tributa et metalla et ceterae servientium poenae, quas in aeternum per-
65 ferre aut statim ulcisci in hoc campo est. Proinde ituri in aciem et maiores vestros et posteros cogitate!"

An Account of the Germans.   (*Germania*, xvi.–xix.)

Nullas Germanorum populis urbes habitari satis notum est, ne pati quidem inter se iunctas sedes.[3] Colunt discreti ac diversi, ut[4] fons, ut campus, ut nemus placuit. Vicos[5] locant non in

---

[1] shock.   [2] love.   [3] homes.   [4] according as.   [5] villages.

nostrum morem connexis et cohaerentibus aedificiis; suam quisque domum spatio circumdat, sive adversus casus ignis reme- 5
dium,[1] sive inscitiā aedificandi. Ne caementorum quidem apud
illos aut tegularum[2] usus; materiā ad omnia utuntur informi et
citra speciem[3] aut delectationem. Quaedam loca diligentius
illinunt terrā ita purā ac splendente, ut picturam ac lineamenta
colorum imitetur. Solent et subterraneos specus aperire, eosque 10
multo insuper fimo[4] onerant, suffugium[5] hiemi et receptaculum
frugibus, quia rigorem frigorum eiusmodi locis molliunt, et si
quando hostis advenit, aperta populatur, abdita autem et defossa
aut ignorantur, aut eo ipso fallunt, quod quaerenda sunt.

Tegumen omnibus sagum[6] fibulā[7] aut, si desit, spinā[8] con- 15
sertum. Cetera intecti totos dies iuxta focum atque ignem agunt.
Locupletissimi veste distinguuntur, non fluitante, sicut Sarmatae
ac Parthi, sed strictā et singulos artus exprimente.[9] Gerunt et
ferarum pelles, proximi ripae negligenter, ulteriores exquisitius,
ut quibus nullus per commercia cultus. Eligunt feras, et detracta 20
velamina spargunt maculis[10] pellibusque beluarum, quas exterior
Oceanus atque ignotum mare gignit. Nec alius feminis quam
viris habitus, nisi quod feminae saepius lineis amictibus velantur,
eosque purpurā variant, partemque vestitus superioris in manicas[11]
non extendunt, nudae brachia[12] ac lacertos; sed et proxima pars 25
pectoris patet.

Quamquam severa illic matrimonia,[13] nec ullam morum partem
magis laudaveris. Nam prope soli barbarorum singulis uxoribus
contenti sunt, exceptis admodum paucis, qui non libidine, sed
ob nobilitatem plurimis nuptiis ambiuntur. Dotem non uxor 30
marito, sed uxori maritus offert. Intersunt parentes et propinqui ac munera probant, munera, non ad delicias muliebres quae-
sita, nec quibus nova nupta comitatur, sed boves, et frenatum[14]
equum, et scutum cum frameā[15] gladioque. In haec munera uxor

---

[1] precaution. [2] tiles. [3] show. [4] dung. [5] refuge. [6] cloak. [7] clasp. [8] thorn. [9] outlining.
[10] markings. [11] sleeves. [12] accus. of specif. [13] marriages. [14] bridled. [15] spear.

35 accipitur, atque invicem ipsa armorum aliquid viro affert. Hoc
maximum vinculum, haec arcana sacra, hos coniugales deos
arbitrantur. Ne se mulier extra virtutum cogitationes extraque
bellorum casus putet, ipsis incipientis matrimonii auspiciis ad-
monentur venire se laborum periculorumque sociam, idem in pace,
40 idem in proelio passuram ausuramque. Hoc iuncti boves, hoc
paratus equus, hoc data arma denuntiant; sic vivendum, sic
pereundum; accipere se, quae liberis inviolata ac digna reddat,
quae nurus[1] accipiant rursusque ad nepotes referantur.

Ergo septa[2] pudicitia agunt nullis spectaculorum illecebris,[3]
45 nullis conviviorum irritationibus corruptae. Litterarum secreta
viri pariter ac feminae ignorant. Paucissima in tam numerosa
gente adulteria, quorum poena praesens, et maritis permissa.

---

[1] daughter-in-law. [2] guarded. [3] temptations.

XXV. GAIUS SUETONIUS TRANQUILLUS.

Gaius Suetonius Tranquillus, whose life probably lies between the year 75 and 160 A.D., was a Roman lawyer and writer under the Emperor Trajan, and was for a time private secretary to the Emperor Hadrian. He was a man of wide learning and wrote many works of an encyclopaedic character, some of them in Greek. His more important productions were a biographical work *Viri Illustres*, fragments of which remain; a collection of miscellanies entitled *Pratum*, now lost; and a life of the twelve Caesars (*De Vita Caesarum*) in eight books. His style and manner of treatment are monotonous, yet by the accumulation of details he often gives pictures of great vividness, so that one of the later emperors, Commodus, offended by their graphic power, ordered the book to be thrown to the wild beasts.

The standard text of the *Lives* is that by Roth (Leipzig, 1858) ; and of the fragments, that by Reifferscheid (2d ed. Leipzig, 1890). There is an edition of the first two books of the *Lives* with English notes by H. T. Peck (2d ed. N. Y. 1893). The *Lives* and the remains of the *Viri Illustres* are translated into English in the Bohn Library by Thomson and Forester (London, 1881).

The Golden House of Nero.   (*Nero*, xxxi.)

NERO.
(*Louvre*.)

Non in aliā re tamen damnosior quam in aedificando, domum a Palatio Esquilias usque fecit, quam primo "transitoriam," mox incendio absumptam restitutamque "auream" nominavit. De cuius spatio atque cultu suffecerit haec retulisse. Vestibulum eius fuit, in quo colossus CXX pedum staret ipsius effigie ; tanta laxitas, ut porticus triplices miliarias haberet ; item stagnum maris instar, circumsaeptum aedificiis ad urbium speciem ; rura insuper, arvis atque vinetis et pascis silvis-

que varia, cum multitudine omnis generis pecudum ac ferarum. In ceteris partibus cuncta auro lita,[1] distincta gemmis unionum-que[2] conchis erant; cenationes[3] laqueatae tabulis eburneis versa-
20 tilibus, ut flores, fistulatis[4] ut unguenta desuper spargerentur; praecipua cenationum rotunda, quae perpetuo diebus ac nocti-bus vice mundi circumageretur; balineae marinis et albulis[5] fluentes aquis. Eius modi domum cum absolutam dedicaret, hactenus comprobavit, ut se diceret quasi hominem tandem habi-
25 tare coepisse.

PALACE OF THE CAESARS.
(*Restoration by Benrenuto*)

Praeterea incohabat piscinam a Miseno ad Avernum lacum, contectam porticibusque conclusam, quo quidquid totis Baiis calidarum aquarum esset converteretur; fossam ab Averno Os-tiam usque, ut navibus nec tamen mari iretur, longitudinis per
30 centum sexaginta milia, latitudinis, quā contrariae quinqueremes commearent. Quorum operum perficiendorum gratiā quod ubi-que esset custodiae in Italiam deportari, etiam scelere convictos non nisi ad opus damnari praeceperat.

---

[1] overlaid.　[2] pearls.　[3] dining rooms.　[4] having pipes.　[5] sulphurous.

Ad hunc impendiorum [1] furorem,[2] super fiduciam imperii, etiam
spe quādam repentinā immensarum et reconditarum opum impul-   35
sus est ex indicio equitis Romani pro comperto [3] pollicentis the-
sauros antiquissimae gazae,[4] quos Dido regina fugiens Tyro
secum extulisset, esse in Africā vastissimis specubus [5] abditos,
ac posse erui parvulā molientium [6] operā.

The Madness of Caligula.   (Calig. xviii. foll.)

Munera[7] gladiatoria, partim in amphitheatro Tauri partim in
Septis, aliquot edidit, quibus inseruit catervas Afrorum Campa-
norumque pugilum ex utrāque regione electissimorum. Neque
spectaculis semper ipse praesedit, sed interdum aut magistrati-
bus aut amicis praesidendi munus iniunxit. Scaenicos ludos et   5
assidue et varii generis ac multifariam fecit, quandam et noctur-
nos, accensis totā urbe luminibus. Sparsit et missilia[8] variarum
rerum, et panaria[9] cum obsonio viritim [10] divisit; quā epulatione
equiti Romano contra se hilarius avidiusque vescenti partes suas
misit, sed et senatori ob eandem causam codicillos.[11] quibus prae-   10
torem eum extra ordinem designabat. Edidit et circenses plurimos a mane ad vesperam, interiectā modo Africanarum venatione
modo Troiae decursione, et quosdam praecipuos, minio [12] et chrysocollā [13] constrato Circo, nec ullis nisi ex senatorio ordine aurigan-
tibus. Commisit et subitos, cum e Gelotianā apparatum Circi   15
prospicientem pauci ex proximis maenianis postulassent.

Novum praeterea atque inauditum genus spectaculi exco-
gitavit. Nam Baiarum medium intervallum ad Puteolanas moles,
trium milium et sexcentorum fere passuum spatium, ponte con-
iunxit, contractis undique onerariis navibus et ordine duplici ad   20
anchoras conlocatis, superiectoque aggere terreno ac directo in

---

[1] expenditure.   [2] frenzy.   [3] as real.   [4] treasures.   [5] caves.   [6] on the part of the laborers.
[7] shows.   [8] things to be scrambled for.   [9] baskets of bread.   [10] to each man.   [11] letters patent.
[12] vermilion.   [13] green.

Appiae viae formam. Per hunc pontem ultro citro commeavit
biduo continenti, primo die falerato[1] equo insignisque querceā[2]
coronā et caetrā et gladio aureāque clamide,[3] postridie quadriga-
25 rio habitu curriculoque biiugi famosorum[4] equorum, prae se
ferens Dareum puerum ex Parthorum obsidibus, comitante prae-
torianorum agmine et in essedis[5] cohorte amicorum. Scio plerosque existimâsse, talem a Gaio pontem excogitatum aemulatione
Xerxis, qui non sine admiratione aliquanto angustiorem Helles-
30 pontum contabulaverit[6]; alios, ut Germaniam et Britanniam,
quibus imminebat, alicuius inmensi operis fama territaret. Sed
avum meum narrantem puer audiebam, causam operis ab interi-
oribus aulicis[7] proditam quod Thrasyllus mathematicus[8] anxio
de successore Tiberio et in verum nepotem proniori affirmâsset,
35 "non magis Gaium imperaturum quam per Baianum sinum
equis discursurum." . . .

Compluribus cognominibus adsumptis (nam et "Pius" et
"Castrorum Filius" et "Pater Exercituum" et "Optimus Maximus Caesar" vocabatur). Cum audiret forte reges, qui officii
40 causā in urbem advenerant, concertantes apud se super cenam
de nobilitate generis, exclamavit: εἷς κοίρανος ἔστω, εἷς βασιλεύς.[9]
Nec multum afuit quin statim diadema sumeret speciemque[10]
principatus in regni formam converteret. Verum admonitus[11] et
principum et regum se excessisse fastigium,[12] divinam ex eo
45 maiestatem asserere sibi coepit; datoque negotio ut simulacra
numinum religione et arte praeclara, inter quae Olympi Iovis,
apportarentur e Graeciā, quibus capite dempto suum imponeret,
partem Palatii ad Forum usque promovit,[13] atque aede Castoris et
Pollucis in vestibulum transfiguratā, consistens[14] saepe inter fra-
50 tres deos, medium adorandum se adeuntibus exhibebat; et quidam eum Latiarem Iovem consalutârunt. Templum etiam numini

---

[1] caparisoned. [2] of oak leaves. [3] cloak. [4] blooded. [5] war-chariots. [6] bridged over.
[7] courtiers. [8] astrologer. [9] Let there be a single prince, a single king! [10] nature. [11] advised.
[12] grandeur. [13] extended. [14] taking his stand.

suo proprium et sacerdotes et excogitatissimas hostias instituit.
In templo simulacrum stabat aureum iconicum,[1] amiciebaturque
cotidie veste, quali ipse uteretur.   Magisteria sacerdotii ditissi-
mus quisque et ambitione et licitatione maxima vicibus com-   55
parabant.[2]   Hostiae erant phoenicopteri,[3] pavones, tetraones,[4]
numidicae,[5] meleagrides,[6] phasianae,[7] quae generatim per singulos dies immolarentur.   Et noctibus quidem plenam fulgen-
temque lunam invitabat assidue in amplexus, interdiu vero cum
Capitolino Iove secreto fabulabatur, modo insusurrans[8] ac prae-   60
bens in vicem aurem, modo clarius nec sine iurgiis. . . .

Nihilo reverentior leniorve erga senatum, quosdam summis
honoribus functos ad essedum sibi currere togatos per aliquot
passuum milia, et cenanti modo ad pluteum[9] modo ad pedes
stare succinctos linteo[10] passus est; alios cum clam interemisset,   65
citare[11] nihilo minus ut vivos perseveravit, paucos post dies
voluntaria morte perisse mentitus.[12]   Consulibus oblitis de natali
suo edicere abrogavit magistratum, fuitque per triduum sine
summa potestate res publica.   Quaestorem suum in coniuratione
nominatum flagellavit, veste detracta subiectaque militum pedi-   70
bus, quo firme verberaturi insisterent.

Simili superbia violentiaque ceteros tractavit ordines.   Inqui-
etatus fremitu gratuita in circo loca de media nocte occupantium,
omnes fustibus abegit; elisi[13] per eum tumultum viginti amplius
equites Romani totidem matronae, super innumeram turbam cete-   75
ram.   Scaenicis ludis, inter plebem et equitem causam discor-
diarum serens, decimas[14] maturius dabat, ut equestria ab infirmo
quoque occuparentur.   Gladiatorio munere, reductis interdum
flagrantissimo sole velis, emitti quemquam vetabat remotoque
ordinario apparatu, tabidis[15] feris vilissimos senioque confectos   80
gladiatores quoque paegniarios[16] patres familiarum notos sed

---

[1] life-size.   [2] secured.   [3] flamingoes.   [4] moor fowls.   [5] bustards.   [6] guinea hens.   [7] pheasants.
[8] whispering.   [9] the head of his couch.   [10] towel.   [11] invite.   [12] pretending.   [13] crushed.
[14] money orders.   [15] decrepit.   [16] make-believe.

insignes debilitate aliquā corporis obiciebat.   Ac nonnumquam horreis[1] praeclusis, populo famem indixit.

Saevitiam ingenii per haec maxime ostendit.   Cum ad saginam 85 ferarum muneri praeparatarum carius pecudes compararentur, ex noxiis laniandos[2] adnotavit et custodiarum seriem recognoscens,

POLLICE VERSO.
(*From the painting by Gérôme.*)

nullius inspecto elogio,[3] stans tantum modo intra porticum mediam, "a calvo ad calvum"[4] duci imperavit.   Votum exegit ab eo, qui pro salute suā gladiatoriam operam promiserat, spec- 90 tavitque ferro dimicantem, nec dimisit nisi victorem et post multas preces.   Alterum, qui se periturum eā de causā voverat, cunctantem pueris tradidit verbenatum[5] infulatumque[6] votum

---

[1] public granaries.   [2] to be torn in pieces.   [3] label.   [4] neck and crop.   [5] decked with garlands.
[6] and with fillets.

reposcentes per vicos agerent, quoad praecipitaretur ex aggere.
Multos honesti ordinis, deformatos prius stigmatum notis, ad
metalla[1] et munitiones viarum aut ad bestias condemnavit, aut   95
bestiarum more quadripedes[2] caveā coercuit, aut medios serrā[3]
dissecuit; nec omnes gravibus ex causis, verum male de munere
suo opinatos, vel quod numquam per genium suum deierāssent.
Parentes supplicio filiorum interesse cogebat; quorum uni valitudinem excusanti lecticam misit, alium a[4] spectaculo poenae   100
epulis statim adhibuit atque omni comitate ad hilaritatem et
iocos provocavit. Curatorem munerum ac venationum, per con-
tinuos dies in conspectu suo catenis[5] verberatum, non prius occidit quam offensus putrefacti cerebri odore. Atellanae poetam ob
ambigui ioci versiculum mediā amphitheatri harenā igni crema-   105
vit. Equitem Romanum obiectum feris, cum se innocentem pro-
clamāsset, reduxit, abscissāque linguā rursus induxit. . . .

Nec minore livore ac malignitate quam superbiā saevitiāque
paene adversus omnis aevi hominum genus grassatus est.[6] Sta-
tuas virorum inlustrium, ab Augusto ex Capitolinā areā propter   110
augustias in Campum Martium conlatas, ita subvertit atque
disiecit ut restitui salvis titulis non potuerint, vetuitque posthac
viventium cuiquam usquam statuam aut imaginem nisi consulto
et auctore se poni. Cogitavit etiam de Homeri carminibus abo-
lendis "cur enim sibi non licere." dicens, "quod Platoni licuis-   115
set, qui eum e civitate quam constituebat, eiecerit?" Sed et
Vergilii ac Titi Livi scripta et imagines paulum afuit quin ex
omnibus bibliothecis amoveret, quorum alterum ut nullius ingenii minimaeque doctrinae, alterum ut verbosum in historiā
neglegentemque carpebat. De iuris quoque consultis, quasi sci-   120
entiae eorum omnem usum aboliturus, saepe iactavit, "se meher-
cule effecturum ne quid respondere possint praeter eum."

XXVI. PUBLIUS AELIUS HADRIANUS.

HADRIAN.
(*British Museum.*)

Publius Aelius Hadrianus was born at Rome in 76 A.D. and died in 138. He was of Spanish ancestry and related to the Emperor Trajan, by whom he was brought up, and whom he succeeded in the year 117 A.D. With the exception of the last years of his reign, when he became suspicious and cruel, he devoted himself to the material and intellectual good of his subjects, by the promulgation of humane laws, and especially by the numerous magnificent architectural works which he planned and carried out. He spent several years in travel, visiting all parts of the Empire, and founded or aided many institutions of learning. He sought everywhere the society of men of letters, and was especially fond of Athens and Alexandria, where he was constantly engaged in discussion with the philosophers. His own writings were of a desultory character and seem never to have risen above the level of dilettanteism, though often clever and full of wit. Apart from decrees, there remain to us only short fragments, epistolary and epigrammatic. There is a life of Hadrian in German by Gregorovius (Stuttgart, 1884).

The Retort Courteous.

(Quoted by Spartianus, *Vit. Hadr.* 16.)

Floro poetae scribenti ad se:
    Ego nolo Caesar esse,
    Ambulare per Britannos,
    Latitare [1] per Germanos,
    Scythicas pati pruinas, [2] —

---

[1] sneak around. [2] frosts.

MAUSOLEUM OF HADRIAN IN ROME (CASTLE OF ST. ANGELO).

rescripsit [Hadrianus]:
    Ego nolo Florus esse,
    Ambulare[1] per tabernas,[2]
    Latitare per popinas[3]
    Culices[4] pati rotundos.   10

The Departing Soul.

(Quoted by Spartianus, *Vit. Hadr.* 27.)

    Animula, vagula, blandula,
    Hospes comesque corporis,
    Quae nunc abibis in loca,
    Pallidula, rigida, nudula,
    Nec ut soles dabis iocos?   5

---

[1] hang around.   [2] taverns.   [3] bar-rooms.   [4] fleas.

XXVII. THE LAST WILL AND TESTAMENT OF A LITTLE PIG. (TESTAMENTUM PORCELLI.)

This *jeu d'esprit* is of unknown authorship and uncertain date; but as it is mentioned by St. Jerome (*Comment. in Is.* xii. introd.), it must have been written earlier than the fourth century A.D. The oldest MS. containing it is of the ninth century. St. Jerome says that it was repeated by the boys in schools, where it excited much laughter. It is evidently intended for children, the language of the preliminary paragraph being unmistakably that of the nursery tale; though some editors have supposed it to be the work of a lawyer, and written merely to burlesque the legal forms of a will. It has been edited by Moritz Haupt (*Opuscula*, ii. 178); and the text is printed by Bücheler in his smaller edition of Petronius (Berlin, 1886). See Notes.

"M. Grunnius Corocotta[1] porcellus testamentum fecit. Quoniam manu meā scribere non potui, scribendum dictavi.

CUTLER'S SHOP.

"Magirus cocus dixit 'Veni huc, eversor domi, solivertiator,[2] fugitive porcelle, et hodie tibi dirimo vitam.' Corocotta porcellus dixit: 'Si qua feci, si qua peccavi, si qua vascella pedibus meis confregi, rogo, domine coce, vitam peto, concede roganti.' Magirus cocus dixit 'Transi, puer, affer mihi de cocinā cultrum. ut hunc porcellum faciam cruentum.' Porcellus comprehenditur a famulis, ductus sub die XVI Kal. Lucerninas.[3] ubi abundant cymae,[4] Clibanato et Piperato[5] consulibus. Et ut vidit se moriturum esse, horae spatium petiit et cocum rogavit ut testamentum facere posset. Clamavit ad se suos parentes, ut de cibariis[6] suis aliquid dimitteret eis. Qui ait:

---

[1] Marcus Grunter Pigskin.   [2] devastator of the earth, i.e. rooter.   [3] the Kalends of Candlelight.   [4] young cabbages.   [5] Pott and Pepper.   [6] provisions.

"'Patri meo, Verrino Lardino,[1] do lego dari[2] glandis[3] modios 20
XXX, et matri meae Veturinae Scrofae do lego dari Laconicae
siliginis modios XL, et sorori meae Quirrinae[4] in cuius votum[5]
interesse non potui, do lego dari hordei[6] modios XXX. Et de
meis visceribus dabo donabo sutoribus saetas,[7] rixoribus capitinam,[8] surdis auriculas, causidicis et verbosis linguam, bubulariis 25
intestina, isiciariis[9] femora, pueris vesicam,[10] puellis caudam,

SACRIFICE OF A PIG.

cursoribus et venatoribus talos,[11]
latronibus ungulas.[12] Et nec
nominando coco legato dimitto
popiam[13] et pistillum quae me- 30
cum attuleram de Tebeste usque
ad Tergeste: liget sibi collum
de reste.[14] Et volo mihi fieri
monumentum aureis litteris scriptum : " M. GRUNNIUS COROCOTTA 35
PORCELLUS VIXIT ANNIS DCCCC ·
XC · VIIII · S[15] · QUOD SI SEMISSEM
VIXISSET, MILLE ANNOS IMPLES-
SET." Optimi amatores mei vel consules vitae, rogo vos ut cum
corpore meo bene faciatis, bene condiatis de bonis condimentis 40
nuclei,[16] piperis, et mellis, ut nomen meum in sempiternum
nominetur. Mei domini vel consobrini[17] mei, qui in medio
testamento interfuistis, iubete signari.'

"Lardio[18] signavit. Ofellicus[19] signavit. Cyminatus[20] signavit. Lucanicus[21] signavit. Tergillus[22] signavit. Celsinus sig- 45
navit. Nuptialicus signavit.

"Explicit.[23] testamentum porcelli sub die XVI Kal. Lucerninas Clibanato et Piperato consulibus feliciter."

---

[1] Boarleigh Bacon.   [2] I give and bequeath.   [3] acorns.   [4] Peggy.   [5] wedding.   [6] barley.
[7] bristles.   [8] headpiece.   [9] sausage makers.   [10] bladder.   [11] knuckle-bones.   [12] hoofs.   [13] ladle.
[14] rope.   [15] and a half.   [16] nutmeg.   [17] cousins.   [18] Bacon.   [19] Cutlet.   [20] Kraut.   [21] Mincer.
[22] Flitch.   [23] = *explicitum*

XXVIII. AULUS GELLIUS.

Aulus Gellius, a writer of miscellanies who flourished in the second century A.D., was probably of Roman birth, though little is known of his life,
except that he spent some time at Athens pursuing various studies, the results
of which are embodied in his only work, entitled *Noctes Atticae*, in twenty
books, of which the eighth is lost except the chapter-headings. The *Noctes
Atticae* is a great scrap-book consisting of unrelated extracts from Roman
and Greek authors, especially archaic writers, with his own comments. The
importance of the collection is in the light it often throws on questions of
history, grammar, antiquities, and literature, and in its preservation of quotations from Greek and Roman authors whose works have perished. The chief
edition of this text is that by Hertz, 2 vols. (Berlin, 1883–5). There is a poor
translation into English by Beloe (London, 1799).

A Woman Hater. (i. 6.)

Verba ex oratione Metelli Numidici, quam dixit in censurā[1] ad populum, cum
eum ad uxores ducendas[2] adhortaretur; eaque oratio quam ob causam repre-
hensa et quo modo defensa sit.

Multis et eruditis viris audientibus legebatur oratio Metelli
Numidici, gravis ac diserti viri, quam in censurā dixit ad populum de ducendis uxoribus, cum eum ad matrimonia capessenda[3]
hortaretur. In eā oratione ita scriptum fuit: si sine uxore
5 [vivere] possemus. "Quirites, omni eā molestia careremus; sed
quoniam ita natura tradidit, ut nec cum illis satis commode, nec
sine illis ullo modo vivi possit, saluti perpetuae potius quam
brevi voluptate consulendum est."
Videbatur quibusdam, Q. Metellum censorem, cui consilium
10 esset ad uxores ducendas populum hortari, non oportuisse de
molestiā incommodisque perpetuis rei uxoriae confiteri, neque id
hortari magis esse quam dissuadere absterrereque; set contra in
id potius orationem debuisse sumi dicebant, ut et nullas plerum-

---

[1] censorship.   [2] marrying.   [3] enter upon.

que esse in matrimoniis molestias adseveraret et, si quae tamen
accidere nonnumquam viderentur, parvas et leves facilesque esse   15
toleratu diceret maioribusque eas emolumentis et voluptatibus
oblitterari easdemque ipsas neque omnibus neque naturae vitio,
sed quorundam maritorum culpā et iniustitiā evenire. Titus
autem Castricius recte atque condigne Metellum esse locutum
existimabat. " Aliter," inquit, " censor loqui debet, aliter rhetor. 20
Rhetori concessum est, sententiis uti falsis, audacibus, versutis,[1]
subdolis,[2] captiosis,[3] si veri modo similes sint et possint movendos
hominum animos qualicumque astu[4] inrepere.[5] " Praeterea turpe
esse ait rhetori, si quid in malā causā destitutum atque inpro-
pugnatum relinquat. " Sed enim Metellum," inquit, " sanctum   25
virum, illā gravitate et fide praeditum cum tantā honorum atque
vitae dignitate apud populum Romanum loquentem, nihil decuit
aliud dicere quam quod verum esse sibi atque omnibus videbatur,
praesertim cum super eā re diceret, quae cotidianā intellegentiā
et communi pervolgatoque vitae usu comprenderetur. De molestiā 30
igitur cunctis hominibus notissimā confessus fidem[6] sedulitatis[7]
veritatisque commeritus, tum denique facile et procliviter, quod
fuit rerum omnium validissimum atque verissimum, persuasit,
civitatem salvam esse sine matrimoniorum frequentiā non posse."

Socrates and Xanthippe. (i. 17.)

Quantā cum animi aequitate toleraverit Socrates uxoris ingenium intractabile ;
atque inibi, quid M. Varro in quādam saturā de officio mariti scripserit.

Xanthippe, Socratis philosophi uxor, morosa admodum fuisse
fertur et iurgiosa,[8] irarumque et molestiarum muliebrium per
diem perque noctem scatebat.[9] Has eius intemperies in maritum Alcibiades demiratus, interrogavit Socraten, quaenam ratio

5 esset, cur mulierem tam acerbam domo non exigeret. "Quoniam," inquit Socrates, "cum illam domi talem perpetior, insuesco et exerceor, ut ceterorum quoque foris petulantiam et iniuriam facilius feram."

Secundum hanc sententiam quoque Varro in saturā Menippeā,
10 quam de officio mariti scripsit "Vitium," inquit, "uxoris aut tollendum aut ferendum est. Qui tollit vitium, uxorem commodiorem praestat, qui fert sese meliorem facit." Haec verba Varronis "tollere" et "ferre" lepide[1] quidem composita sunt, sed "tollere" apparet dictum pro "corrigere." Id etiam apparet,
15 eius modi vitium uxoris, si corrigi non possit, ferendum esse Varronem censuisse, quod ferri scilicet a viro honeste; vitia enim flagitiis leviora sunt.

The Ring Finger. (X. 10.)

Quae eius rei causa sit, quod et Graeci veteres et Romani anulum hoc digito gestaverint, qui est in manu sinistrā minimo proximus.

ANULUS.

Veteres Graecos anulum habuisse in digito accepimus sinistrae manus, qui minimo est proximus. Romanos quoque homines aiunt sic plerumque anulis usitatos. Causam esse huius rei Apion in libris Aegyptiacis hanc dicit, quod insectis apertisque humanis corporibus, ut mos in Aegypto fuit, quas Graeci "ἀνατομάς" appellant, repertum est, nervum quendam tenuissimum
ab eo uno digito, de quo diximus, ad cor hominis
10 pergere ac pervenire; propterea non inscitum[2] visum esse, eum potissimum digitum tali honore decorandum, qui continens et quasi conexus esse cum principatu cordis videretur.

ANULUS.

---

[1] nicely. [2] silly.

Some Superstitions. (X. 12.)

De portentis fabularum, quae Plinius Secundus indignissime in Democritum philosophum confert,[1] et ibidem de simulacro volucri columbae.

Librum esse Democriti, nobilissimi philosophorum, de vi et naturā chamaeleontis eumque se legisse Plinius Secundus in naturalis historiae vicesimo octavo refert, multaque vana atque intoleranda auribus deinde quasi a Democrito scripta tradit, ex quibus pauca haec inviti meminimus, quia pertaesum[2] est: 5 accipitrem avium rapidissimum a chamaeleonte humi reptante, si eum forte supervolet, detrahi et cadere vi quādam in terram ceterisque avibus laniandum sponte suā obiicere sese et dedere. Item aliud ultra humanam fidem: caput et collum chamaeleontis si uratur ligno, quod appellatur "robur," imbres et tonitrus fieri 10 derepente, idque ipsum usu venire, si iecur eiusdem animalis in summis tegulis uratur. Item aliud, quod hercle an ponerem dubitavi, ita est deridiculae vanitatis, nisi idcirco plane posui, quod oportuit nos dicere, quid de istius modi admirationum fallaci inlecebrā sentiremus, quā plerumque capiuntur et ad perniciem 15 elabuntur ingenia maxime sollertia, eaque potissimum, quae discendi cupidiora sunt. Sed redeo ad Plinium. Sinistrum pedem ait chamaeleontis ferro ex igni calefacto torreri cum herbā, quae appellatur eodem nomine chamaeleontis, et utrumque macerari[3] unguento conligique in modum pastilli[4] atque in vas[5] 20 mitti ligneum et eum, qui id vas ferat, etiamsi is in medio palam versetur, a nullo videri posse.

His portentis atque praestigiis a Plinio Secundo scriptis non dignum esse cognomen Democriti puto; vel illud quale est, quod idem Plinius in decimo libro Democritum scripsisse adseverat, 25 aves quasdam esse certis vocabulis et earum avium confuso sanguine gigni serpentem; eum qui ederit linguas avium et conloquia interpretaturum.

[1] attributes. [2] wearied, disgusted (impers.). [3] steeped. [4] lozenge, roll. [5] vessel, box.

Multa autem videntur ab hominibus istis male sollertibus[1]
30 huiuscemodi commenta[2] in Democriti nomen data, nobilitatis
auctoritatisque eius perfugio utentibus. Sed id, quod Archytam
Pythagoricum commentum esse atque fecisse traditur, neque
minus admirabile neque tamen vanum aeque videri debet. Nam
et plerique nobilium Graecorum et Favorinus philosophus, memo-
35 riarum veterum exsequentissimus, affirmatissime scripserunt,
simulacrum columbae e ligno ab Archytā ratione quādam dis-
ciplināque mechanicā factum volasse; ita erat scilicet libramentis
suspensum et aurā spiritus inclusā atque occultā concitum.

Milo's Strange Death.   (xv. 16.)

De novo genere interitus Crotoniensis Milonis.

Milo Crotoniensis, athleta inlustris, quem in chronicis scriptum est Olympiade LXII primum coronatum esse, exitum habuit
e vitā miserandum et mirandum. Cum iam natu grandis artem
athleticam desisset iterque faceret forte solus in locis Italiae
5 silvestribus, quercum vidit proxime viam patulis in parte mediā
rimis hiantem.[3] Tum experiri, credo, etiam tunc volens, an
ullae sibi reliquae vires adessent, inmissis in cavernas arboris
digitis, diducere et rescindere quercum conatus est. Ac mediam
quidem (partem) discidit divellitque; quercus autem in duas
10 diducta partes, cum ille, quasi perfecto quod erat conixus, manus
laxâsset, cessante vi rediit in naturam manibusque eius retentis
inclusisque stricta denuo[4] et cohaesa, dilacerandum hominem feris
praebuit.

The Story of Arion.   (xvi. 19.)

Sumpta historia ex Herodoti libro super fidicine[5] Arione.

Celeri admodum et cohibiti oratione vocumque filo[6] tereti[7] et
candido[8] fabulam scripsit Herodotus super fidicine illo Arione.

---

[1] skilled.   [2] fictions.   [3] gaping.   [4] back again.   [5] lute-player.   [6] style.   [7] polished.   [8] clear.

"Vetus" inquit, "et nobilis Arion cantator[1] fidibus[2] fuit. Is
loco et oppido Methymnaeus, terrā atque insulā omni Lesbius
fuit. Eum Arionem rex Corinthi Periander amicum amatumque
habuit artis gratiā. Is inde a rege proficiscatur, terras inclutas[3]
Siciliam atque Italiam visere. Ubi eo venit auresque omnium
mentesque in utriusque terrae urbibus demulsit,[4] in quaestibus
istic et voluptatibus amoribusque hominum fuit. Is tum post
ea grandi pecuniā et re bonā multā copiosus Corinthum instituit
redire, navem igitur et navitas, ut notiores amicioresque sibi,
Corinthios delegit." Sed eos Corinthios, homine accepto navique
in altum provectā praedae pecuniaeque cupidos, cepisse consilium
de necando Arione. Tum illum ibi, pernicie intellectā, pecuniam
ceteraque sua, ut haberent, dedisse, vitam modo sibi ut parcerent,
oravisse. Navitas precum eius harum commiseritum esse illac-
tenus,[5] ut ei necem adferre per vim suis manibus temperarent,[6]
sed imperavisse, ut iam statim coram desiliret praeceps in mare.
"Homo" inquit "ibi territus, spe omni vitae perditā, id unum
postea oravit, ut, priusquam mortem obpeteret, induere[7] permit-
terent sua sibi omnia indumenta[8] et fides capere et canere
carmen casus illius sui consolabile. Feros et immanes navitas
prolubium[9] tamen audiendi subit; quod oraverat, impetrat.
Atque ibi mox de more cinctus, amictus ornatus stansque in
summae puppis foro,[10] carmen, quod "orthium" dicitur, voce
sublatissimā cantavit. Ad postrema cantus cum fidibus ornatuque
omni, sicut stabat canebatque, iecit sese procul in profundum.
Navitae, hautquaquam dubitantes, quin perisset, cursum, quem
facere coeperant, tenuerunt. Sed novum et mirum et pium
facinus contigit." Delphinum repente inter undas adnavisse
fluitantique[11] esse homini subdidisse et dorso super fluctus edito
vectavisse incolumique eum corpore et ornatu Taenarum in terram
Laconicam devexisse. Tum Arionem prorsus ex eo loco Cor-

---

[1] musician. [2] lute. [3] renowned. [4] charm. [5] = in so far. [6] refrain. [7] put on. [8] garments.
[9] inclination. [10] gangway. [11] floating.

iuthum petivisse talemque Periandro regi, qualis delphino vectus
35 fuerat, inopinanti sese optulisse eique rem, sicuti acciderat,
narravisse. Regem istaec parum credidisse, Arionem, quasi
falleret, custodiri iussisse, navitas inquisitos, ablegato[1] Arione,
dissimulanter interrogâsse, ecquid audissent in his locis, unde
venissent, super Arione? eos dixisse, hominem, cum inde irent,
10 in terrâ Italiâ fuisse eumque illic bene agitare et studiis delecta-
tionibusque urbium florere atque in gratiâ pecuniâque magnâ
opulentum fortunatumque esse. Tum inter haec eorum verba
Arionem cum fidibus et indumentis, cum quibus se in salum
eiaculaverat, extitisse, navitas stupefactos convictosque ire infi-
15 tias[2] non quisse. Eam fabulam dicere Lesbios et Corinthios
atque esse fabulae argumentum, quod simulacra duo aënea ad
Taenarum viserentur, delphinus vehens et homo insidens.

---

[1] removet.   [2] *ire infitias* = deny.

XXIX. EARLY CHRISTIAN HYMNS.

CHAMBER IN THE ROMAN CATACOMBS.

The Latin hymns of the early Christian Church are interesting as literary compositions and also for their metrical structure, as showing a reversion to the older system of verse in which accent and rhyme prevail instead of syllabic quantity. Such had always been the case with the purely popular poetry of the Romans, with whom the elaborate system of prosody found in classical literature was always an artificial thing; and so it was natural that the hymns of the early Church, being written for the people, should display the same characteristics as are found in the folk-verse. No hymns of which the authors' names are known are found earlier than the first part of the fourth century, after which time St. Hilary and St. Ambrose led the way in this species of composition, in which they were followed by Prudentius (350–410), Sedulius, about the same time, Venantius Fortunatus (530–609), Gregory the Great (540–604), the Venerable Bede (673–735), and many others.

Of the three specimens given here, the first is by St. Ambrose (340–397), who was chosen Bishop of Milan in 374. The second, the immortal *Dies Irae*, is of unknown authorship and uncertain date, though it has often been ascribed to the Franciscan, Thomas of Celano. The third is by St. Bernard.

For a good account of the Latin hymns, with sketches of the best known Latin hymn-writers, reference may be made to Archbishop Trench's *Sacred Latin Poetry* (London, 1874), and to Duffield's *Latin Hymn Writers* (New York, 1888). A fine collection of Latin hymns is that by Cardinal Newman, *Carmina Ecclesiae* (London, 1876); as also that of the German scholar, Mone, *Hymni Latini*, 3 vols. (1853–55). Considerable information on special points is to be found in Julian's *Dictionary of Hymnology* (New York, 1888). For further discussion see the Notes.

I.

Veni, redemptor gentium,
Ostende partum Virginis;
Miretur omne saeculum:
Talis decet partus Deum.

5 Non ex virili semine,
Sed mystico spiramine,
Verbum Dei factum est caro,
Fructusque ventris floruit.

     *   *   *   *   *

Procedit, e thalamo suo,
10 Pudoris[1] aulâ regiâ,
Geminae gigas substantiae,
Alacris ut currat viam.

Egressus eius a Patre,
Regressus eius ad Patrem,
15 Excursus usque ad inferos,
Recursus ad sedem Dei.

Aequalis aeterno Patri,
Carnis tropaeo cingere,
Infirma nostra corporis
20 Virtute firmans perpeti.

Praesepe[2] iam fulget tuum,
Lumenque nox spirat novum,
Quod nulla nox interpolet
Fideque iugi luceat.

---

[1] modesty. [2] home.

II.

Dies irae, dies illa
Solvet saeclum in favillā,[1]
Teste David cum Sibyllā.

Quantus tremor est futurus,
Quando Iudex est venturus,   5
Cuncta stricte discussurus!

Tuba, mirum spargens sonum
Per sepulcra regionum,
Coget omnes ante thronum.

Mors stupebit et natura   10
Cum resurget creatura,
Iudicanti responsura.

Liber scriptus proferetur,
In quo totum continetur,
De quo mundus iudicetur.   15

Iudex ergo cum sedebit,
Quidquid latet apparebit,
Nil inultum remanebit.

Quid sum, miser, tum dicturus
Quem patronum rogaturus,   20
Cum vix iustus sit securus?

Rex tremendae maiestatis
Qui salvandos salvas gratis,
Salva me, fons pietatis!

---

[1] cinder.

25 Recordare, Iesu pie,
Quod sum causa tuae viae ;
Ne me perdas illā die !

Quaerens me sedisti lassus,
Redemisti crucem passus ;
30 Tantus labor non sit cassus !¹

Iuste Iudex ultionis,
Donum fac remissionis,
Ante diem rationis.²

Ingemisco³ tanquam reus,
35 Culpā rubet vultus meus ;
Supplicanti parce, Deus !

Qui Mariam absolvisti,
Et latronem exaudisti,
Mihi quoque spem dedisti.

40 Preces meae non sunt dignae,
Sed tu bonus fac benigne
Ne perenni cremer⁴ igne !

Inter oves locum praesta,
Et ab haedis⁵ me sequestra,
45 Statuens in parte dextrā.

Confutatis maledictis,
Flammis acribus addictis,
Voca me cum benedictis.

Oro supplex et acclinis,⁶
50 Cor contritum quasi cinis,
Gere curam mei finis.

---

¹ wasted. ² reckoning. ³ bewail. ⁴ burn. ⁵ goats. ⁶ bending toward thee.

III.

Ut incundas cervus [1] undas
Aestuans desiderat.
Sic ad rivum Dei vivum
Mens fidelis properat.

Sicut rivi fontis vivi   5
Praebent refrigerium,[2]
Ita menti sitienti
Deus est remedium.

Quantis bonis superponis [3]
Sanctos tuos, Domine: 10
Sese laedit, qui recedit
Ab aeterno lumine.

Vitam laetam et quietam
Qui te quaerit, reperit;
Nam laborem et dolorem   15
Metit,[4] qui te deserit.

Pacem donas. et coronas
His qui tibi militant;
Cuncta laeta sine metá[5]
His qui tecum habitant   20

—

[1] stag. [2] refreshment. [3] endow. [4] reaps. [5] end.

SUGGESTIONS FOR COLLATERAL READING.

———✦———

The following works will be found especially useful as collateral and supplementary reading: —

BIBLIOGRAPHY.

KELSEY. Fifty Topics in Roman Antiquities, with References. Boston, 1891.

[A judicious and suggestive syllabus of the subject of Roman life, with a list of the most accessible books of reference.]

LANGUAGE.

ALLEN. Remnants of Early Latin. Boston, 1880.

[A convenient collection of specimens of the earliest remains of Latin, from non-literary sources, with good notes, and a short introduction.]

HARRINGTON AND TOLMAN. Early Latin Fragments. (In Preparation.)

[To be published in 1895 by American Book Company.]

EGBERT. Introduction to the Study of Latin Inscriptions. (In Press.)

[To be published in 1895 by American Book Company.]

MERRY. Selected Fragments of Roman Poetry. Oxford, 1891.

[A representative selection from existing fragments of the epic, dramatic, and satiric poets, from the earliest times to the Augustan Age.]

HISTORY.

SHUCKBURGH. A History of Rome to the Battle of Actium. London and New York, 1894.

[An interesting narrative of Roman history, based upon the most recent investigations.]

BURY. A History of the Roman Empire from its Foundation to the Death of Marcus Aurelius (B.C. 27–A.D. 180). London and New York, 1893.

[This work takes up the story of Rome at the point where Mr. Shuckburgh leaves it. The book is admirably written, in accordance with the best authorities, and contains some special chapters on the development of Roman literature and the various phases of Roman life.]

BARING-GOULD.   The Tragedy of the Caesars.   2 vols.   London, 1892.

[A suggestive account of the personality of the first six Caesars, written with considerable freshness and originality.   The text is sumptuously illustrated with reproductions of the most famous likenesses of the emperors and their immediate associates.]

LITERATURE.

TEUFFEL, SCHWABE, AND WARR.   A History of Roman Literature.   2 vols. London, 1891–92.

[A work essentially for reference, rather than for reading.   It is indispensable to the advanced student of Latin; giving a minute account of the original sources of information regarding the writers of Latin literature, and a very complete bibliography of all standard works, especially the German, including monographs, dissertations, and programmes.]

CRUTTWELL.   A History of Roman Literature from the Earliest Period to the Death of Marcus Aurelius.   London and New York, 1886.

[A very pleasantly written account of Latin literature, with some interesting paragraphs on the language.   It is probably better adapted to excite the interest of the student than any work of the kind in English, and is independently written from the author's own standpoint.]

ROMAN LIFE AND CUSTOMS.

FRIEDLÄNDER.   Darstellungen aus der Sittengeschichte Roms in der Zeit von August bis zum Ausgang der Antonine.   3 vols.   Leipzig, 1888–90.

[A treasure-house of information about the details of Roman life, Roman society, usage, and custom, with references to the sources from which this knowledge is drawn.]

PRESTON AND DODGE.   The Private Life of the Romans.   New York and Boston, 1894.

[A popular account of the subject, drawn from good authorities, and written in an interesting style.   The text is illustrated by a number of cuts.]

INGE.   Society in Rome under the Caesars.   London and New York, 1888.

[This little book was originally written as an essay, in competition for the Hare Prize at the University of Cambridge.   While making no pretensions to originality, it is a well-written and convenient condensation of the facts set forth in more elaborate works, and will be found accurate and instructive.]

DYER.   Pompeii: Its History, Buildings, and Antiquities.   New edition.   London, 1875.

[So many problems of archaeology are solved by the discoveries at Pompeii as to make the records of this buried city of extreme interest to every student of Roman life.   This work in a single volume gives a good account of the excavations prior to 1875, and is illustrated by plans, maps, and cuts.]

LANCIANI.   Ancient Rome in the Light of Recent Excavations.   Boston and New York, 1888.

> [A most fascinating account of the city of Rome, with especial reference to the new light that has been thrown upon its topography, architecture, history, and society, by excavations made during the past twenty years. It is written with a wealth of special knowledge and a charm of style that make it unique among works of archaeology. It is beautifully printed, and is made especially interesting by its carefully selected illustrations, one hundred in number.]

GUHL AND KONER.   The Life of the Greeks and Romans.   Last edition of the English translation.   New York, 1878.

> [An account of Greek and Roman life as illustrated by the external objects that have been preserved to modern times. A great many cuts and diagrams give additional value to the text. A new German edition of this standard work appeared in 1893.]

LECKY.   A History of European Morals.   Vol. I.   New York and London, 1884.

> [A work of unusual power and value, written with great charm of style, and dealing with its subject in a scientific and philosophical spirit. A vast amount of minute and curious knowledge is embodied in its pages; and the foot-notes supplement the text with references and quotations of much interest to the student.]

NOTES.

I. POPULAR SONGS, CHARMS, ETC.

PAGE **13. lalla.** A natural sound made in soothing children. It is the same as the Swedish *lulla*, " to hum," and its elements occur in the English *lull, lullaby*, and in the historical nickname *Lollards* applied to the followers of Wyclif, originally meaning "the droners," or "chanters" (Skeat). So the Germans call the vocabulary of the nursery *Lallwörter*. The word is not here the imperative of *lallo*, "to babble" (Gk. λαλεῖν), but only a soothing sound formed from the repetition of the syllables *la, la, la*.

lacta. "Take your milk."

Terra pestem teneto. From Varro's treatise *De Re Rustica*, i. 2. 27, where it is quoted. The person using this charm is to sing it over twenty-seven times, to touch the ground, and to spit, — spitting being regarded by the Romans as having some special medical virtue. Thus epilepsy is cured by spitting on the patient (Plaut. *Capt.* iii. 4. 23; Pliny, *H. N.* x. 23. 33 and xxviii. 4. 7). Compare Christ's cure of the blind man in the Gospel of St. John ix. 6.

Habeat scabiem, etc. Reconstructed by L. Müller from the scholiast Porphyrio on Horace, *Ars Poetica*, 417. It is the Roman equivalent of the modern "Devil take the hindmost." The goal-post which marks the end of the race is supposed to be the speaker of the line.

Huat hanat huat. Probably mere gibberish, like the famous "Hocus pocus tontus talontus" of the mediaeval jugglers, though like that it may have been corrupted from an actual formula. Many of the old liturgies used by the Roman priests had become so twisted out of their original sound as to be unintelligible even to those who used them in their rites (Quintil. i. 6. 40). This particular *cautio*, or charm, is quoted by Cato in his agricultural treatise, 160.

14. Hiberno pulvere, etc. An old saw quoted by Festus, p. 93. It is like "A green Christmas makes a fat churchyard," and "A dirty spring makes a golden harvest," etc.

camille. The *camilli* were boys employed in religious rites and services, especially by the Flamen Dialis and at Roman marriages, something like the acolytes of the Roman Catholic Church. The word, which is a very old one, is of uncertain etymology. See Hartung, *Die Religion der Römer*, i., p. 157 ; ii., p. 71.

Quod habes ne habeas, etc. From Plautus, *Trinummus*, 350, where it is given as a popular gibe against misers, and dog-in-the-mangers generally.

pote. Sc. *est.*

bene esse. "To have a good time." Colloquial expression.

Heia, viri, etc. A boating song, of uncertain age, found in a Berlin MS. of the eighth century. There is frequent mention in the ancient writers of the *nauticus cantus* (e.g. Cic. *Nat. Deor.* ii. 35) of boatmen at the oar; and the practice of singing at work also appears to have been general. Thus Varro, cited by Nonius (56), speaks of the vine-dressers singing at the vintage, and the *sarcinatrices in machinis*, which one would like to translate, "the seamstresses over their sewing machines." For the spirited lines given here, see Bährens, *Poet. Lat. Min.* iii. 167, and Peiper in the *Rheinisches Museum*, xxxii. 523.

nostrum. Agreeing with the second *heia*, "our yoho."

vago pondere. "Their shifting mass."

corus. Also written *caurus;* the *argestes* of the Greeks and the *mistral* of modern Provence. The northwest wind. See Gell. ii. 22.

Dulcis amica veni, etc. This very curious poem is found in MSS. of the eleventh century, but in the main is probably of much older date. Goldast ascribes it to a certain Albius Ovidius Iuventinus, but this personage appears to be a sort of mediaeval Mrs. Harris, and the authorship is in reality quite unknown. The Romans seem to have been greatly interested in the capacity of the Latin language to imitate in its vocabulary the sounds made by the various birds and beasts, and took pride in the number of expressive mimetic words (onomatopoeias) which it possessed. In one of the works of Suetonius, entitled *Pratum* (see p. 163), he brought together all these imitative verbs ; and though the *Pratum* as a whole has not come down to us, this particular chapter has been preserved, and may be found in Reifferscheid's collection of the fragments of Suetonius (pp. 247–254). It is probable that the missing portions of Varro's treatise, *De Lingua Latina*, contained a still earlier collection of the same kind. Spartianus relates that the Emperor Geta used to get together the teachers of language, and ask them to give him lists of these imitative words, quoting from earlier writers their authority for using them (Spart. *Geta*, 5). The subject of onomatopoeias is again taken up by Polemius Silvius, in the fifth century, in his *Laterculus;* showing that it possessed a continuous interest for students of language. There are also two short poems of similar character, entitled respectively *De Voce Hominis Absona* (Bährens, *Poët. Lat. Min.* v., p. 368) and *De Philomela* (id. ibid., pp. 368–370). It is reasonable, therefore, to suppose that the poem given in our text is of earlier origin than the period to which its oldest MS. is assigned, and that it is possibly based upon the chapters of Suetonius. Its mediaeval modifications, however, are made evident by the single word *drosca* (line 11), which is not Latin, but German (*throsca, droschel, drossel,* Eng. *throstle, thrush*), and which serves as a sort of ear-mark to show that the poem was worked over in some German monastery.

The superior richness of the Latin in onomatopoeias, as compared with the English, will be seen in attempting to translate the poem. For many of the Latin verbs there are no English equivalents whatsoever. The poem has been edited by Nodier in the Appendix to his *Dictionnaire des Onomatopées Françaises* (2d ed., Paris, 1828), and by Lemaire in his *Bibliotheca Classica Latina*, vol. cxl. See, for criticism, comment, etc., Ebart, *Allgemeine Geschichte der Literatur des Mittelalters im Abendlande*, vol. ii.; Löwe, in the *Rheinisches Museum*, vol. xxxiv., pp. 493–496; Wackernagel, *Voces Variae Animantium* (Basel, 1869); and a paper by H. T. Peck, on "Onomatopoetic Words in Latin," in the *Classical Studies in Honour of Henry Drisler*, pp. 226–239 (New York and London, 1894).

15. vocum discrimina. "Distinct sounds." So in line 47.

odis. Gk. ᾠδή.

glottorat. Another form is *gloctorat.* The word refers to the clattering of the stork's huge bill, and not, as Lewis and Short seem to think, to the bird's voice. Compare Ovid, *Met.* vi. 97:

> *Ipsa sibi plaudat crepitante ciconia rostro,*

a passage which also refutes Mayor's explanation of *crepitat* in Juv. i. 116, though, curiously enough, he quotes it in support of his own view.

ciconia. The stork's bill. Roman boys bent up their fingers in imitation of this, as a gesture of mockery and contempt, much like the modern placing of the thumb upon the nose and spreading the fingers. This gesture was called *ciconia*, and is mentioned by Persius (i. 58) and by St. Jerome. Another gesture of insult was the thrusting out of the middle finger (*digitus infamis*), for making which sign at one of his officers the Emperor Caligula was assassinated.

pessimus et passer. "The sparrow, the rascal."

chaere. The Greek salutation χαῖρε, with which parrots were regularly taught to greet those who entered the house (Pers. *Prol.* 8).

16. omne quod audit ait. So Ovid, *Met.* v. 299, *Institerant ramis imitantes omnia picae;* and Pers. *Prol.* 9.

panther amans. "The rutting panther." The more usual Latin form is *panthera.* Pliny derived the word from πᾶν + θήρ, and explained it as given because the characteristics of all beasts are found united in the panther. From this popular etymology a number of curious fables arose, for which see Wright's *Popular Traditions in Science*, p. 82.

pia . . . ovis. "The faithful sheep."

sordida. "Greedy."

rite. "As is their wont," "usually"; i.e. the dog makes a variety of sounds, but barking is the most characteristic of them. Naturalists tell us that the wild dog has only one or two notes as against the whine, whimper, howl, yelp, and bark of the domesticated animal.

rana coaxat. Aristophanes, in his play, the *Frogs*, represents the frog's croak by κοάξ; and the Latin *coaxo* (also written *quaxo*) may be borrowed from it. Cf. Fest., p. 288, Müll. From the Latin form is the French verb *coasser*.

17. Pessuli. The lover is supposed to stand outside the house of his mistress, and adjure the bolts and bars to slip aside and let him in. Similar compositions are common in Latin literature. Hor. *Odes*, iii. 10.

ludii barbari. *Ludii* (also *ludiones*) are acrobats. He wishes the bolts fairly to leap from their sockets in their eagerness to let him.

nihili. Genitive of value.

mille, mille, mille. Sung by the soldiers of Aurelian. The verse is trochaic tetrameter catalectic, but based on accent, and not on syllabic quantity. Thus the penult of the words *homo*, *bibat*, and *habet*, is in each regarded as long because the accent lengthens it, just as in English. See T. H. Key's chapter on accent in his *Language, its Origin and Development*, p. 442 (London, 1874), where he cites this passage. Another specimen is found in the verses of Hadrian given on p. 171.

The repetition of the *mille* is a primitive trick of emphasis, like the children's "ever and ever and ever so long ago." Cf. Dryden's "Fallen, fallen, fallen, fallen, fallen from his high estate." This principle of repetition, as a device for giving greater force to what is said, lies at the base of various figures of rhetoric (anaphora, epizeuxis, epistrophe, symploce, epanalepsis, anadiplosis, epanadiplosis, epanados, polyptoton, paregmenon, paronomasia, alliteration, synonyma, parechesis, etc.), and explains reduplication and other forms of dynamic change in the making of words.

II. TOMB INSCRIPTIONS.

18. The sarcophagus of Lucius Cornelius Scipio, of which an illustration is given in the text, was found in the family tomb of the Scipios, on the Appian Way, not far from the Porta Capena of Roman times, and was removed to the Vatican Museum by Pope Pius VII. In it the bones of Scipio were found in 1780, in very good preservation. They were removed to Padua, and there interred at the expense of a Venetian, Signor Quirini. The tomb itself is still one of the sights of Rome, and is shown to visitors, who grope about its various dark and dismal chambers by the light of a taper. The Scipio of the sarcophagus was consul in B.C. 298, and was the great-grandfather of Scipio Africanus, who conquered Hannibal (B.C. 202). The inscription is in Saturnian verse.

perlege. "Read it to the end."

sepulcrum hau pulcrum pulcrae. A sort of parechesis, like Cicero's *pleniore ore, fortunatam natam*, etc.

19. horunc. i.e. *horum + ce.*

incessu. Compare Vergil's famous *vera incessu patuit dea* (*Aen.* i. 405).

lanam fecit. The spinning of wool was the typical occupation of a Roman matron. The *mater familias* sat in the *atrium* of the house spinning among her maids; and so Lucretia, when Tarquin met her.

Dum vixi bibi libenter. A line that reminds one of honest Iago's ditty : —

> " And let me the canakin clink, clink,
> And let me the canakin clink :
> A soldier's a man
> And life's but a span, —
> Why then let a soldier drink ! "

Salvius et Eros dant. Salvius and Eros are the slaves or freedmen who have caused the stone to be erected.

III. QUINTUS ENNIUS.

20. impudentes arioli. The ancient representatives of the ingenious persons who in modern times advertise to impart (for a small sum) their knowledge of a sure way to make a fortune, or who write books on "The Secret of Success."

monstrant viam. The blind are leaders of the blind.

dracumam. Lengthened form of *drachmam*, like *Alcumena* for *Alcmena* ; *mina* for *mna*, etc. The drachma was worth about eighteen cents.

Haece locutus vocat. Aulus Gellius (xii. 4) cites these lines from the eighth book of the *Annales* as giving an ideal picture of a true and loyal friend, — the perfect type of an intimate. He adds that Lucius Aelius Stilo, Varro's great teacher, used to say that Ennius had here drawn with accuracy a fine picture of himself. Notice the roughness of the hexameters in this passage and in the speech of Pyrrhus given below, — the continual neglect of the final *s* (*locutu'*, *lassu'*, *rebu'*, *malu'*, *doctu'*, *facundu'*, *contentu'*, *scitu'*, *commodu'*), the long penult in *dederītis*, the synizesis in *eorundem*, etc.

21. O Tite tute Tati, etc. The most famous alliterative line in Latin, as the most famous alliteration in Greek is the line from the *Oedipus Tyrannus* of Sophocles (line 371), in which Oedipus taunts the seer Tiresias with his blindness : —

> τυφλὸς τά τ' ὦτα τόν τε νοῦν τά τ' ὄμματ' εἶ.

Curiously enough each involves the repetition of the letter *t*. The alliteration in the line of Ennius, is, however, rather a childish and meaningless jingle. Some writers have tried to trace a sort of principle in the choice of letters in Latin alliterative lines. Thus Munro in his introduction to Lucretius thinks that

the repetition of *v* is used to produce the effect of wailing (see in the present
volume, p. 34, line 67); that the repetition of *p* conveys the idea of effort and
force, etc., but this seems rather fanciful. The earlier and later Roman writers
are fond of alliteration, but those of the Augustan Age use it very sparingly.
See Ebrard, *Alliteration in d. lat. Sprache* (Bayreuth, 1882); Bötticher, *De
Alliterationis apud Romanos Vi et Usu* (Berlin, 1884); and Cruttwell, pp.
238, 239.

The Titus Tatius of the line is the Sabine king who undertook to avenge the
rape of the Sabine women. See p. 103.

Nec mi aurum posco. The Epirote King Pyrrhus, the Cœur de Lion of
antiquity, who waged war on the Romans from B.C. 280–275 in a spirit of knightly
adventure, is represented in these lines as refusing to accept money as a ransom
for the prisoners that he had taken, but as freely giving them up without a price.
The chivalrous and martial spirit of the king is finely indicated in the lines which
are given by Cicero in his *De Officiis*, i. 12.

dederītis. This long penult is common in the older prosody. The general
tendency in the development of Latin prosody is toward the shortening of long
vowels; *i.e.* toward lightness and grace. Thus Ennius has more long vowels
than Lucretius, and Lucretius than Vergil.

vitam cernamus. A sort of condensed expression for the more regular *de
vita cernamus*, or *pro vita cernamus*. The accusative must be explained as an
accusative of specification.

Nemo me decoret. Twice quoted by Cicero (*De Amicit*. 20; *Tusc. Disp.* i.
15), who thinks it a fine and manly assertion by the poet of his own greatness,
like that of Horace in the famous ode beginning *Exegi monumentum aere perennius*.

dacrumis. Older form of the more usual *lacrimis* (Gk. δάκρυμα).

IV. TITUS MACCIUS PLAUTUS.

22. Advorsum venire, etc. The stage setting shows the front of the house
of Philolaches. Philolaches, Philematium, and others are beginning a drinking-
bout (*comissatio*), reclining upon couches in the Graeco-Roman fashion. Callidamates, who has been dining not wisely but too well elsewhere, enters with
unsteady steps, leaning upon Delphium, who directs his course as well as she can.

temperi. Adverbial form = *tempore*.

hem, tibi imperatum est. "There! those are your orders."

illi. For *illic*, the latter being the stronger (deictic) form with the emphatic
suffix -*ce*.

comissatum. Supine, to denote purpose after a verb of motion. From
κωμάζω, "to revel," and not connected with *committo*.

Philolachetem. This name is declined *Philolaches*, genitive, *Philolachē-tis*, or *Philolachis*. Cf. line 1. The proper names in Plautus are usually indicative of the characters who bear them, like those in Thackeray. Thus, *Philolaches*, the spendthrift (φιλός + λάχος from λαχεῖν) is "one fond of his inheritance"; Callidamates, the lover of women, is "the one subdued by beauty" (κάλλος + δαμάω); Philematium, the loving mistress of Philolaches, is "little kiss," "Küsschen" (φιλημάτιον). Notice that the names and scenes of Roman comedies are Greek, it being forbidden to depict Roman personages on the stage except in the dignified *fabulae praetextae*, or historical dramas. Thus Naevius, a contemporary of Plautus, was imprisoned and then exiled for the liberties he took with leading statesmen like the Metelli. This fate is guardedly mentioned with sympathy in the *Miles Gloriosus*, 211 : —

> Os columnatum poetae esse inaudivi barbaro
> Quoi bini custodes semper totis horis occubant.

Actors (*histriones*) and theatrical people generally received summary treatment at Rome. The former were Greeks, freedmen, or slaves, and were legally classed as *infames*, being coupled with gladiators and prostitutes. The praetor might at any time have them whipped without a formal trial, and they often suffered banishment. Nevertheless, as time went on, though their legal status was little improved, they gained in social standing, and some of them, like Aesopus, and Roscius the friend of Cicero, were universally respected and esteemed. "Stars" like these received large sums for their services. Aesopus left a fortune of 20,000,000 sesterces ($800,000); and Roscius was paid at the rate of 1000 denarii ($175) for each performance. (See Cic. *Pro Roscio*, 8, § 23 ; Macrobius, *Sat.* iii. 14.)

23. Ecquid. "At all."

moratus. From *mos, mores.*

licet. "You may."

Duce. Four verbs regularly omit the final *e* in the imperative, — *dic, duc, fac,* and *fer,* — but the fuller form is found in all except *fer.*

amabo. A colloquial expression like *sis* (*si vis*), *sultis* (*si vultis*), etc.

ocellus . . . mel meum. Other familiar terms of endearment are *melilla* (dimin. of *mel*), *mea vita, anima, meus pullus passer* ("my chick-sparrow"), *mea columba* ("dovey"), *passercula* (dimin. of *passer*), *anaticula* ("duckey") *vitellus* ("my little calf"), *pullulus* ("chickabiddy"), *mus* ("mousey," — also curiously enough, a term of abuse, "you rat!" in Petron. 58), *curculum* ("sweetheart"), and a variety of similar epithets, — zoölogical, botanical, and physiological.

sed et hoc, sc. *bracchium.* He has hold of her arm.

cedo. Emphatic imperative of *dare : ce + da.* The plural form is *cette* (*ce + date*).

Hem tene. "Come now! hold on."

anime mi. Said to Philematium, by whose side he is reclining.

Accuba, i.e. on a couch by the table.

Quin. *Quî + ne;* literally "how not." *Ne* is here the early negative = the later *non.*

eumpse. Earlier and more logical accusative of *ipse* (*is + pse*). Afterward the suffix *pse* was regarded as a part of the stem and the case-ending placed after the whole.

24. Lusiteles. The name (λύειν + τέλη), "one who pays his dues," fits the character. Lusiteles is the good young man who never does anything wrong, and who, as here, solemnly reckons up the profit and loss of every transaction of life. The soliloquy put into his mouth in this passage, is, however, quite Shakspearian.

simitu. "All at the same time " = *simul.*

expetessam. Present subjunctive of the intensive verb *expetesso.*

rei. "Business," "money-getting." Some one has wittily said that the word *res* is a check signed in blank so that one may write into it any meaning that he wishes.

reus. The defendant in a suit is *reus;* the plaintiff, *accusator.*

rem. Here "case "; a legal term.

25. cuppes. " Sweet-toothed." *Cuppedia,* and sweetmeats, dainties. The Forum Cupedinis was the Huyler's of ancient Rome. (Varro, *L. L.* v. 146.)

saviis. *Savium* is the old word for a kiss (φίλημα), and denotes the kiss of passion; *osculum,* the kiss of pure affection. After the time of Catullus (see notes to p. 42), *basium* is the usual word (French, *baiser;* Old Eng., *buss*).

si audes. *Audeo* contains the root of *avidus,* and hence the phrase *si audes* (usually syncopated to *sodes*) is equivalent to *si vis,* — "won't you."

ille cuculus. "That goose."

fiat. " All right."

sumpti. As many as eighteen nouns of the fourth declension are occasionally found with the genitive form of the second declension. Most of these are verbal nouns, and the second declension genitive probably comes from confusion with the neuter of the perfect participles used substantively.

nuntii, renuntii. "Messengers back and forth."

apage. "Begone." Gk. ἄπαγε.

te nil utor. "I have no use for you."

Larem coronā. Callicles is coming out of his house, and as he does so, turns and calls out to his wife who is within, and invisible to the audience. As he utters the fourth line, he shuts the door. The *lar,* or image of the household god, in early Roman times stood in the front part of the house, — the *atrium,* or general reception-room. Afterward, it was removed to the private apartments, and even to the kitchen. He tells his wife to put a garland upon the image, the day being a festival of some sort.

26. edepol. Roman men swore by Hercules; women, by Castor; both sexes, by Pollux. The form *edepol* is probably *ah deus Pol*. See Gellius, xi. 6.

ut valet. "How is her health?" *Ut* here = *quo*.

siquid mihi malist. "If I have any piece of bad luck."

victuraquest. "And she's going to live (forever)."

nupta sit . . . ducam. A woman is said *nubere;* a man, *ducere*.

Vin conmutemus. "Would you like us to make a swap?" *Vin = visne.*

faxo. Future perfect for *fecero*.

ne. Not the negative, but a particle of affirmation like the Greek *ναί*.

nanctu's. From *nanciscor*, and = the more used *nactus*, the participle here retaining the nasal of the present indicative.

nota mala res optumast. "Better to bear the evils that we have, than fly to others that we know not of."

hoc. The object of *animum advorte*, which taken together make a new verb in sense.

V. CATO THE CENSOR.

27. vilici. The steward or overseer in charge of a *villa rustica*. Such a *villa* had two courts, an outer and an inner. At the entrance to the outer court the *vilicus* had his office, so as to watch the slaves as they went in and out. Near by was the kitchen where the slaves gathered after the day's work was over. Above both courts were the little sleeping-rooms (*cellae*) of the slaves; and underground, in a kind of cellar, was the *ergastulum*, or slave-prison, where the refractory ones were punished by being kept in chains (*vincti*). The inner court was occupied by the stables, cattle-pens, etc. (*bubilia, equilia, ovilia*). It will be seen, therefore, that the *villa rustica* was a combination of farm-house, slave-quarters, and stable. See Varro, *Res Rustica*, i. 11–13; Columella, i. 4, 5 foll.

Feriae. The holidays of various sorts, especially the Feriae Sementivae or Paganalia (at seed-time), the Compitalia (see below), and the vintage festival, the Feriae Vindemiales, in October.

familiã. The slave family; a noun cognate with *famulus*, "a servant," from the Oscan *famel*.

gratiam referat. "Show his gratitude," "express his appreciation."

siet. An old optative form, originally *esiet*. Cf. the Greek εἴην (ἐσίην, etc.).

exerceat. "Keep busy."

Compitalibus. The Compitalia, or Ludi Compitalicii, was an annual festival in honor of the Lares Compitales, or deities presiding over the cross-roads (*compita*). On the occasion of this feast, all slaves were released from work, and allowed to do as they pleased.   After the time of Augustus, the Compitalia were held twice a year (May 1 and Aug. 1), but in Cato's time, in the winter. See Gellius (x. 24).

credat.   " Give credit."

28. Duas aut tres familias.   Here *familiae* has its modern sense.   He is not to be a general borrower or lender, but may have neighborly relations of the sort with two or three families in the vicinity.

putet.   The verb *putare* means originally " to prune," " clear away," i.e. of vines, — a sense retained in the English " amputate " (*ambi + putare*) ; thus, " to clear up," " arrange," " settle," applied to accounts ; lastly, and following naturally from the preceding, " to reckon," " calculate," " think."   It is a good illustration of the process by which a word referring to a purely physical action gradually takes on a metaphysical meaning.

politorem.   " A farm laborer."   This and the two preceding words refer to hired workmen as opposed to slaves.

Parasitum.   " Hanger-on."

scibit . . . dormibit.   In early Latin the ending -*bo* as a future suffix is found in all four conjugations.   This future formation occurs only in Latin and Keltic, and is one of the facts adduced by Schleicher to prove that at one time there was a Latino-Keltic period ; i.e. that the Latin and Keltic branches of the Indo-European family were still united after the Hellenic and other kindred peoples had separated from them.   See Schleicher in the *Rheinisches Museum* for 1859.   All this, however, belongs to the ancient history of linguistics.

cubitum.   Supine.

modios.   The *modius* was closely equivalent to the English peck, contained sixteen *sextarii* or pints.

conpeditis.   " To the chain-gang."

P. IIII.   *Pondo quattuor*, — *pondo* being an indeclinable noun regularly used with numerals.   It was originally the ablative of a second-declension noun, *pondus*, and meant " by weight," " by the pound."

ficos esse coeperint.   *Esse* is here *edere.*

congios.   The *congius* was about six pints English.

II S.   i.e. *duos et semissem*, " two and a half."   In Vitruvius and other writers, *semis* is usually indeclinable.

Saturnalibus.   A famous Roman festival in honor of Saturn, held in the latter part of December.   In city and country alike, it was a season of absolute relaxation and mirth, resembling in many respects the carnival of modern Italy, while some of its usages survive in our Christmas customs.   It was, for slaves especially, a season of merriment, for they were excused from all ordinary labor, allowed to wear the liberty cap, to speak with entire freedom, and according to some Roman writers were treated to a banquet at which they wore their masters' clothes, and were even waited on by them.

summa vini. "The whole amount of wine."

pro portione. "Proportionally," i.e. to the severity of the labor assigned them.

Oleae caducae. Olives that fell to the ground ; opposed to *oleae tempestivae*, those that duly ripen and are picked.

29. hallecem et acetum. The brine and vinegar in which the olives have been kept.

S. I. i.e. *sextarium unum*, "one pint."

P. III S. Of three and a half pounds of wool.

centones. Garments composed of patchwork. Hence arose the literary term *cento*, applied to a poem made up of lines and half lines of other poems pieced together, — a species of literary work in which many dilettante engaged during the decline of classical literature. Homer and Vergil furnished the greatest amount of material for these mosaics (*Homerocentones, Vergiliocentones*). Thus, there is a poem of 2343 verses on the life of Christ, wholly composed of bits from Homer dovetailed together, and traditionally ascribed to the Empress Eudocia. Another, on the passion of Christ, is from Euripides, and consists of 2610 verses. From Vergil was drawn the sacred history by Proba Faltonia (in the fourth century A.D.), and a tragedy called *Medea*, the work of Hosidius Geta, of the second or third centuries A.D. Other specimens will be found in the fourth volume of the *Poetae Lat. Minores.* See Borgen, *De Centonibus Homericis et Vergilianis* (Copenhagen, 1828) ; Hasenbalg, *De Centonibus Vergilianis* (Putbus, 1846) ; Delapierre, *Ouvrages Écrits en Centons* (London, 1868) ; id. *Tableau de la Littérature du Centon* (London, 1875).

The passage from Cato shows on the whole a spirit of justice and, in a way, of kindness, toward the slave. He must do his full share of work, but he is to be properly cared for, with no indulgence, to be sure, but with no unnecessary severity. Yet the spirit after all is that of Varro's striking phrase in which he calls the slave *instrumentum vocale*, — a mere utensil which happens to be able to speak. There is not a word that ranks him higher than the cattle, — "something better than his dog, a little dearer than his horse." On slavery among the ancients, see Gurowski, *Slavery in History* (New York, 1860) ; and Wallon, *Histoire de l'Esclavage dans l'Antiquité* (Paris, 1879).

VI. TITUS LUCRETIUS CARUS.

30. Nil igitur mors est. Lucretius thinks that as death is utter annihilation of our own personality, it can bring us no evil of any kind, being merely the negation of everything. Epicurus, the philosophic master of Lucretius, condensed this argument into an epigram. "The thought of death need not trouble us ; for where we are, death is not ; and where death is, we are not." See Ritter,

Hist. of Ancient Philosophy, iv. 87 ; and Zeller, *Stoics, Epicureans, and Skeptics*, ch. 17.

ad nos neque pertinet hilum. " And concerns us not a whit."

aegri. Genitive after *nil*.

fuere. The subject is *homines*, to be supplied.

utrorum. i.e. the Carthaginians or the Romans. " Men were uncertain to the dominion of which one of the two all human possessions were to fall."

cadendum . . . esset. Impersonal, the agent being expressed by the dative *omnibus humanis.*

ubi non erimus. " When we shall cease to exist." Nothing concerned us before we came into being, and so nothing will concern us after we cease to be.

omnino. " At all."

31. **nostro de corpore.** To be taken with *distractast.*

comptu. A word found only here.

Pertineat. The *nec* in line 18 modifies this verb.

retinentia. i.e. the matter of which we are now composed may again unite and form another similar human being, but as the identity has been lost, and the chain of conscious continuity has been broken, the new being will have no kinship to its predecessor.

de nobis. " So far as we are concerned." **de illis.** " So far as they are concerned."

cum respicias. " Whenever you consider."

semina. The seeds of things ; "atoms." Other expressions of Lucretius for the atoms are *elementa (prima), primordia, corpora prima, genitalia corpora, exordia rerum*, etc.

ut nunc sum. *ut = in quo.* " That these same atoms of which we are now composed were formerly arranged in the same position as they are now."

inter enim iectast. Tmesis for *interiecta.* Tmesis is more and more frequent the nearer one gets to the primitive stages of both Greek and Latin, because one is thus getting nearer to the period of those languages when the prepositions were adverbs. Ennius even separates compound nouns into their original elements: e.g. *saxo cere comminuit brum (cerebrum comminuit) ;* and *Massili portabant iuvenes ad litora tanas (Massilitanas).*

vitai pausa. " A cessation of life."

ab sensibus. " Dissociated from sensations," i.e. as non-sentient matter.

Debet enim . . . esse. " For he must exist."

misere si forte aegreque futurumst. " If perchance one is to be unhappy and wretched."

id quoniam mors eximit. " Since death takes this away from us ; " i.e. the time when one can be wretched.

probet. Syncopated for *prohibet.*

neque hilum differre. " And that it makes not the slightest difference."

ullo tempore. i.e. whether he has been born at one time rather than another, since it comes to the same thing in the end.

mors inmortalis. A very striking expression, — the one thing that is deathless is death itself.

tellus quod dura creâsset. Lucretius regarded life as inherent in certain combinations of atoms, and thought that when the earth was young it teemed with vital energies which produced spontaneously all possible forms of life, — that out of the warm soil came not only herbage, trees, and all kinds of vegetation, but also living creatures. Birds broke forth from the eggs that had been found within the earth. Little children crept out of the hollows near the surface. All sorts of monstrosities were also produced. There were those which had no feet, others with no heads; eyeless and mouthless creatures came into being. But only those able to maintain themselves lived; for the law of nature is the survival of the fittest. This crude form of the doctrine of evolution was first taught by Empedocles, of Agrigentum, who flourished in the fifth century B.C., and whom Lucretius greatly admired (i. 716–733). See Winnefeld, *Die Philosophie des Empedocles* (Rastatt, 1862), and the account in Mayor's *Sketch of Ancient Philosophy* (Cambridge, 1881).

The picture of the gradual dawnings of civilization as given by Lucretius is very interesting, and shows great ingenuity and penetration. Man goes to school to Nature. He discovers fire by seeing lightning kindle a conflagration, or by observing flame produced when the branches of trees rub together in the forest. The use of metals was learned when burning forests melted them, and they ran into cavities on the earth's surface. Planting and grafting were also acquired by observation. Men began to sing when they tried to imitate the sounds of the birds. The wind blowing through the hollow reeds first suggested the flute and the pipe. The medical art was learned from sick animals that sought out by instinct the herbs that were able to effect a cure. Language developed gradually by the exercise of a power inherent in men and animals alike.

32. molirier. Archaic infinitive = *moliri.*

novitas florida. "The blooming youth."

scibant = *sciebant.*

arbita. Same as *arbuta.*

Umida saxa. This repetition is called by the rhetoricians Epizeuxis.

33. sibi valere. To be his own master, — "lord of himself, that heritage of woe."

silvestria. "In the woods."

subus. Scanned in the archaic fashion *subu'*. See notes to p. 21.

palantes. "Roaming about."

erat curae. Sc. *illis.*

Spumigeri suis. *Sus* is here masculine, as often.

intempestā nocte. "At the dead of night."

34. Viva videns vivo, etc. A famous alliterative line. See notes to p. 21.
minas ponebat = *deponebat.*

Nec poterat quemquam, etc. This and following are two very striking
lines.

Improba navigii ratio. The Latin races have never been fond of seafaring,
and Latin literature abounds in passages that display a dread of the seas, and a
belief that the gods intended them to be absolute barriers between the lands they
separate. A familiar expression of this thought is found in the famous ode of
Horace to Vergil (i. 3, 21–26).

amicitiem. Rare form of the fifth declension.

35. omnimodis. Illogically formed on the analogy of *multimodis* (used on
p. 31, line 27), for *omnibus modis.*

At varios linguae sonitus, etc. The Lucretian theory of language is that
man has the faculty of evolving language just as he possesses other faculties that
are gradually developed by necessity and practice. This is just as true of
animals as of men, only the former, having no complex or abstract ideas to
express, need only the limited vocabulary of cries and howls. In the beginning,
man's vocabulary was equally limited, for his range of thought was little greater
than that of the beasts ; but as his mind developed beyond theirs, so his power
of speech correspondingly grew. There was in the primitive speech a peculiar
appropriateness in the name to the thing. Epicurus says : "The natures of men
in the case of each people, experiencing peculiar feelings and having peculiar
ideas, *expelled the air accordingly,* thus expressing different feelings and ideas
differently."

This is in reality the theory of phonetic types (the "ding-dong theory"),
advocated in recent years by Heyse and Max Müller. A simple statement of it
is as follows: Just as a piece of metal rings differently when struck by different
substances, so man rings differently, so to speak, when struck by different emo-
tions, desires, and ideas. It is curious that the advocates of this theory do not
see that it is only the onomatopoetic theory over again, stated in the form
of a simile ; for the onomatopoetic theory covers not only such words as are
imitative of *sound,* but those that are inherently appropriate to whatever they
describe. Thus Vergil's line descriptive of the flight of a dove, —

> Radit iter liquidum celeres neque commovet alas,

is just as truly onomatopoetic with its recurrent liquids and vowels as his won-
derful mimetic description of a cantering horse : —

> Quadrupedante putrem sonitu quatit ungula campum.

For a fuller discussion, see Häckel, *Natural History of Creation,* ii. 300 ; Dar-
win, *Descent of Man,* i. 52–60 ; Heyse, *System der Sprachwissenschaft;* Max
Müller, *Science of Language,* i., ch. 9 ; Diebitsch, *Sittenlehre des Lucretius*

(Ostrowo, 1886); Whitney, *Life and Growth of Language*, pp. 120, 282, 294–298; Strong, Logeman, and Wheeler, *Introd. to the Study of the History of Language*, pp. 157–169 (London and New York, 1891).

utilitas. A favorite term in the Epicurean philosophy, denoting the general adaptation of means to end, — "expediency," "convenience."

ad gestum. Language is therefore a sort of verbal gesture. See Aulus Gellius, x. 4.

infantia. From *in*, negative, and *fari*, "to speak."

vim. In writers before the time of Cicero, *utor, fruor, fungor*, and their compounds occasionally govern the accusative instead of the ablative.

pantherarum. See notes to p. 16.

auxiliatum. A word found only here. Lucretius is especially fond of verbal nouns of the fourth declension.

putare aliquem tum nomina distribuisse. Cf. Genesis, ii. 20.

inde. Pronominal adverb. "From him."

36. rebus . . . apertis. By things that are open to every one's observation.

canum Molossûm. The Molossian hounds of Epirus are everywhere spoken of as the finest and sturdiest for hunting large game.

Et catulos blande, etc. "And when they begin to lick their whelps tenderly with their tongues, or when they fondle them with their paws, and charging on them with open mouth, threaten to swallow them, while their teeth menace them in pretense."

baubantur. An onomatopoetic word found only here.

37. Corvorum. Professor Kelsey refers, for an account of the ancient mystery connected with the raven, to an article in the *Popular Science Monthly*, vol. xviii., pp. 45–56, entitled "A Flock of Mythological Crows."

fulgēre. Here of the third conjugation.

rami stirpesque teruntur. The ancients produced fire by rubbing together sticks prepared for the purpose and known as *igniaria* (Gk. πυρεῖα). These were (1) a block of soft wood with a hollow in it; and (2) a bit of hard wood which was whirled around in the hollow of the block until the friction produced sparks which were, in early times, caught on a tinder made of dried grass, but later on a kind of sulphur matches (*ramenta sulpurata*), such as were used down to the early part of the present century, before lucifer matches were invented. The *igniaria* were so inconvenient to use that they were generally employed only for kindling fire for sacred purposes, e.g. for relighting the fire in the Temple of Vesta when by any chance it became extinguished. For ordinary needs, the more convenient flint and steel were employed, and mention is also made of burning-glasses (Plutarch, *Numa*, 9). For an account of primitive methods of producing fire, reference may be made to Tylor's *Early History of Mankind*, p. 237 (London, 1865), and a paper by Dr. M. H. Morgan in the *Harvard Studies in Classical Philology*, vol. i. (Boston, 1890).

Haec ratio quondam morborum, etc. This great plague which devastated Athens is described by Thucydides in his second book, and by Hippocrates (*De Morbis Popularibus,* bk. iii.). It is also mentioned by Diodorus Siculus (xii. 7), who ascribes the appearance of the disease to an excess of rain in the hot months, to a lack of proper food, — the preceding harvests having failed, — and to unnatural absence in this year of the customary cool north winds (*Etesiae*). See also Häser, *Geschichte der epidemischen Krankheiten* (Jena, 1867).

Cecrops. Cecrops and Pandion (line 6) were early kings of Attica.

38. vis in cor. i.e. into the stomach, which the early physicians called by the name for heart (καρδία). Compare our term " heart-burn " for a form of dyspepsia.

singultus. " Retchings," " belchings " (Gk. λύγξ κενή).

nervos. " The muscles."

coactans. " Contracting."

sacer ignis. Erysipelas, known in modern times as " St. Anthony's fire," because in the pestilential epidemic of 1089 in France, it was reputed that many were cured by the intercession of St. Anthony. It is fairly probable that the epidemic of 1089 and that in Athens were identical in character, neither being erysipelas, but rather a form of *raphania*, — a disease caused by eating the ergot of rye produced in damaged grain, such as the Athenians must have had owing to the poor harvests of the preceding year and the wet, unhealthful summer in which the plague broke out. The symptoms as described by Lucretius and others are strongly suggestive of ergotism.

40. fida canum vis. "The faithful dogs." This statement corresponds with that of Thucydides (ii. 50).

animam ponebat. Here *ponebat = deponebat.* So *animam agere* and (line 94) *animam amittebat.*

VII. GAIUS VALERIUS CATULLUS.

Passer. Sparrows were favorite pets of the Romans. Other birds so kept were doves, ducks, jackdaws, parrots, and quails, the last being used for fighting, like game-cocks.

42. deliciae. " The darling." Plural of excellence.

Quicum. *Qui* is here an ablative of the form of the third declension. Other third declension forms of the relative are *cuius* (*cuis*), *cui, quem, quibus.*

meae puellae. Lesbia, on whose identity with Clodia, mentioned in the biographical note, see a paper by Professor Alfred Gudeman in the *American Journal of Philology,* x. 3.

tristes. " Gloomy."

Vivamus, mea Lesbia, atque amemus. "The key-note of the whole poem is struck in the first word" (Merrill). Live and enjoy life, is the dominant thought; yet there is an undercurrent of pathos in the exquisite lines that finds expression in the *Nox est perpetua una dormienda*. The more intense the *joie de vivre*, the more agonizing the thought that we must leave it all; and the recollection of this is always the skeleton in the Epicurean closet.

severiorum. Intensive comparative; men who are too old to sympathize with the love of pleasure.

unius assis. Genitive of value. The *as* was worth about a cent.

43. basia. The word occurs first here. See notes to page 25. The modern Dutch writer of Latin verse, Jan Everard, better known as Johannes Secundus (1511–1536), wrote a series of short poems entitled *Basia*, each descriptive of a kiss. In graceful expression and voluptuous warmth of sentiment, these very famous productions are not unworthy of comparison with the lines of Catullus. The last edition of them appeared at Leyden, in 1821.

deinde usque. "And then straight on."

fecerīmus. See notes to page 21, *dederīmus*.

Disertissime Romuli nepotum. This poem was written to thank Cicero for some favor done to Catullus. Some editors have regarded the complimentary expressions contained in it as ironical, but for no reason that is obvious to the exoteric mind. On the other hand, Caesar was greatly disliked by Catullus, who attacked him in two of his poems, without much effect, however, for Caesar made no reply to his abuse, and with a sort of contemptuous cynicism, sent him an invitation to dinner.

Collis O Heliconii. This poem was written in honor of the wedding of one Manlius Torquatus, identified by some editors with the L. Manlius Torquatus who was one of the Pompeian party and fell in battle in B.C. 47. His bride was Vinia Arunculeia. It is a sort of epithalamium, but not written to be sung as epithalamia usually were, by a choral band outside the chamber of the newly married couple.

The wedding day of a Roman pair was chosen with great care, so that it might not fall on any unlucky day or upon a day for any reason inappropriate. The whole month of May, for instance, was considered unlucky for weddings, and there was a Roman proverb, *Mense Maio malae nubent*. The early days of March and also of June were likewise regarded as unsuitable for marriage, and so the Kalends, Ides, and Nones of every month. The conventional wedding-dress was a pure white robe (*tunica*) fastened by a woolen girdle. The bride's hair was done up in six braids, and adorned with a garland of flowers gathered by herself. The bridal veil was of vivid flame-color (*flammeum*). The ceremony was simple. Some married lady, a friend of the pair, led them to one another; they joined hands, a prayer was offered to the deities who presided over marriage, and a sacrifice offered. Then followed the wedding banquet, which began in the afternoon. When night came on, the bride was seized, and with a pretence of violence was taken from her mother and carried to her husband's house, escorted by a procession headed by musicians playing the flute, and by an attendant with a lighted torch. Songs were sung on the way. By the side of the young wife walked two boys whose father and mother were still living (*patrimi et matrimi*), and behind her were borne a spindle and thread to symbolize her matronly duties. The bridegroom scattered walnuts (*spargere nuces*) among the street boys as a sign that he had now put away all childish things. At the house, the bride anointed the door-posts with oil and fat, and having decorated them with ribbons, was carefully lifted over the threshold lest she should stumble (a bad omen) in entering. In the *atrium* of the house, where stood the marriage-bed (*lectus genialis*), her husband welcomed her to their home, and with him she offered a prayer to the gods. Three coins were brought by her, one of which she gave to her husband (symbolizing her dowry), one she gave to the household Lares, and one she dropped into the street for the Lares Compitales. (See notes to p. 27.) On the day after the wedding, the husband gave a dinner (*repotia*), at which the bride received her husband's relatives, who then brought their wedding presents. On wedding rings, see text on page 176. A fuller account of the Roman ceremonies will be found in Becker's *Gallus*. For the symbolism involved in the various rites, see Maine, *Early Law and Custom* (London, 1883); McLennan, *Studies in Ancient History* (London, 1876); and Westermarck, *History of Human Marriage* (London, 1891).

Cultor, Uraniae genus. Hymen, god of marriage, is variably called the son of the muse Urania, of Terpsichore, and of Bacchus and Venus. The song opens with an apostrophe to him. *Cultor = incola.*

Hymenæe Hymen. Gk. Ύμὴν Ύμέναιε. The god of marriage.

44. Luteum. The red yellow of flame.

Pelle humum pedibus. i.e. in dancing.

Idalium. A mountain in Cyprus sacred to Venus.

Phrygium iudicem. Paris, who acted as judge in the first beauty-show on record, awarding the prize to Venus.

alite. Literally "bird," so many omens being drawn from the flight of birds. See notes to p. 114.

45. in modum. "In unison," "rhythmically."

zonulā soluunt sinus. The bride wore a girdle (*zona*, dimin. *zonula*) which the husband removed. Hence *zonam solvere = nubere.* Notice the diaeresis in *soluunt.*

captat aure maritus. The husband stands at the door of his house, waiting eagerly to catch the distant music that will announce the approach of the procession escorting his bride.

puellulam. A double diminutive, the primary form being the obsolete *puera* (fem. of *puer*), then *puella, puellula.* Catullus is fond of diminutives, and his use of them gives his lines a tinge of colloquialism, since their formation characterized the popular Latin as they do the popular Spanish of to-day.

Viden. *Videsne.*

Splendidas quatiunt comas. "The torches toss their tresses of flame."

Flere desine. Said to the bride who weeps as all women feel inclined to do at a wedding, whether their own or another's.

46. Tollite o pueri, faces. The procession is now about to depart.

conlocate. i.e. in the *lectus genialis.*

caelites. "The celestials."

Bona Venus. "Kindly Venus."

47. Vesper adest. A second epithalamium possibly on the same marriage as the preceding, though there is nothing in the verses themselves to show this.

innuptae. = *virgines.*

contra. On their side of the *pingues mensae*, opposite the youths.

Oetaeos. Mt. Oeta between Thessaly and Aetolia.

Noctifer. The evening star.

perniciter. From *pernix, pernitor*, and not connected with *pernicies*, which is from *pernĕco.*

palma. The palm of victory.

alio . . . alio. "To one theme . . . to another."

48. avellere natam. Referring to the symbolical show of violence in taking the bride from her mother. See introductory note, pp. 205, 206.

49. Ut flos in saeptis. A very famous passage often quoted and often imitated. Readers of the *Heart of Midlothian* will recollect its citation by Reuben Butler to the Duke of Argyll. Professor Merrill cites from Robinson Ellis the imitation by Ben Jonson in *The Barriers*, and by Robert Browning in *The Ring and the Book*, iii. 233 foll.

Ut vidua. The old simile of the vine and the elm, the ivy and the oak, that has since done yeoman's service in the mouths of sentimentalists.

nudo. "Treeless."

contingit summum radice flagellum. Inversion for *contingit radicem flagello.*

50. iuvenci. i.e. between the rows of vines.

par conubium. A marriage with her social equal. The adjective *par* refers to rank, *aequalis* to age.

Chommoda. The smart set at Rome at various times pursued fads of different kinds with an exaggerated enthusiasm not unknown in modern days. At one time everything Greek was in fashion; at another time everything Etruscan, just as in our own country the fashionable world was affected with Gallomania during the palmy days of the Second Empire, and with Anglomania after 1871. This poem of Catullus satirizes the affectation of a young Hellenomaniac. The Latin language had none of the aspirated consonants so common in the Greek, — *ch*, *ph*, *th*, — and the rough breathing *h* played no great part in its word-formation. In fact, the general tendency was to drop it as an initial letter (cf. the ordinary forms *arena*, *anser* with the older *harena*, *hanser*), and as a matter of fact, *h* did finally become a silent letter as in modern Spanish, and is practically lost in Italian. The prevailing fondness for everything Greek, however, led to the Graecizing of many words. Thus, Quintilius mentions such forms as *chorona*, *praecho*, *chenturio* (i. 5, 19 foll.). Several words definitely retained the aspirated consonant and fixed it in the language, as *pulcher*, *Cethegus*, *triumphus*, and *Carthago*, for the older *pulcer*, *Cetegus*, *triumpus*, *Cartago* (Cic. *Or.* 160), just as we now in English universally but incorrectly write *rhyme* instead of *rime*, having been misled by the analogy of *rhythm* into thinking it a word of Greek origin. Later, when *h* became a silent letter, the wildest confusion prevailed in the orthography of the Romans. Arrius, in the present epigram, was simply a fashionable young person who aspirated at random in his attempt to ape the Greeks. Sir Theodore Martin's translation of the epigram is so clever as to deserve quotation : —

> " Whenever Arrius wished to name
> ' Commodious,' out ' chommodious ' came:
> And when of his intrigues he blabbed,
> With his ' hintrigues ' our ears he stabbed ;
> And thought, moreover, he displayed
> A rare refinement when he made
> His *h*'s thus at random fall
> With emphasis most guttural.
> When suddenly came news one day
> Which smote the city with dismay,
> That the Ionian seas a change
> Had undergone, most sad and strange ;
> For, since by Arrius crossed, the wild
> ' Hionian Hocean ' they were styled! "

quantum poterat. " As loud as he could." He was naturally anxious that every one should realize how thoroughly " good form " he was.

leniter et leviter. Other swells mispronounced as he did, but in quiet tones, and did not stun the ears.

VIII. CAESAR.

53. Druidum. The etymology of this word is uncertain. It has been connected with the Greek δρῦς, "oak," with the Saxon *dry*, "magician," with the Irish *drui*, " a sacred person," and with other words; but no derivation has met with general acceptance. The origin of the Druids is likewise a matter of conjecture. Their doctrines, which closely resemble those of Pythagoras, indicate an Eastern origin, but nothing is known with regard to their first appearance on the stage of European history, the first and most detailed account that we possess being this short digression of Caesar. His account, with some further details furnished by the elder Pliny, form practically the sum of our knowledge of the institution and its workings. The order gradually decayed in Gaul, but maintained for some time its influence in Britain, where the chief monuments still exist in the remains of altars, etc., which show considerable skill in mechanics. Among the best discussions of Druidism are those of Jean Reynaud, *L'Esprit de la Gaule* (Paris, 1866); Barth, *Ueber die Druiden der Kelten* (Erlangen, 1828) ; and Rhys, *Celtic Heathendom* (London, 1888).

54. in finibus Carnutum. Probably near the present town of Dreux. Anglesea was the headquarters in Britain.

loco consecrato. The oak was their sacred tree, and oak groves, sometimes surrounded by stone walls, formed the temples.

in Britannia reperta. But the Welsh tradition says that they entered Gaul from the remote East.

Graecis litteris. Characters, not the language.

transire ad alios. It is not known whence the Druids derived this theory. Cf. Lucan, i. 450.

mundi. Like κόσμος = order.

55. homines immolant. As no instances of this practice are recorded at this period, it has been judged that it had passed out of existence as an institution in Caesar's time. Livy (xxii. 57) records a similar practice on the part of the Romans.

simulacra. These images seem to have been permanent ones, but no details can be gleaned from this vague description.

Mercurium, etc. The identification of these gods is in some cases uncertain. The Gallic divinities are called by the names of the Roman gods whose attributes they appear to possess. Jupiter is probably *Taranis ;* Mercury, *Teutates ;* Mars, *Hesus ;* Apollo, *Belenis.*

exstructos tumulos. Probably the cairns, topped with a flat stone, on which the Druidical fires were lighted.

numero . . . noctium finiunt. The Germans had the same custom, Tac. *Germ.* 11. So the Jewish and the Puritan Sabbaths began at nightfall. Cf. our *fortnight, sennight, twelfth-night.*

56. vitae necisque potestatem. The *paterfamilias* originally had absolute power, including that of life and death, over the *familia.* It was customary to inflict capital punishment only after condemnation by a family tribunal, and he was not criminally responsible for the abuse of this power. In later times this legal absolutism was limited to the right of administering moderate chastisement. The *patria potestas* included the right of repudiating a new-born child, and of selling children into slavery. Until the time of Augustus, the *filius familias* was incapable of holding property in his own name.

ROM. LIFE — 14

57. Hercyniae silvae. Embracing the Black Forest, Odenwald, Thüringer-wald, Erz- and Riesengebirge, and part of the Carpathians.

Helvetiorum. Between the Jura Mountains, the Rhine, and Lake of Constance, the Rhone, and Lake Geneva.

Nemetum. West of the Rhine. Their capital was Noviomagus, now Speier.

Rauricorum. Near Basle.

Dacorum et Anartium. In the southeast provinces of modern Austria, beyond the Theiss.

bos. The reindeer or bison. The statements of these chapters are evidently derived from mere hearsay and misconception.

58. accidunt arbores. Possibly derived from the common expedient of covering pits with light material which gives way under the tread of an animal. See below *foveis*, etc.

IX. PUBLILIUS SYRUS.

59. Absentem laedit. A thought similar to that involved in the appeal from Philip drunk to Philip sober.

Amans quod suspicatur, etc. A foreshadowing of the Shaksperian description of the "green-eyed monster which doth mock the meat it feeds on."

Bis gratum est. etc. A variation of the familiar *bis dat qui cito dat,* which is found in Publilius Syrus in another place in the form *bis dat qui dat celeriter.*

Bona nemini hora, etc. This line is the converse of the English proverb "It's an ill wind that blows nobody good."

Bonus animus laesus, etc. "Beware the fury of a patient man" (Dryden). This is again given by Publilius in another form: *Furor fit laesa saepius patientiā.*

Discipulus est, etc. Cf. Henry Ward Beecher's remark that "one's foresight is never as good as one's hindsight."

Ducis in consilio, etc. Cf. "Better an army of stags with a lion for a leader than an army of lions led by a stag."

60. Fortunam citius reperias, etc. "Easy come, easy go."

Malum est consilium, etc. "Consistency is the vice of fools."

Non pote non sapere, etc. A maxim agreeable to the teachings of Socrates and Herbert Spencer.

Stultum facit Fortuna, etc. Another form of the more familiar proverb, *Quem perdere vult Deus prius dementat.*

Voluptas e difficili data, etc. "Sweet is pleasure after pain." (Dryden.)

Ubi peccat aetas maior, etc. "As the old cock crows, the young one learns."

X. MARCUS TULLIUS CICERO.

62. This extract serves to show the wide range of matter admitted in argument before a Roman court, as well as to exhibit the perfection of Cicero's style when applied to a congenial subject. The speech was delivered in court in the year 62 B.C., in defense of Cicero's friend, the poet Archias, a native of Antioch, who had acquired Roman citizenship under the *Lex Plautia Papiria* in 89 B.C., but whose claim to its possession had been attacked by a certain Gratius. The legal argument is but a small part of the oration, the remainder being devoted to an exposition of the charms and value of literature.

63. **tempestivis conviviis.** Beginning early and lasting till late. The usual hour for the *cena* was three o'clock.

64. **quaedam.** " What I may call ; " *quidam* is often so used by Cicero.

hunc . . . Africanum. The younger, as being nearer in time.

C. Laelium. The friend of P. Cornelius Scipio, and the chief speaker in the dialogue *Laelius* (*De Amicitia*), which takes its name from him.

M. Catonem. Nepos calls him *cupidissimus litterarum.* He began the study of Greek at an advanced age. Cicero's treatise *De Senectute* is called for him *Cato Maior.* The treatise was written about 45 B.C., when Cicero was 62 years old. Scipio, Aemilianus, and Laelius are supposed to visit Cato the Censor, and, wondering at his cheerfulness and activity at 84, request him to show them how to bear the weight of years so easily. Cato complies, refutes the charges usually brought against old age, and fortifies his position by instances of illustrious men of all periods. The purity of style and dignity of treatment have always made it a favorite work, though it is full of false logic and special pleading.

Non cani. *Saepe grandis natu senex nullum aliud habet argumentum quo se probet diu vixisse praeter senectutem* (Seneca, *Tranq.* iii. 7).

65. **certo in loco.** Special seats of honor were reserved for ambassadors and distinguished guests.

nostro collegio. i.e. the college of augurs, of which Cicero was a member. The augurs formed the authorized medium for learning the will of the gods, which in Rome was sought in the flight of birds and in omens, not, as in Greece, through oracles. Augurship was commonly supposed to owe its origin to Romulus, who appointed a college of three augurs, answering to the number of the early tribes (Cic. *De Repub.* ii. 9, 16). Livy, on the other hand, refers the institution of augurs to Numa, to whom the origin of most religious customs was attributed, as the Jewish rites were all attributed to Moses. The college consisted of six members after the time of Numa, all patricians. The number was increased to nine by the addition of five plebeians (300 B.C.) to fifteen by Sulla, and to sixteen by Julius Caesar. The augurs were elected for life. The only distinction in the college was that of age, and the only pay of the members consisted in the privileges accorded to other priests, — special places at the games and festivals, and exemption from military service and certain civil duties.

66. In the year 62 b.c., during the celebration of the mysteries of the Bona Dea at the house of Julius Caesar, P. Clodius, a dissolute young patrician, gained admission disguised in female costume. He was discovered, but escaped, and at his trial for sacrilege, set up a plea of alibi, which was disproved by the evidence of Cicero, who thus incurred the enmity of Clodius. The latter became tribune in 58, and introduced an enactment forbidding fire and water (the usual formula of banishment) to any one who had put Roman citizens to death without a trial. Although this law was aimed at Cicero, he was not mentioned by name, but, thoroughly frightened, he went into voluntary exile at the advice of his friends. On the day of his departure, Clodius carried a law banishing him by name, and prohibiting him from living within 400 miles from Rome. Cicero journeyed to Thessalonica, where he lived in security at the house of his friend Cn. Plancius. This letter, written on his journey, shows the weaker side of his character. For a time he lost all courage, and indulged in unmanly lamentations and regrets, suspecting his friends, and trying by various artifices to regain the favor of those whom he had offended. In the following year a decree was passed sanctioning his recall, and he returned to Rome in September of 58 b.c.

S. P. D. The form of the Roman letter differs in several respects from that used in modern correspondence, particularly in the combination of salutation and signature, and in the absence of complimentary phrases, such as "yours truly," and the like. The normal order of the address is the nominative case of the name of the writer, the dative of the person addressed, and the letters S. D. (*salutem dicit*). This formula was capable of variation corresponding to the degree of intimacy of writer and recipient, by the addition of *suus, dulcissimus,* or some endearing epithet, by the use of a diminutive, or by the more cordial *plurimam* added to *salutem.* All these variations are exhibited in the address of the present letter. The body of the letter does not differ greatly from modern forms, except in the "epistolary use" of the historical tenses based on the time of reading, where we use the present based on the time of writing. The close is apparently abrupt, — *vale,* or *cura ut valeas,* followed by the date (sometimes preceded by *data,* agreeing with *epistula* understood), and the place, usually in the locative or ablative.

The ordinary materials for brief correspondence were tablets of wood or ivory, fastened together in sets of two or more, and coated with wax, upon which the writing was scratched with the *stilus.* For longer communications, papyrus was used, upon which the writing was done with ink (*atramentum*) made of soot and gum, the pen being a split reed (*calamus*). This rude writing equipment made it impossible to conduct a large correspondence except by means of slaves, to whom the letters were dictated (*librarii, servi a manu, amanuenses).* Letters were first securely tied with thread (*linum*), wax was dropped upon the knot and impressed with the seal of the sender, which to some degree took the place of the autograph signature.

As there was no public postal service, the delivery of letters was accomplished by special messengers or by the hand of travellers, until imperial time, when a sort of system was established (*cursus publicus*) for the use of officials and those who could secure special permission to employ its facilities. See Rothschild, *Histoire de la Poste aux Lettres* (Paris, 1875).

minus vitae cupidi. A weak regret that he had not committed suicide.

legis improbissimae. The Clodian Law which exiled Cicero.

XI. PUBLIUS VERGILIUS MARO.

70. Copa. This lively genre piece belongs, if genuine, to Vergil's earlier efforts. It is an invitation to a friend to escape the heat of the day in a shady resort, enjoying fruit and wine in good company. The youth of the poet is seen in the spirit of the poem, which shows much greater vivacity than his later compositions. There is a separate edition of the poem with notes by Leo (Berlin, 1891).

taberna. Literally, a hut formed of planks, then a shop, and especially a wine-shop by the roadside, which the Roman landlords were in the habit of erecting to dispose of the produce of their estates.

Maenalio. The Arcadian mountain Maenalus, the favorite haunt of Pan, was so celebrated that the Roman poets frequently use the adjective for "Arcadian" or "pastoral."

cado picato. The newly made wine was first poured into a large gourd-shaped butt (*dolium*) smeared with pitch, and usually let into the ground. Here it was allowed to ferment for a year, when, for purposes of sale or use, it was poured (*diffundere*) into *amphorae* or *cadi*, which were also pitched, and, if the wine was to be preserved for a longer period, were corked with clay and the mouth pitched.

serta. Garlands made by stitching blossoms upon thin strips of linden bark.

71. Acheloïs. A water-nymph, the daughter of Acheloüs, the river-god.

caseoli. The Roman cheeses were usually eaten in a fresh state like cream cheese or pot-cheeses, but were also pressed and hardened into ornamental shapes in boxwood moulds.

tuguri custos. i.e. Priapus. See note to p. 90.

cicadae. Identical with the American "locust," so-called. At Athens a golden cicada (τέττιξ) was worn in the hair as an ornament, it being regarded as a creature sprung from the earth like the early inhabitants of Attica, according to the legend. The cicada was also kept in cages like canaries at the present day.

vitro. It has been asserted that glass was more generally used and for a greater variety of purposes among the ancient peoples than in our own time. It is at least certain that its use among the Romans was very general. Glass of Phoenician importation occurs at Tarquinii in cemeteries of the eighth century B.C. The word *vitrum* is first used by Lucretius (iv, 604, vi, 991), but the substance is constantly referred to as a well-known object by poets of the Augustan age (cf. Verg. *Aen.* vii. 759 ; Hor. *Carm.* iii. 13, 1). Italy was for a long time supplied from the manufactories of Phoenicia and Egypt; but in Pliny's day glass factories had been established in Italy, Spain, and Gaul. The workmanship of the specimens seen in the large museums ranks in skill and delicacy with that of the best modern artists. Glass was familiar in nearly all its modern applications, including its use for window panes, as has been shown by discoveries at Pompeii and Herculaneum. The aedile Scaurus, B.C. 58, con-structed the *scena* of his theater in three tiers, the lower of marble, the upper of gilded wood, and the middle largely of glass. (Pliny, *Hist. Nat.* xxxvi. 189.) See Fröhner, *La Verrerie Antique* (Paris, 1879).

strophio. A twisted chaplet or garland. See note on *serta* above.

talos. The *talus*, originally knuckle-bone or ankle-bone, was also the name given to dice, which were at first only the natural bone. The *tali* had four long sides and two small ends. Two of the long sides were broad and two narrow. One of the broad sides was convex, the other concave, while of the narrow sides one was flat, the other indented. In playing, four *tali* were used, emptied from a dice-box (*fritillus*). The lowest throw (*canis, canicula*) was four aces ; the highest was that called *Venus*, in which the numbers cast were all different, their sum amounting to fourteen. This throw was also called *Basilicus*, because by obtaining it the king of the feast was appointed (Hor. *Carm.* i. 4, 18 ; ii, 7, 25). See Becq de Fouquières, *Les Jeux des Anciens*, pp. 325-356.

Laocoön. The Laocoön group of the Rhodian school of Greek sculpture once stood, according to Pliny, in the palace of Titus. It was found in 1506 in the baths of Titus. The restoration of the right arm, which was lacking when the group was discovered, has been severely criticised. For a noble description of the group, see Byron, *Childe Harold*, iv. 160. Vergil, in writing this passage, probably had in mind the statue. For a criticism of the Laocoön group, see Perry's *Greek and Roman Sculpture*, pp. 520 foll. (London, 1882).

Tenedo. A small island in the Aegean off the coast of Troas. To this island the Greek fleet withdraw in order to induce the Trojans to think that they had departed (*Aen.* ii. 21).

72. Ardentesque oculos. Accusative of specification.

73. Harpyiae. The Harpies (ἁρπάζω, "to snatch") had been sent by the gods to torment Phineus in Thrace. He was delivered from them by the Argo-nauts, who drove them to the Strophades. To the two mentioned by Hesiod (Aëllo and Ocypete), Vergil adds a third, Celaeno. Dante (*Inferno*, xiii. 10) gives the following description : —

> " There do the hideous Harpies make their nests,
> Who chased the Trojans from the Strophades,
> With sad announcement of impending doom :
> Broad wings have they, and necks and faces human,
> And feet with claws, and their great bellies fledged."

74. Misenus. The pilot of the fleet of Aeneas. He was drowned and buried near Cumae on a promontory, which from him was called Misenum.

Dardanios. " Trojan " ; descended from Dardanus, one of the founders of the Trojan line.

Danaïs. " Greek " ; from Danaüs, an ancient king of Argos.

Iliacos. " Trojan " ; of Ilium, the city of Ilus, son of Dardanus.

Penates. The Penates, originally the guardians of the storeroom (*penus*), together with Vesta and Lar, were the household gods of the Romans. Their altar was the hearth of the house, on which were sculptured the figures of the two Penates with that of the Lar.

75. Ithaca. Now Thiaki, a small rocky island in the Ionian Sea, famed as the birthplace of Ulysses.

Ulixi. The name of the great Greek hero of the Trojan War, Odysseus, appears in Latin in the forms Ulysses, Ulyxes, and Ulixes.

Cyclopis. " Round-eyed." In works of art, the Cyclopes are represented as giants with one eye in the forehead. They were the sons of Uranus and Gaea, and were cast into Tartarus by their father. After assisting Cronus to the sovereignty of the gods, they were put again into prison by him, and at last freed by Zeus, for whom they forged the lightning. The Cyclopes were later imagined as assistants of Vulcan, and placed in Sicily under Aetna. Polyphemus was said to be the son of Poseidon and Thoösa. Later legends make him the unsuccessful lover of the nymph Galatea, for which story see Gay's *Acis and Galatea*; Proctor's *Death of Acis*; Robert Buchanan's *Polypheme's Passion*; and Austin Dobson's *Tale of Polypheme*.

76. Phoebeae lampadis. " The torch of Phoebus," i.e. the sun.

Monstrum horrendum. The halting, heavy sound produced by the elisions and spondees of this line represents the laboring movements of the blinded giant. Browning (*Waring*. iv.) has made strange use of these lines : —

> " As long I dwell on some stupendous
> And tremendous (Heaven defend us !)
> Monstr' — inform, — ingens — horrend — ous
> Demoniaco seraphic
> Penman's latest piece of graphic."

lavit inde cruorem. A very bold stroke or thoughtlessness on Vergil's part. Bathing a wound in sea water is hardly a natural proceeding, and neither Polyphemus nor Vergil probably knew anything of antiseptic medicine.

77. Aetnaeos fratres. The Cyclopes, who were supposed to inhabit the caves of the mountain.

obscuri. The entrance to the infernal regions was begun at break of day.

Ditis. Dis (= Dives) pater. The ruler of the lower world, worshipped by the Romans, and corresponding to the Greek Pluto or Hades.

Orci. A peculiar divinity of the dead, created by popular belief. Like Hades, his name was used to denote the lower world. With this description, compare that in Spenser's *Faery Queen*, vii. 21-25.

78. Eumenidum. The goddesses of vengeance (Gk., *Erinyes*), variously called the daughters of Gaea, or of Nyx (Night) and Skotos (Darkness), who punish all transgressions. Their name, Eumenides ("the kindly ones") springs from the familiar unwillingness to speak plainly of things of ill omen.

Multaque praeterea. "These several mixed natures, the creatures of imagination, are not only introduced with great art after the dreams, but, as they are planted at the very entrance and within the very gates of these regions, do probably denote the wild deliriums and extravagances of fancy which the soul usually falls into when she is just upon the verge of death" (Addison, *Tatler*, No. 154).

Centauri. A savage race, dwelling in the district near Pelion and Ossa in Thessaly, who were destroyed in a war with their neighbors, the Lapithae. They are represented as half horse, half man.

Briareus. One of the *hecatoncheirae*, huge monsters with a hundred arms; son of Uranus and Gaea, "called by men Aegaeon, by the gods Briareus" (Hom. *Il.* i. 403).

belua Lernae. A monster with nine heads which ravaged the country of Lerna near Argos. The slaying of the monster was the second of the labors of Heracles.

Chimaera. A fire-breathing monster, the fore part of whose body was that of a lion, the middle that of a goat, and the hind part that of a dragon. It ravaged Lycia, and was finally killed by Bellerophon. The Chimaera was probably the fanciful personification of a volcano of the same name in Lycia.

Gorgones. Three frightful beings, daughters of Phorcys and Ceto, with wings, brazen claws, enormous teeth, and serpents instead of hair. The best known of the Gorgons, Medusa, was killed by Perseus with great difficulty, as the sight of her head turned every one who looked upon it into stone. The head was placed by Athena in the centre of her shield.

Cocyto. "River of Wailing." (Gk. κωκύω.) A river in Epirus, a tributary of the Acheron, and, like the latter, supposed to be connected with the lower world, or a river of the lower world. Homer makes it a tributary of the Styx, and Vergil in this passage represents the Acheron as flowing into the Cocytus.

Charon. The son of Erebus and the Styx, a dark and grisly old man, who ferried the souls of the departed across the river of the lower world. His fare, an obolus, was placed in the mouth of the dead person.

79. Tendebant. A wonderfully pathetic line, often quoted in literature.

Navita. i.e. Charon. *Navita = nauta.*

O virgo. The Sibyl.

olli. Archaic form for *illi.* Cf. the pronominal adverb *olim.*

Stygiam paludem. Styx, daughter of Oceanus and Tethys, was the first of the immortals to help Zeus against the Titans, and in return was made the goddess by whom the most solemn oaths were sworn. As a river, Styx is described as a branch of Oceanus flowing in the lower world.

Nec datur, etc. "This was probably an invention of the heathen priesthood to make the people extremely careful of performing proper rites and ceremonies to the memory of the dead" (Addison).

80. Cerberus. To increase the horror, some poets gave him a hundred heads (Hor. *Carm.* ii. 34), others fifty, but he is usually portrayed with three, the middle head being that of a lion, with a wolf's head on one side and an ordinary dog's head on the other.

> "Cerberus, monster cruel and uncouth,
>   With his three gullets like a dog is barking
>   Over the people that are there submerged.
>   Red eyes he has, and unctuous beard and black,
>   And belly large, and armed with claws his hands;
>   He rends the spirits, flays and quarters them."
>
> (Dante, *Inferno*, vi. 13.)

Minos. A mythical king of Crete, son of Zeus and Europa. On account of the murder of his son at Athens, he undertook an expedition against Attica, and compelled the Athenians to send him once every nine years seven boys and seven girls to Crete to be devoured by the Minotaur. He appears in later times as a judge of the dead, with Aeacus and Rhadamanthus.

81. Phlegethon. "River of Burning." (Gk. φλέγω.) A river of the lower world, a tributary of the Acheron.

Tisiphone. One of the Furies. See note on Eumenidum, to p. 78.

Teucrûm. The Trojans, as descendants of Teucer, the most ancient king of Troy, son of Scamander and the nymph Idaea.

Hecate. A Greek deity, sometimes confused or associated with Persephone, sometimes identified with the moon goddess. As a goddess of the night, she gradually became a deity of ghosts and magic. She was represented as haunting graves and crossways, where offerings of eggs, fish, and onions were made to her on the last day of the month. In art she is usually represented by three statues placed back to back, each one with special attributes.

Avernis. Now Lago di Averno, a lake near Cumae, filling the crater of an extinct volcano. Near it was the cave of the Cumaean Sibyl, through which Aeneas descended to the lower world.

Rhadamanthus. Brother of King Minos of Crete, who, in consequence of his justness in life, was made a judge in the lower world.

agmina saeva sororum. The Furies.

82. praeceps. Adjective used as a noun.

Titania pubes. The Titans, offspring of Uranus and Gaea (Heaven and Earth).

Salmonea. Salmoneus was a Thessalian who emigrated to Elis and built the town of Salmone. He deemed himself equal to Zeus, ordered sacrifices made to him, and imitated the thunder and lightning. He was slain by a thunderbolt and punished in the lower world.

Aere et cornipedum. Imitative line.

Tityon. Tityus, a giant of Euboea, offered violence to Latona or Artemis, and was slain by her arrows. Cast into Tartarus, he lay stretched over nine acres, with vultures or snakes devouring his liver.

Terrae omniparentis. Cf. the notes to p. 31.

Lapithas. A savage race, neighbors of the Centaurs. They were said to be the inventors of bits and bridles for horses.

Ixiona. Ixion was the king of the Lapithae, who treacherously murdered his father-in-law, and when purified and taken to heaven by Zeus, attempted to win the love of Hera. A phantom resembling her was created by Zeus, and by it Ixion became the father of Centaur. As a punishment for his ingratitude, he was chained to a wheel which rolled perpetually.

Pirithoüm. The son of Ixion. When he was celebrating his marriage with Hippodamia, an intoxicated Centaur insulted the bride. This gave rise to the battle with the Centaurs, who were defeated. Perithoüs was tormented in Hades for having attempted to abduct Proserpina.

83. clienti. "A dependent."

Theseus. The great legendary hero of Attica, son of King Aegeus of Athens, who figured in almost all the great heroic expeditions. He took part in the Argonautic expedition, slew the Minotaur, and assisted Pirithoüs in his attempt to carry off Proserpina, for which he was kept in the lower world until delivered by Heracles.

Phlegyas. The son of Ares and father of Ixion and Coronis, the latter of whom became by Apollo the father of Aesculapius. Having in revenge set fire to the god's temple, he was slain by Apollo and condemned to punishment in the lower world.

Non. mihi si linguae, etc. An imitation of Hom. *Il.* ii. 489.

XII. GAIUS CILNIUS MAECENAS.

84. Debilem facito manu. These curious lines, written in the trochaic measure of *Yankee Doodle*, were apparently composed by Maecenas in one of his most effeminate moods. He was a sufferer from what would now be styled nervous prostration, and resorted to various devices to get a little sleep to restore the tone of his unstrung nerves. Soft music was played while he tossed upon his couch, and an artificial waterfall plashed in his palace to soothe him to slumber. The frantic love of life displayed in this passage quoted by Seneca is at once pathetic and repulsive.

quate. "Make my glairy teeth chatter."

si sedeam cruce. Referring to the instrument of torture known as the *eculeus* or "colt" (cf. the Italian *cavaletto*), — a sort of seat with a sharp point, astride of which the victim was placed with heavy weights attached to his feet.

XIII. QUINTUS HORATIUS FLACCUS.

86. Emirabitur. A word found only here.

tabulā votivā. The temples of Isis especially were thus adorned. Compare the custom, common in Italy, of adorning the shrines of saints with crutches, etc., of those who have been cured.

Babylonios. Cicero's writings show a widespread belief at Rome, even before the time of Horace, in the Chaldean astrology. Through it mathematics and astronomy became objects of suspicion, and the Senate repeatedly passed resolutions *de pellendis magis, Chaldaeis, mathematicis, astrologis, ceterisque maleficis;* cf. Tac. *Ann.* ii. 27, 32, 69; xii. 52; *Hist.* i. 22, etc. Horace himself was free from this superstition.

carpe diem. A famous phrase.

87. Integer vitae. This ode, beginning with the praises of virtue, and at the close making enjoyment the sum of all wisdom, while apparently containing contradictory sentiments, is in accord with Horace's practise *ridendo dicere verum.*

Fusce. Aristius Fuscus, a friend of Horace, of whom not much is known. He is mentioned again in *Sat.* i. 9.

Syrtes. The modern gulfs of Sidra and Cabes.

Hydaspes. A tributary of the Indus, now the Jhelûm.

Lalagen. "The prattler." (Gk. λαλεῖν.) See note to p. 13.

Daunias. Daunia was a part of Apulia, whose inhabitants were renowned for their military spirit.

Iubae. King of Mauritania, which he received in exchange for his paternal

kingdom of Numidia, when the latter was made a Roman province. He wrote
many works, and is cited by Pliny as an authority on natural history.

Arida. "Parched."

pigris. "Sluggish"; i.e. frozen.

Iuppiter. The name of the god is frequently used to designate his realm,
the bright sky; e.g. *sub Iove*, under the open sky.

Chloë. This poem may be compared with Longfellow's *Maidenhood*, of
which it is the ancient prototype.

88. Tempestiva. "Old enough."

Fons Bandusiae. The locality has been much disputed, but is now known
to have been near Venusia. Horace gave the same name to a fountain on his
Sabine farm. The festival of the *Fontinalia* was celebrated on Oct. 13. Liba-
tions of wine were offered, garlands were placed about the fountains, and the
blood of a sacrificed kid was allowed to flow into the springs.

vitro. See note on *vitro*, p. 71.

mero. "Unmixed wine," opposed to *mulsum*.

Lascivi. "Playful."

Caniculae. The star Sirius. The *Dies Caniculares* were proverbial with the
Romans, as the dog-days with us.

Nescit. = *nequit*. Cf. Eng. *can* = the Scotch *ken* (know); and the use of
French *savoir* in the same sense.

nobilium fontium. Hippocrene, Arethusa, Castalia, etc.

Lymphae. An improperly Graecized form for the true Latin *lumpae*, like
our *rhyme* for *rime*.

89. Maecenas, summoned to Brundusium on affairs of state in 37 B.C., took
with him several friends, among them Horace, on the trip of which this satire
gives a humorous description. The journey was made leisurely, sixteen or
seventeen days being consumed on the road between Rome and Brundusium,
312 miles. This satire has been put to use by Becker in the journey scene in
his *Gallus*.

Aricia. Now Riccia, about 16 miles from Rome; celebrated for the grove
and temple of Diana on the Lacus Nemorensis (now Nemi) with the spring of
Egeria.

Hospitio. Inns (*deversoria*) existed in Rome as early as the second century B.C. The taverns erected on the highroads by neighboring land owners
(see note on *taberna*, p. 70) were supplemented, as traffic increased, by stations
for changing horses (*mutatio*) and for night quarters (*mansio*). The cook
shops (*popinae*) and taverns (*cauponae*) were not frequented by the better
classes, although the gilded youth of Rome had their special taverns, in which
they held the Roman equivalent for the German Kneipe. The occupation of
innkeeper (*caupo*) belonged to the most despised professions (cf. l. 4, *cauponibus
malignis*). The interior arrangement of the inns corresponded probably to that

of the present Italian *osterie*, and then, as now, the nature of the house was indicated by signs. So, for example, Pompeii had its "Elephant House," Rome its "Cock Tavern," in the Forum, Lyons its "Inn to Mercury and Apollo," etc.

Heliodorus. Nothing further is known of him.

Forum Appi. Founded by Appius Claudius, 43 miles southeast of Rome, when he made the Appian Way. From this place a canal led through the Pomptine Marshes to Anxur.

altius . . . praecinctis. "To more active travellers"; referring to the habit of girding up the garments for greater ease in exercise.

Iam nox . . . parabat. Mock-heroic.

90. pueri. Cf. the French use of *garçon* and "boy" = "slave" in our Southern States.

convicia. *Con* + *vox.*

Ingerere. Historical infinitive.

palustres. = *in paludibus.*

viator. See the article by Ashmore in *Classical Studies in Honour of Henry Drisler* (N.Y. 1894).

pastum. Supine.

dolat. Literally "hews," "cuts at him."

quartā . . . horā. Until about 290 B.C., the time of midday was announced to the consuls by a servant (*accensus*), who watched till the sun reached a particular opening in the south side of the Forum. After the introduction of sun-dials (*solaria*) and water-clocks (*clepsydrae*), the daylight and darkness were divided into twelve hours each, the hours, of course, varying in length with the season of the year.

pransi. The Romans had in early times three meals — breakfast (*ientaculum*) at 9, the principal meal (*cena*) at 12, and the *vesperna* in the evening. Later a different arrangement became customary; lunch (*prandium*) was substituted at 12 for the *cena*, which was then taken about 3, after the bath. The *cena*, originally a very simple meal, became, after the second century B.C., a very elaborate one, sometimes prolonged over the whole latter part of the day. Masters and servants originally took their meals in common in the *atrium*; later, special dining-rooms (*triclinia*) were built. Napkins (*mappae*) were introduced in the reign of Augustus. No knives or forks were used; the meats were cut up by a special slave (*scissor*).

Anxur. A Volscian city, later called Tarracina by the Romans.

Priapum. Priapus, the Greek god of fruitfulness. His statue, set up in Roman gardens, seemingly served as a scarecrow.

Maluit esse deum. Cf. the magnificent piece of sustained irony, Isaiah, chap. xliv. 9–17.

novis hortis. On the Esquiline Hill.

commune sepulcrum. The eastern slope of the Esquiline, outside the

Servian rampart, was in early times the Potter's Field of Rome. Within the city, no burials could take place ; *hominem mortuum, inquit lex in duodecim, in urbe ne sepelito neve urito* (Cic. *De Leg.* ii. 23, 58). See Lanciani, *Ancient Rome,* chap. iii. ; and *Pagan and Christian Rome,* chap. vi. The place was acquired by Maecenas, who laid it out in gardens (cf. *novis hortis,* l. 6) and built there a handsome house.

91. Heredes . . . sequeretur. The usual inscriptions were H. M. H. N. S. = *hoc monumentum heredes ne sequatur,* or H. M. Ad H. N. Trans. (*transito*), i.e. the burial place did not form a part of the inheritance, and hence could not be sold by the heirs.

Aggere, etc. The Servian agger. See note on *commune sepulcrum* above.

quae versant. Note the impressive effect of the indefinite.

Umbrae. "Shades." Cf. Shakespeare's witch-scene in *Macbeth.*

92. dentes. According to Epod. 5, 47, she had *dentem lividum.*

caliendrum. "(False) headdress," i.e. "wig."

Accurrit quidam. Propertius has been suggested as the bore, but he was more than ten years younger than Horace, and therefore hardly more than a child when this satire was written.

Num quid vis. A usual formula preliminary to saying farewell, as seen in various passages in Plautus ; cf. *num quid nunc aliut me vis* (*Mil. Glor.* 1086).

quendam non tibi notum . . . longe cubat. These circumstances are touched upon as likely to discourage the bore from accompanying him.

Caesaris hortos. On the Ianiculum, bequeathed to the Roman people by Julius Caesar (Suet. *Iulius,* 83).

pluris. Genitive of value.

Varium. L. Varius, an epic and tragic poet, the friend of Horace, Vergil, and Maecenas. After the death of Vergil, he was directed by Augustus to revise the *Aeneid.*

93. quis membra . . . mollius. "Who can shake a leg more neatly ? "

Est tibi mater. Probably an ancient equivalent of the modern impertinence, " Does your mother know you're out ? "

Sabella. Sabinum was traditionally a witch-country.

quando . . . cunque. Tmesis.

Vestae. The temple stood on the south side of the Forum, north of the Palatine. Horace and his companions had walked along the Via Sacra, past the (later) Arch of Titus, and had reached the tribunal of the praetor, which reminded the bore of his lawsuit.

vadato. Probably ablative absolute = *vadimonio dato,* corresponding to the similar absolute uses *sortito, testato* and *intestato, auspicato,* etc.

94. stare. Technical legal term.

propero. Colloquial indicative where strict Latinity (the Latinity of literature) would demand the subjunctive.

sodes. = *si audes*. *Audeo* contains the root of *aridus*. "If you please."

Maecenas quomodo tecum. "How does Maecenas stand with you?" A flattering way of putting it, as though Horace were the great man and Maecenas the humble follower.

Nemo dexterius. A delicately veiled sneer at Maecenas. The bore is feeling for Horace's true sentiments towards Maecenas, and trying to draw him out.

sic habet. = *sic se res habet*, οὖτως ἔχει.

deducam. *Deducere* is a technical term used of clients escorting their *patronus* home ; *prosequi* is to escort him from his house to the Forum, etc.

dissimulare . . . ridere. Historical infinitives.

95. tricesima sabbata. Many ingenious explanations of these words have been given, but it is altogether unlikely that Fuscus had any special Jewish feast in mind, but trumped up the excuse as a part of the practical joke on Horace.

oppedere. A coarse word belonging to the colloquial language.

surrexe. Colloquial contraction for *surrexisse*.

Archiacis. "Made by Archias," an otherwise unknown maker of inexpensive furniture.

imperium fer. "Put up with my ordering."

Moschi. According to the scholiast, a rhetorician from Pergamum, accused of poisoning.

nato Caesare. The birthday may be either that of Julius Caesar, July 12, or that of Augustus, Sept. 23. *Aestivam noctem* below would seem to indicate the former.

96. paupertate. Not exactly "poverty," for which the word is *egestas*, but narrow means.

toral. The covering of the *lectus*.

mappa. See note on *pransi* to p. 90.

par pari. A Latin form of our proverb "Birds of a feather flock together." So in Cic. *De Senectute* (3, 7), *Pares autem, vetere proverbio cum paribus facillime congregantur*.

umbris. Additional guests not invited by the entertainer, but brought by invited guests. Cf. *Sat.* ii. 8. 22.

quanti. Genitive of price.

Fallacem. Because the resort of fortune-tellers, rogues, and cheats.

pueris tribus. A very small number. Cf. *Sat.* i. 3, 12, where ten slaves are mentioned as very few.

echinus. A word originally meaning a sea-urchin ; here probably a salt-cellar. So in the Third Satire Horace speaks of *concha salis*.

dormitum. Supine of purpose.

Marsya. A satyr flayed by Apollo. His statue stood in the Forum near the praetor's tribunal. The features, distorted after his punishment by Apollo, seemed to express disgust for the usurious Novius.

97. Ad quartam. Eight to nine o'clock. He probably does not mean that he *slept* so late, for he calls one who sleeps to the first hour (*Epist.* i. 17, 6), or after daylight (*Epist.* i. 18, 34), a late sleeper. These quiet hours of the early morning he uses for his studies. Cf. *lecto aut scripto* below.

lusum trigonem. A favorite game of ball at Rome which required special dexterity with the left hand. Note that *lusum* is not a noun, but a participle, and render "after the game of ball is over."

durare. Infinitive used for a *quin* clause.

O matre pulchrā filia pulchrior. It is not clear from the ode who the beauty was whom Horace here tries to propitiate, but she is supposed to be one Tyndaris, daughter of Gratidia or Canidia, who had been ridiculed by Horace (cf. *Sat.* i. 8). Tradition makes her to have been a Neapolitan flower-girl.

Latoë. = Apollo, son of Latona. For the sentiment cf. Juvenal's *mens sana in corpore sano*, p. 145.

Nunc est bibendum. An ode celebrating the taking of Alexandria and death of Cleopatra (30 B.C.).

Saliaribus . . . dapibus. The feasts of the Salii, or priests of Mars, were proverbial for their richness.

Tempus erat. The tense is at first sight peculiar. "Now *was* the time"; i.e. we were right in waiting for the present time; it really was the proper moment.

98. Tendit Apollo. i.e. relaxation is necessary. "All work and no play makes Jack a dull boy." "It's a long lane that has no turning."

imminuit dies. Here *dies* = *tempus.*

99. Exegi monumentum. So Ennius in the lines given on p. 21; so, too, Ovid.

Libitinam. Venus as a death goddess.

fortibus et bonis. Not the ablative of the agent, which would require the preposition *ab*, but the ablative of source — "from the brave and good."

Credat Iudaeus Apella. The Jews were regarded by the Greeks and Romans as excessively superstitious. This quotation is used very much like our "Tell that to the marines!"

100. Quidquid delirant. *Quidquid* is the accusative of specification.

Dimidium facti. "A thing begun is half done."

Oblitusque meorum, etc. Imitated in Pope's line, "the world forgetting, by the world forgot."

adire Corinthum. According to Gellius (i. 8, 4), the proverb οὐ παντὸς ἀνδρὸς ἐς Κόρινθον ἐσθ' ὁ πλοῦς originated because *frustra iret ad Corinthum ad Laïdem, qui non quiret dare quod posceretur.* The sense, of course, is that only the wealthy can indulge in expensive luxuries.

Hinc illae lacrimae. An expression first used by Terence (*Andria*, 126), and then by Cicero (*Pro Caelio*, 23).

101. Nescit vox missa reverti. Cf. *volat irrevocabile verbum* (*Epist.* i. 18, 71).

XIV.   PUBLIUS OVIDIUS NASO.

103. The prose account of this tradition is given in Livy, i. 9.

viduos. *Viduus* and *caelebs* are used of both unmarried men and widowers.

vela. Awnings, in place of roofs, were stretched over the whole theater as a protection against sun and rain. The rings to which the awnings were fastened may still be seen in the Colosseum.

scena. Originally "bower," as in Verg. *Aen.* i. 164 ; then applied to the stage decorated as described in the preceding line.

plausus. The system to which applause was later reduced is seen in the following passage from Suetonius (*Nero*, 20). "At the same time he chose young men of the equestrian order and above five thousand robust young fellows from the common people, on purpose to learn various kinds of applause, called *bombi* (booming, humming), *imbrices* (clapping with hollowed hands ; *imbrex*, gutter-tile), and *testae* (clapping with flat hands ; *testa*, tile). They were divided into several parties, and were remarkable for their fine heads of hair, and were extremely well dressed, with rings on their left hands. The leaders of these bands had 40,000 sesterces allowed them." The ancient *claque*.

104. commoda. Gifts made to soldiers on their discharge from service.

Annae Perennae. The goddess of the returning year. Her festival was celebrated near the junction of the Arno and the Tiber, on the Ides of March.

advena. Because considered an Etruscan river.

Nestoris annos. Nestor had lived through three generations of men.

Forsitan audieris. Venus tells Adonis how Atalanta was overcome in a foot-race by Hippomenes, son of the Boeotian king Megareus, and great grandson of Neptune.

105. teque viva carebis. Atalanta was transformed into a lioness, and so lost her own form while still alive (*Met.* x. 698).

106. Aonio. = Boeotian. The name Aonia was given to that part of Boeotia, near Phocis, in which Mt. Helicon and the fountain of Aganippe were situated. Hence the Muses are called *Aonides*.

Onchestius. The father of Megareus was Onchestus, son of Neptune.

107. nollem visa fuissem. *Ut* is omitted after *nolo*.

108. Schoeneïa. She was the daughter of the Boeotian king Schoeneus.

109. For Ovid's banishment, see Introduction, p. 101.

Ausoniae. Originally the district about Cales and Beneventum ; later extended to near Italy. It was also called Opica.

110. exstinctos focos. The hearth typified the family life, and its extinction the desertion of the home. So the sacred fire of Vesta symbolized the life of Rome.

Parrhasis. = *Parrhasia.* Calisto, daughter of Lycaon, king of Arcadia, transformed by Hera into a bear, and afterwards placed as a constellation in the heavens.

apta. Lucky for starting, as determined by an astrologer.

limen tetigi. The most unlucky omen on beginning a journey. So the bride was carried across the threshold of her father's and of her husband's home to avoid the possibility of such an ill omen. See p. 206.

111. Scythia. A vague term in ancient geography, sometimes meaning Scythia, properly so called, sometimes an indefinite name for modern Mongolia and Tartary.

Theseā . . . fide. The proverbial friendship of Theseus and Pirithoüs; cf. Hor. *Carm.* iv. 7, 27. *Nec Lethaea valet Theseus abrumpere caro Vincula Pirithoo.*

Metus. King of Alba, punished in this manner for treachery by Tullus Hostilius (Livy i. 2, 8).

XV. TITUS LIVIUS.

113. Et supererat multitudo. "And (this was a natural expedient, for) the number of inhabitants was too great." This use of *et*, equivalent to the elliptical καὶ γάρ (*et . . . enim*), is a favorite one with Livy.

avitum malum. Referring to the seizure of Numitor's kingdom by his brother Amulius.

inde. The *cause* of the strife; the *occasion* is given in the next sentence.

aetatis. A recognition of the rights of primogeniture.

114. tutelae. "Under whose protection these regions were."

auguriis. *Mihique ita persuasi, Romulum auspiciis, Numam sacris constitutis, fundamenta iecisse nostrae civitatis* (Cic. *De Nat. Deor.* iii. 5).

templa. As here used, *templum* is any spot consecrated by the augural ritual; cf. Livy, i. 18, 6 (*Numa*) *ab augure . . . deductus in arcem, in lapide ad meridiem consedit. . . . Declaratus rex, de templo descendit.*

conditoris nomine appellata. An etymological impossibility. Roma or Ruma meant originally "River-town" (Gm. *Stromstadt*, Corssen).

Palatium. Originally a "feeding place," "pasture," from the root of *pasco.*

Euandro. (Εὔανδρος, "Good-man.") A mythical prince who, before the Trojan War, led a Pelasgian colony from Arcadia and founded a city Pallanteum on the hill afterwards called Palatium. He introduced the worship of Pan = Faunus; cf. Verg. *Aen.* viii. 51.

Herculem . . . Geryone. The tenth labor of Hercules was to steal the cattle of Geryon, a three-headed monster on the island of Erytheia. He was supposed to have come to Italy on his return with the cattle.

Cācus. Described as a half-human, fire-breathing monster. His name was confounded by the Italian Greeks with κἄκός, without regard to the quantity of the first syllable, in contrast with the good Evander.

115. Cum hostes adessent. The Etruscans already had possession of the Ianiculum, which formed a natural bulwark toward Etruria.

Pons Sublicius. Remains of this earliest of Roman bridges are still to be seen. It was built by Ancus Martius in 639 B.C., and was entirely of wood, iron being unknown at the time of the construction, nor was iron allowed in any subsequent restoration. For the horror of iron, see Lanciani, *Ancient Rome*, p. 41 f.

in statione. "In command of the guard."

116. Tiberine pater. Cf. Verg. *Aen.* viii. 72, *Tuque, o Thybri tuo genitor cum flumine sancto,* and Macaulay's lines: —

> " O Tiber, father Tiber, to whom the Romans pray,
> A Roman's life, a Roman's arms take thou in charge this day ! "

118. iuberem macte virtute esse. = *dicerem " macte virtute esto."* *Macte* is the vocative of the adjective *mactus*, from an obsolete *mago = augeo;* and is formulaic, being used even with the accusative (Florus, ii. 18, 16).

XVI. GAIUS PETRONIUS [ARBITER].

119. The selection given here forms a part of the famous episode known as "Trimalchio's Dinner Party" (*Cena Trimalchionis*). The narrator of the story is one Encolpius, who tells how he and his friend Ascyltus with a boy, Giton, are invited to dinner by a rich old upstart named Trimalchio. Trimalchio had been born a slave, but had won his freedom by no very nice practices, and had subsequently accumulated an immense fortune in trade. He is now a shrewd, vulgar, conceited old fellow, with some gleams of kindness and good feeling, but utterly ignorant of social usages and destitute of tact. His guests are, for the most part, persons of his own kind. The conversation put into their mouths by Petronius gives us valuable specimens of the colloquial, ungrammatical Latin (*sermo plebeius*) spoken by the uneducated and often non-Roman people of the mercantile class. The scene of the *Cena* is probably laid in Puteoli. See a valuable paper by H. W. Haley in the *Harvard Studies in Classical Philology*, iii. 1–40.

nivatam. "Cooled with snow." The ancients kept snow in pits and used it as we do ice.

paronychia. Παρωνυχία in classical Greek means a felon or whitlow, but here it means the thin loose skin about the nails.

acido cantico. "A shrill song."

triclinium. "The table."

patris familiae. For the older form *patris familias*, which possesses the genitive ending in *-s* of the first declension in Greek.

gustatio. A sort of preliminary course intended to whet the appetite. It usually consisted of shell-fish, olives, eggs, mushrooms, radishes, etc., and the drink served with them was wine mixed with honey (*mulsum*). To serve so elaborate a *gustatio* as Trimalchio gave them was an exhibition of ignorance of the niceties of gastronomy.

Trimalchionem. The name signifies "thrice effeminate" from μαλάσσω, Lat. *malacus*, *malchio* (Mart. iii. 82).

locus novo more primus. The usual number of guests was nine, arranged as follows : —

```
                        lectus medius
                  ┌────────────────────────┐
                  │ imus   medius  summus   │
        ┌─────────┼──── 6     5     4 ──────┼─────────┐
 lectus │ summus  │     7           3       │ imus    │ lectus
 imus   │ medius  │     8           2       │ medius  │ summus
        │ imus    │     9           1       │ summus  │
        └─────────┴──────────────────────────────────┘
```

The place of honor was no. 6. The master of the feast usually reclined at no. 7. At Trimalchio's dinner, the host, instead of putting some guest into the honorable place, takes it himself, probably because, as he politely tells them later on, he does not consider the present company as entitled to any great civility. Mau, however, regards *primus locus* as referring to the place marked 1 on the diagram, citing the use of πρῶτος in Plutarch, *Quaest. Conviv.* i. 3.

promulsidaria. *Promulsis* is another name for the *gustatio.*

120. Corinthius. i.e. of Corinthian brass, greatly valued by the ancients.

bisaccio. A word found only here.

Syriaca pruna. The black plums and the scarlet pomegranate seeds represented coals of a fire under the silver gridiron, as though the sausages were still broiling on the hearth.

glires. Dormice were regarded by the Romans as great delicacies. Pliny (*H. N.* viii. 82) tells us that at one time the censor, in an effort to suppress luxurious living, forbade dormice, oysters, and imported birds to be eaten. Rules for cooking dormice are given by Apicius, viii. 9. See Friedländer, *Sittenge-schichte Roms*, iii. 29. 6.

papavera. "Spices."

ad symphoniam. "To the sound of music."

laticlaviam mappam. He marked his napkin with the broad purple stripe (*latus clavus*), the badge of high rank. Trimalchio was a *Sevir Augustalis*, an office usually given to freedmen, and regarded it in his reverence for official rank as a mighty honor. Only senators were allowed to wear the *latus clavus* on the tunic, so Trimalchio puts one on his napkin.

anulum grandem subauratum. Only knights were entitled to wear a golden ring (*ius anuli*). Trimalchio does not dare to violate the law, but manages to evade it in part. He wears two rings, both of which appear to be gold when seen at a distance ; but one is only gilded, and the other is sprinkled with little iron stars so as not to be wholly golden.

pinnā argenteā. Martial (xiv. 22) called a toothpick *dentiscalpium*. Ordinarily they were made of the stalks of the mastic tree (*lentiscus*) or of quills.

dentes perfodit. A revelation of his breeding, which is accentuated by his remark that it is a great bore for him to be present, and that his guests have greatly inconvenienced him.

121. absentivos. Old form with *-os* for the later *-us*, retained like many other archaisms in the plebeian Latin.

calculis. The game was probably the game of *latrunculi*, closely resembling our checkers or draughts. An account of it may be found in Falkener's *Games Ancient and Oriental* (London, 1892).

omnium textorum dicta. "All kind of Billingsgate," the weavers (*textores*) being taken as typical of the great unwashed. Cf. Martial, xii. 59. 6.

repositorium. = *ferculum*.

mehercules. For the more common *mehercle*. Seneca, however, has *mehercules* more than forty times (Friedländer).

concepti sint. Sc. *pulli*.

coclearia. "Spoons." The *coclear* had a sharp point on one end, for eating oysters, snails, etc., and a bowl on the other end for eating eggs (Mart. xiv. 121). The *ligula* more closely resembled our spoon.

selibras. "Half a pound." After *plus*, *minus*, and *amplius* the *quam* may be omitted without changing the construction. Hence the accusative case here instead of the ablative.

toralia. A hanging attached to the front of a couch or sofa depending from above the mattress to the floor. It was commonly white in color and was usually of some material that could be washed. The *toralia* of Trimalchio with their elaborate embroideries are therefore another instance of his ostentation.

subsessores. Huntsmen who lie in wait for the game.

pilleatus. The *pilleus* was the liberty-cap, and was set on the head of a newly made freeman. Trimalchio explains to his guests presently that the boar had already been served up at a previous dinner the day before, and having been sent off by the guests untouched, was now decorated like a slave just dismissed from bondage. A mild joke of Trimalchio's.

scrofam. A dainty bit of table decoration.

122. apophoreti. Usually in the neuter *apophoreta* (ἀποφόρητα). Presents for the guests to take home with them. The fourteenth book of Martial's Epigrams consists of 223 couplets, each of which is supposed to be enclosed with a souvenir, as a sort of motto.

polymitā. From πολύμιτος, "woven with many threads."

debet esse. "He must be a thoroughly worthless slave."

At non Trimalchio. "But not so Trimalchio."

123. botulus. *Botulus* is a vulgar Latin word, reappearing in the French *boudin* and English "pudding." Cf. Gell. xvi. 7. 11.

Gaio feliciter. Sc. *eveniat* or *vertat*. When the emperor and empress entered the theater, the people used to rise and exclaim *Domino ac dominae feliciter* (Sueton. *Domit.* 13).

lacunaria. In the most magnificent houses at Rome, the panels of the ceiling were arranged to shift their position and display different scenes to the guests. Sometimes they would open and let a shower of roses fall. See the passage from Suetonius given on p. 164; and cf. Mayor's note on Juvenal, i. 56.

alabastris. "Scent-bottles."

more vulgato. "In the usual way."

minimā vexatione. "On the slightest pressure."

crocum. The Romans made great use of saffron, both as a condiment for food and to give a perfume to their wines. In the amphitheater, concealed pipes, at frequent intervals, sprayed the spectators with saffron-water. By refined persons, however, saffron was regarded much as musk is to-day, and rose-water and violet were preferred.

mappas implevimus. i.e. to carry away. This was a not uncommon custom at Rome (Mart. ii. 37 ; vii. 20).

124. Lares bullatos. The *bulla* was a globe of metal, often of gold, worn by free-born children, who on coming of age consecrated it to the Lares. The children of freedmen wore *bullae* made of leather. It was regarded as a sort of amulet.

Dii propitii. sc. *sint*. A sort of grace after meat. For another clever description of a parvenu's dinner, see the account given by Horace (Sat. ii. 8) of how the snob Nasidienus entertained Maecenas.

Forte dominus Capuam, etc. This extract is one of the stories told by Trimalchio's guests during the dinner.

persuadeo hospitem. Plebeian Latinity for *hospiti*.

fortis tamquam Orcus. "As bold as the devil."

Apoculamus. A word found only in Petronius, where it occurs again in ch. 66. The meaning is clear, but the derivation is doubtful. Some derive it from *ab + oculus*, comparing the low Latin *aboculus* whence the French *aveugle ;* so that *apoculare (= aboculare)* would mean "to get out of sight" (Bücheler). More probably it is from the low word *culus*, so that *apoculare* will exactly represent the French *reculer* (low Latin *rinculare*).

gallicinia. From *gallus + cano ;* cf. Hor. *Sat.* i. 10, *sub galli cantum.* The plural seems to occur only here.

facere. sc. *se. = ire.* A late Latin use. So in Tertullian, *Pall.* 3 : *ad illum ex Libyā Hammon facit.*

respexi ad comitem. The use of *ad* is post-classical ; exactly our "looked back *at.*"

Mihi anima in naso esse. "My heart was in my mouth." Editors compare Anacreon's κραδίη δὲ ῥινὸς ἄχρις ἀνέβαινε (Bergk, 7) ; *esse* is the historical infinitive.

lupus factus est. The belief in werewolves is older than recorded history, and is one of the primitive manifestations of a general belief in metempsychosis. Herodotus (iv. 105) says of the Neuri, a semi-Scythian people, that it is reported that "once every year each Neurian becomes a wolf for a few days, and then is restored again to the same form as before." Vergil in the Eighth Eclogue says : —

> His ego saepe lupum fieri et se condere silvis
> Moerim . . . vidi.

Pliny the Elder (*H. N.* viii. 34) speaks of the common belief in lycanthropy, but says that it is a mere superstition, and ridicules those who entertain it. Plautus twice mentions the *versipelles* (*Amphitr.* Prol.; *Bacch.* iv. 4, 10). Pomponius Mela repeats the Herodotean story about the Neuri (ii. 1). In modern times, the belief has been widely diffused, and the legends of the Black Forest populate it with these gruesome inhabitants. The notion probably arose from cases such as that of the "wolf-boys" of India like Mowgli the *Shikarri* immortalized by Rudyard Kipling in *Many Inventions* and the *Jungle Book.* See Herz, *Der Werwolf* (1862); Baring Gould's *Book of Werewolves* (1865) ; and K. F. Smith in the *Publications of the Mod. Lang. Assoc.* for 1894.

Qui mori. Sc. *debuisset ;* or *mori* may be the historical infinitive.

125. genios. The *genius* of a person is put by the Romans for the person himself, as here.

126. Lolliam Paulinam. The granddaughter of the immensely rich M. Lollius, whose fortune she inherited. She was first married to C. Memmius Regulus, but the Emperor Caligula fell in love with her, divorced her from her husband, and married her himself. His passion for her did not, however, last very long, for he soon repudiated her. When Claudius was emperor, Lollia intrigued to win his favor, but her successful rival Agrippina procured her banishment, and finally her death.

Gai principis. Caligula.

smaragdis margaritisque. Emeralds and pearls were the favorite jewels of the Romans, though the opal, amethyst, and ruby were much admired. Julius Caesar gave to Servilia, the mother of Brutus, a pearl worth $240,000. The famous pearl which Cleopatra dissolved and drank was one of a pair valued at $400,000. The ancients probably knew of the diamond, but, as the art of cutting and polishing it had not yet been learned, did not greatly value it. All the gems were imitated by the ancient jewelers in paste and crystal. For a full account of gems in classical times, see Middleton, *The Engraved Gems of Classical Times* (London, 1891 ; Blümner, *Technologie*, iii. 227 foll. ; and Murray. *Handbook of Greek Archaeology*, pp. 40–50, 146–173 (London, 1892).

quadringenties HS. Sc. *centena milia.* A sum equal to $1,600,000. The sign IIS. stands for IIS (*duo et semis*), the sestertius having been originally worth two and a half *asses.* The value of the sestertius may be roughly reckoned at four cents.

partae. From *pario.*

regum muneribus. i.e. by presents extorted from kings.

127. Curius aut Fabricius. Two typical old heroes of the days of Rome's simplicity.

fercula. The litters on which were carried in the triumphal processions the spoils of the victorious general. Occasionally captives of great distinction were so paraded.

unam imperii mulierculam accubantem. "This little bit of a woman, the head of the empire, at table."

In morsu. "In case of a bite."

edendum. Sc. *caput.*

pollici. Sc. *pedis.* Cf. the French *doigt de pied.*

quae abscissa dimissa sit. "Which, after having it cut off, has been let go."

limus. "A slime." This seems to be a dim foreshadowing of the Pasteur treatment.

lytta. (λύττα.) Hence the Gk. verb λυττάω "to rave" Pliny's superstition

about the *lytta* has endured down to the present century, and puppies are still
occasionally "wormed" to prevent hydrophobia. What are supposed to be
worms, however, are really white pustules beneath the tongue.

Saliuntur. "Are salted."

128. scholae. The various schools of medicine.

litteras scire. "To have some learning." So *litteras nescire* is a proverbial
phrase "to be a fool." A fuller account of the theory of Herophilus is given
by Pliny in xi. 88. The notion was that there was a normal rate of pulse beat
for persons of each age, a variation from which indicated that something was
wrong.

mutata. Sc. *schola*.

inter initia. "At first."

contrariā medicinā. Pliny elsewhere (xix. 7) says that Antonius Musa
cured Augustus of a severe illness by prescribing lettuce which his former phy-
sician had forbidden him to eat. Suetonius (*Aug.* 81) relates that he treated
Augustus for abscesses with cold applications.

apud principes. In their practice any people of importance.

imputavit principibus. Regarded it as a favor to the emperor; lit. "set it
down to the account of the emperor." A business phrase used of recording a
debt due to one's self.

ad eam aetatem. "Up to their time."

eloquentiae assectator. "A professor of oratory."

Iatronicen. "Conqueror of physicians" (Gk. ἰατρονίκης).

129. ephemeride. "Almanac."

Senecae stipulatio. Seneca speaks of this treatment approvingly in two
letters (*Epist.* 53 and 83).

turba se medicorum periïsse. Supposed to be a translation of a line of
Menander: —

Πολλῶν ἰατρῶν εἴσοδος μ' ἀπώλεσεν.

flatu. "The puffing."

insignia. "Some striking facts."

ius Quiritium. "The full right of Roman citizenship."

compito Acilio. "The Acilian four-corners." A part of the city.

130. Opicos. Used by the ancients as we use the word "Vandals." The
Opici or Osci were one of the early Italian peoples, rude and uncultivated, whence
their name became proverbial.

quae nunc nos tractamus. Pliny is, in this part of his work, treating of
medicine as the pharmacopoeia.

Augebo providentiam. "I will glorify their foresight."

ad Graecos transfugae. In adopting their language for writing medical works. An instance of a Roman medical author who wrote in Greek is Sextus Empiricus.

131. credatur. Impersonal. "Credence is given."

For a full account of ancient medicine, see Watson, *The Medical Profession in Ancient Times* (New York, 1856); Daremberg, *Histoire des Sciences Médicales* (Paris, 1870–73); and Berdoe, *Origin and Progress of the Healing Art* (London, 1893).

XVIII. MARCUS FABIUS QUINTILIANUS.

132. Chrysippus. The celebrated Stoic philosopher who lived B.C. 280–207.
deforme. "Unseemly."
injuria. "A wrong thing."
illiberalis. "Coarse."
vapulantibus. *Vapulo* is a neuter passive verb like *fio* and *veneo*.
frangit animum. "Breaks the spirit."
133. nimium est. "More than enough."

Quintilian's view of corporal punishment was not the view that generally prevailed at Rome. Martial speaks of the noise made in whipping children, which made the vicinity of a school unpleasant to the residents (xii. 57). Horace has made the severity of his teacher Orbilius proverbial. Verrius Flaccus, the tutor of the grandchildren of the emperor Augustus, introduced a system of rewards to take the place of a system of punishments, appealing to the ambition rather than to the fears of the children.

in sipario. The drop curtain in a theater was called *siparium*, the principal curtain, *aulaeum*.

nudum. Not "naked," a sense which the Latin word does not usually have, but stripped of the outer garment. So, too, γυμνός in Greek.

in nervo. The *nervus* was an arrangement for confining criminals something like the stocks, being made of wood and having holes for the feet (Plaut. *Asin.* iii. 2, 5).

hoc illam viginti annis audio. A joke that is still hard worked by the newspapers.

134. Stoicus. The Stoics and the Epicureans were the philosophic antipodes of one another; and both schools frequently filled out their discussions of abstract principles with personal abuse.

XIX. MARCUS VALERIUS MARTIALIS.

135. Nil istic quod agat, etc. "There is nothing there for a third cough to do."

Non amo te, Sabidi, etc. This very famous epigram is the original of one equally famous in English, — that written by Tom Brown on Dr. John Fell, Dean of Christ Church, Oxford, about 1670.   It runs as follows : —

> "I do not like thee, Dr. Fell,
> The reason why I cannot tell;
> But this I know and know full well,
> I do not like thee, Dr. Fell."

A still earlier imitation in English is found in Thomas Forde's *Virtus Rediviva* (1661) : —

> "I love thee not, Nell,
> But why I can't tell;
> Yet this I know well,
> I love thee not, Nell."

It seems probable that Brown's epigram was imitated from this rather than directly from Martial.

136. Continuis vexata madet, etc.   This epigram has been made over in modern times and used by the newspaper funny men against the milkman.

copo. Plebeian form of *caupo*, the diphthong disappearing in the long vowel.

Emptis ossibus. Artificial teeth seem to have been made and used by the Romans at a very early period. Cicero (*De Legibus*, ii. 24) quotes an old law which forbade the placing of gold in tombs except that used in the artificial teeth. Martial has other hits on the same subject, e.g. that given on p. 137.

Cerussata. The *cerussa* (ψιμύθιον in Greek) was a face enamel prepared by exposing lead to the fumes of vinegar. It was very largely used by Roman woman as was rouge (*fucus*) and other cosmetics. A description of the making up of a woman's face is given by Plautus in the *Mostellaria*, i. 3 ; and a fragment (*Medicamina Faciei*) ascribed to Ovid treats learnedly of the whole subject. From these and other sources we learn that Roman ladies enameled their skins, rouged their cheeks, touched up their lips with scarlet (*minium*), stained the eyebrows black with antimony, darkened the lids with a preparation of soot (ἄσβολος), traced over the veins with blue, and used patches (*splenia*) to heighten the fairness of their complexion by contrast. See Böttiger's *Sabina*, i. pp. 24 foll. (3d ed. revised by Fischer, Munich, 1878).

comatus. i.e. by wearing a wig (*galerus, capillamentum*), which was a very common thing at Rome, as were all the arrangements of false hair (switches, bangs, chignons, "rats") that are usually supposed to be modern.

Issa est purior osculo columbae. This pretty little poem may be compared with that of Catullus to Lesbia's sparrow, given on p. 42.

virum. "A mate."

137. olent . . . myrrham. A sort of cognate accusative.

XX. DECIMUS IUNIUS IUVENALIS.

138. tibicine. A temporary prop which supports the building as the flute player supports the singer.

frivola. Things half worn out ; rubbish. Derived from *frio, frico.*

Ucalegon. = *neighbor.* The name is borrowed from Vergil's account of the burning of Troy (*Aen.* ii. 311). Vergil gets it from Homer (*Il.* iii. 148).

reddunt. "Pay over ;" i.e. as rent. The word implies giving what is due.

139. Codro. Otherwise unknown.

Proculā. Probably some well-known female dwarf at Rome.

minor. "Too small."

opici. The Opici, or Osci, were an Italian race proverbially rough and uncouth. See the passage from Cato cited by Pliny, and given on p. 130.

Pullati. In mourning, the higher class put on the dress of the next lower. Here the *proceres* do much more in assuming the *tunica pulla*, the ordinary dress of the common people.

differt vadimonia. Puts off the consideration of bail questions.

Euphranoris. Euphranor was distinguished both in sculpture and painting. He was a native of the Corinthian Isthmus. His chief works were produced during the reigns of Philip and Alexander.

Polycliti. Polyclitus, one of the most celebrated sculptors of the ancient world, was an associate of Phidias and Myron. All of his work was in bronze, except the ivory and gold statue of Hera in her temple between Argos and Mycenae.

mediam Minervam. The literary works in the libraries were under her protection.

Persicus orborum lautissimus. "Persian," because the Persians and Orientals generally were regarded as rolling in wealth. Cf. our "nabob." The expression *orborum lautissimus* is best taken as a case of the rhetorical figure Oxymoron ; but *orborum* may be "childless." Asturicus is rich and childless, and hence all flatter him and send him presents, hoping to be remembered in his will.

140. avelli. Middle voice ; "tear yourself away."

Sorae, Fabrateriae, Frusinone. Sora was in Volscian territory, on the Liris, north of Arpinum and Fregellae. Fabrateria lay to the south of Sora, and Frusino to the southwest.

tenebras. "Darkness" for a dark house (*aedes tenebrosas*), by the figure Metonymy, a favorite with Juvenal.

haustu. "By an easy dip."

epulum . . . Pythagoreis. The Pythagoreans were vegetarians, because of their belief that the souls of men passed into animals.

Redarum transitus. Wagons were not allowed to drive through the town before the tenth hour of the day, except loads of building material for public edifices.

mandrae. *Mandra* is originally a halting place, then a cattle pen, and finally the cattle themselves. It is here the objective genitive: "the curses hurled at the team."

Druso. The emperor Tib. Claudius Drusus was famed for his fondness for sleep. Cf. Suet. 8: *quotiens post cibum obdormisceret, quod ei fere accidebat ;* Suet. 33: *in iure dicendo obdormisceret rixque ab advocatis de industria vocem augentibus excitaretur.*

141. Liburno. Liburnians were much used at Rome as litter-carriers. Liburnia lay along the northeastern shore of the Adriatic.

obiter. Physical use of the adverb = *in viā* or *per viam.*

sportula . . . culina. The early custom of occasionally inviting clients to a regular dinner (*cena recta*) gradually gave place to that of presenting to each a portion of food, which being carried away in a small basket (*sporta*) received the name of *sportula.* For the sake of convenience, an equivalent in money was substituted, the usual amount being 100 quadrantes. In this passage portable ovens take the place of baskets, to keep the food warm.

Corbulo. Nero's famous general, Cn. Domitius Corbulo, was *corpore ingens, verbis magnificus* ('Tac. *Ann.* xiii. 8).

saxa Ligustica. The quarries of Luna and Pisa furnished white marble (now called Carrara), used in sculpture, and stone of a bluish tint, which was used only for building purposes.

142. Striglibus. The *strigil* was a flesh scraper used after the vapor bath or the *palaestra* to remove moisture and impurities, and the oil after anointing.

gutto. A small flask containing the oil used for rubbing down the body after bathing.

novicius. "Being new to the business"; i.e. having never died before. A grim joke.

Porthmea. For this passage, see Vergil's description, pp. 78, 79. Beside the fare, costly articles were also laid in the grave with the bodies of the rich. Accounts of the discovery of such articles may be found in Marquardt, *Privatleben der Römer,* and in Lanciani, *Ancient Rome.*

patent vigiles fenestrae. This may be punningly rendered in English, "as many as there are windows up." Cf. *pervigiles popinae,* Sat. viii. 158 ; *vigiles lucernae,* Hor. *Carm.* iii. 8, 14.

coccina laena. The scarlet mantle by which the rich man is recognized.

lampas. A candelabrum with many lights, originally carried before the imperator only.

Candelae. A wax or tallow light with adjustable wick.

143. vapulo. Neuter passive verb like *fio* and *veneo.*

stari. Impersonal: "a halt to be made."

quaero. " Am I to look for you ? "

Pomptina palus. The Pomptine Marshes on the coast of Latium, near Terracina, are formed by several rivers which spread over the plain instead of finding their way to the sea.

Gallinaria pinus. A fir forest near Cumae, a resort of bandits.

uno carcere. The Tullianum, or Mamertine Prison, built by Ancus Marcius. *Carcer ad terrorem increscentis audaciae media urbe, imminens foro, aedificatur* (Livy, i. 33, 8). It was originally a stone quarry called Lautumiae, from which issued a fine spring (*tullius*), the same now shown to visitors as a miraculous feature of St. Peter's prison. The modern and mediaeval name " Mamertine " came from a statue of Mars (Oscan *Mamers*) which formerly stood near it.

144. trutinā. Cf. Hor. *Epist.* ii. 1, 29 : *Romani pensantur eadem Scriptores trutina.*

causidicus. "Pettifogger." The dignified name for a lawyer was *orator* or *patronus.*

praeco. Perhaps " auctioneer."

aera . . . laboranti lunae. *Aeris crepitu, qualis in defectu lunae silenti nocte cieri solet* (Livy, xxvi. 5) ; i.e. to drive away the eclipse.

tunicas succingere. Only men wore such tunics, those of the women reaching to the ankle.

Caedere Silvano porcum. Cato, *De Agric.* 83, describing the sacrifice to Mars Silvanus, adds : *eam rem dirinam rel servus vel liber licebit faciat, mulier ad eam rem divinam ne adsit neve videat quo modo fiat.*

quadrante lavari. Like the Cynic and Stoic philosophers ; for even among men, only the poorest bathed in so inexpensive a manner.

145. enthymema. "An enthymeme," a name given in logic to a formal syllogism of which one member is suppressed ; e.g. " All Romans are brave, and Caesar is a Roman."

quaedam non intellegat. Cf. Martial, ii. 90 : *sit non doctissima coniunx, Sit nox cum somno, sit sine lite dies.*

Palaemonis artem. Q. Remmius Palaemon, the teacher of Quintilian, *docuit Romae, ac principem locum inter grammaticos tenuit.* His yearly income as a teacher amounted to 400,000 sesterces ($16,000).

sit mens sana in corpore sano. Cf. Seneca, *Epist.* 10, 4 : *roga bonam mentem, bonam valitudinem animi, deinde tunc corporis.*

Sardanapali. The last king of the Assyrian Empire of Nineveh, passed his time in effeminacy and luxury, dressed in female attire and unseen by his subjects.

The paraphrase of the last few lines by Dr. Johnson in his *Vanity of Human Wishes* runs as follows : —

> " Still raise for good the supplicating voice,
> But leave to Heaven the measure and the choice.

Safe in his power whose eyes discern afar
The secret ambush of a specious prayer;
Implore his aid, in his decisions rest,
Secure whate'er he gives, he gives the best.
Yet, when the sense of sacred presence fires,
And strong devotion to the sky aspires,
Pour forth thy fervors for a healthful mind,
Obedient passions and a will resigned :
For love, which scarce collective man can fill;
For patience, sovereign o'er transmuted ill;
For faith, that panting for a happier seat,
Thinks death kind Nature's signal of retreat.
These goods for man the laws of Heaven ordain,
These goods he grants who grants the power to gain;
With these celestial Wisdom calms the mind,
And makes the happiness she fails to find.

XXI. GAIUS PLINIUS CAECILIUS SECUNDUS (MINOR).

146. avunculi. Pliny the Elder. See p. 126.

Miseni. A town on the harbor formed by the promontory of the same name. The harbor was the principal station of the Roman fleet in the Tyrrhenian Sea. It was about 20 miles from Pompeii. All along the coast were many handsome villas of the Roman nobility.

147. Campaniae solitus. "Habitual to Campania."

posco librum Titi Livi. This is usually sneered at by the commentators as a bit of priggishness on Pliny's part ; but there is no particular priggishness in his telling of it, for he does not parade it as being necessarily an exhibition of courage. Possibly it was done in the spirit of the philosopher in the haunted house (p. 150) who writes while the ghost is clanking its chains.

ego intentus. Sc. *resto.*

hora prima. Six o'clock.

languidus dies. "The light was still uncertain and rather feeble." This is the earlier meaning of *dies.*

excedere oppido visum. Sc. *est.* "It seemed best to leave the town."

148. effuso cursu. "Headlong flight."

descendere . . . operire. Historical infinitive.

Capreas. Now Capri ; a small island opposite Naples.

Miseni quod procurrit abstulerat. "Blotted out the promontory of Misenum."

orare, hortari, iubere. Historical infinitives.

posse enim iuvenem. Accusative with infinitive depending upon a word of saying implied in the preceding verbs.

149. noscitabant. "They were trying to recognize." The so-called cona-tive use of the imperfect tense.

lymphati. Literally "bewitched by the nymphs" (*lumpae*).

150. donec de avunculo nuntius. Sc. *veniret.*

si digna ne epistulā, etc. A bit of mock modesty.

idolon. Gk. εἴδωλον. Latin names for a ghost are *larva, imago, umbra,* etc.

legit titulum. Advertisements of houses to let began among the Romans with the words EST LOCANDA, which form is retained by the modern Romans at the present time.

iubet sterni. Impersonal.

pugillares. Small tablets that could be held in the hand (*pugillus,* "a handful").

innuebatque digito. "And beckoned with its finger."

151. ceris. From *cera* "wax," used by Metonymy for the waxed pages of the tablets.

publice. "At the public expense." The tale has all the stage-properties of a modern ghost story. The old man beckoning and leading suggests the ghost in Washington Irving's story, *Dolph Heyliger.*

152. A letter addressed by Pliny while governor (propraetor) of the province Pontica to the Emperor Trajan. It gives the earliest information that we have from pagan sources, and is referred to by Tertullian, Eusebius, and St. Jerome.

domine. The word *dominus* originally meant a master in relation to a slave, like the Greek δεσπότης; hence it was not until the Empire had become autocratic that the Roman emperors ventured to allow themselves to be addressed by this title. It was applied, however, to persons in private life as a title of courtesy, exactly as is our English "Master," which has now assumed the form "Mister" on the analogy of its feminine "Mistress." In the Romance languages, and through the various low Latin varieties (*domnus, domna, dominicella*), it becomes the French *dame* (originally both masculine and feminine), *demoiselle,* Spanish *don,* *doña,* Portuguese *dom,* and the Old English *Dan.*

quia cives Romani essent. Who, as being Roman citizens, had the right of an appeal to Caesar, as in the case of St. Paul (Acts, xxv. and xxvi.).

libellus. "An accusation."

153. sacramento. The word *sacramentum* was originally applied to a military oath taken by the Roman soldiers when first enlisted, to be followed presently by the more formal oath, *ius iurandum.* In later usage, however, it is equivalent to *ius iurandum,* and denotes a solemn oath of allegiance and devotion. Hence the Christians applied it to the ceremony of the Lord's Supper as involving a renewed profession of allegiance to the faith.

cibum promiscuum tamen et innoxium. Pliny makes this remark, because the pagan Romans, misunderstanding the language used in the celebration of the Sacrament, had the notion that at the *agapae,* or love feasts, the Chris-

tians ate human flesh and drank human blood. This was only one of the
monstrous stories circulated with regard to them. They were reported to be
guilty of sacrilege, incendiarism, incest, and murder, and Tacitus ascribes to
them *odium humani generis.* Many of these charges were spread by the Jews,
with whom for a long time the Christians were regarded by the Romans as
identical. Hence when Nero sought to find a class of people of whom he could
make scape-goats after Rome had been partly burned, he found the Christians convenient for his purpose, and had them tortured, torn by dogs, and burnt alive
in tunics of papyrus smeared with wax and pitch (*tunical molestae*).

hetaerias. Despotic governments always dread the formation of clubs and
societies, because of the feeling that they may at some time be turned to political
use and made the centers of sedition. Trajan had issued a special rescript forbidding such gatherings, and the weekly meetings of the Christians for worship
appeared to be a violation of the order.

civitates. Here in its rare and generally late Latin sense of "cities." The
remote country districts (*pagi*) retained the old Roman faith longest, and held
out most stubbornly against Christianity ; hence our word "pagan" (*pagani*).
Trajan's reply to this letter directed Pliny to punish such Christians as might
be brought before him, but not to be zealous in seeking them out, and to take
no notice of anonymous accusations.

XXII. GAIUS.

154. dicis gratiā. The phrases *dicis causā* and *dicis ergo* in the same sense
(= λόγου χάριν) also occur. *Dicis*, like *vicis*, is a genitive of which the
nominative is not found.

res mancipi. The word *mancipium* (from *manus + capio*) means "a taking by the hand" ; *res mancipi* are things that are taken possession of by
formal purchase and sale. The genitive is descriptive in its nature.

XXIII. WALL-INSCRIPTIONS.

**155. LABORA ASELLE QVOMODO EGO LABORAVI ET PRO-
DERIT TIBI.** A graffito from the walls of the Palatine, and probably drawn
by some slave who had been made to do a turn at the mill (*pistrinum*) as a
punishment (cf. Terence, *Andria*, i. 2, 28). "Toil on, little ass, as I have
toiled, and much good may it do you ! "

petat. The Romans had various games of ball (*pila*), the most popular being
the triangular game, known as *trigon*, which resembled the English "hand ball."
The following description of the Roman game is quoted (with a few slight modifications) from a recent English writer : —

ROM. LIFE — 16.

" In this favorite game of the Romans, there were no *sides*, but each played for himself; still it was a legitimate game, played for winning and losing. The following description may, as it seems to us, best meet the accounts which we have: There were three players standing in the form of an equilateral triangle. Each player had one ball to start with, and played for his own score. He would wish both his fellow-players to miss their strokes, and drop the ball as often as possible. He might send his ball to either player (presumably there was some rule about sending it fairly within their reach), and he might do so either by catching the ball which came to him and throwing it, or by " fiving " it, so as either to strike it back to the sender (*repercutere*) or sideways to the third player (*expulsare*). Obviously the most disastrous position would be receiving three balls nearly at the same time — if, for instance, his own ball is smartly struck back to him, and almost simultaneously the two others have been sent to him; obviously, also, his easiest position was to receive only one ball at a time with a fair interval before the next."

The winner was probably the player who allowed his ball to drop the fewest times. In the game announced in this inscription Hedysius is probably a professional player (*pilicrepus*) who is challenged by the other three. Two of them play with him at a time. Amianthus signs the notice at the end. See Becq de Fouquières, *Les Jeux des Anciens*, pp. 176-211.

156. Candida me docuit, etc. This is an adaptation of a line of Propertius which runs : —

       Cynthia me docuit castas odisse puellas.

Ad quem. " At whose house." A pentameter line.

Quisquis amat valeat, etc. An hexameter line.

Ianuarias. Sc. *Kalendas . . . rogo.* " I ask the January Kalends for many happy years for us." On the Kalends of January (the first), the Romans exchanged gifts with one another, so that the year might begin with a good omen. These gifts were called *strenae*, whence the modern French *étrennes*. Some of them have been preserved with the formulaic wish *Anno novo faustum felix tibi* (Orelli, *Inscr.* 4306). Poor persons exchanged copper coins, and the rich, gold. The Christian Fathers condemned the practice, as it was associated with the cult of the goddess of good luck, Strenia.

LABYRINTHVS HIC HABITAT. A rough drawing of a labyrinth found on a wall at Pompeii. The writer has, probably in jest, written LABYRINTHVS for the MINOTAVRVS which one would expect, remembering the story of Theseus.

157. Sermo est ille mihi. " That's the talk, to punch holes through his hollow chest."

Quoi . . . non. = *nisi ei.* *Quoi* is archaic and plebeian for *cui.*

The caricature of a soldier, given at the end of the page, was found on the wall of a barrack that had been the quarters of a Roman garrison. The name of Nonius Maximus was written above it, and the same name was repeated in other places accompanied by various insulting epithets. It is thought to be a caricature of a centurion who had made himself unpopular by his severity and strictness. The drawing was made in red chalk.

XXIV. CORNELIUS TACITUS.

158. Agricola having led the Roman troops northward from Britain into Caledonia, the native tribes assailed a portion of his army, and were repulsed. They prepared, however, to renew the struggle, and when Agricola reached the Grampian Mountains, he found the Caledonian host drawn up under its chieftain Galgacus, ready for a decisive battle. Tacitus puts into the mouth of this warrior the spirited harangue given in our text. Such addresses made to an assemblage of troops were technically styled *contiones*.

necessitatem nostram. " Our desperate situation."

spem ac subsidium. Hendiadys = *spem subsidii.*

servientium litora. The shores of Gaul, which had been thoroughly subdued by the Romans.

159. terrarum ac libertatis. This sort of phrase is very characteristic of Tacitus, who is continually coupling concrete and abstract nouns, the effect being regarded as epigrammatic. At the present day, it is usually done for giving a comic effect, as " He was clothed in rage and a long ulster."

recessus ipse ac sinus famae. "Our remoteness and the obscurity of our name " ; *famae* meaning the reports about them.

omne ignotum pro magnifico. A very famous phrase.

infestiores Romani. " And the still more hostile Romans."

ubi solitudinem faciunt, pacem appellant. Another striking phrase which finds its modern equivalent in General Sebastiani's announcement that " order reigns in Warsaw."

alibi servituri. i.e. in the Roman armies abroad.

ager atque annus. "Our yearly produce."

in frumentum. "Grain for tribute."

silvis ac paludibus emuniendis. " In clearing woods and draining marshes."

mancipia. = *servi.* Abstract for concrete.

familiā. The slave family, of course. See notes to p. 27.

ferocia. " High spirit."

Brigantes feminā duce. The allusion is to the great revolt of the Britons under the heroic queen of the Iceni, Boadicea (better Boudicea), in which the Roman colonies at Camulodunum (Colchester) and Londinium (London) were destroyed and 70,000 Romans and their allies were slain. See Tacitus, *Annales*, xiv. 31.

non in poenitentiam laturi. " Ready to sustain our freedom so as not to feel regret."

160. tegit. " Gives shelter."

castella. " Garrisons."

aegra mancipia. In apposition with *senum coloniae*.

in hoc campo. " Rests on this field of battle." The spirit of the whole harangue strikingly resembles that of the immortal lines put by Burns into the mouth of the later Galgacus, Robert Bruce, and beginning " Scots wha hae wi' Wallace bled."

urbes. i.e. no large cities. They had a few small towns (Tac. *Ann.* i. 56).

ut fons placuit. Church and Brodribb note that the modern names of German towns frequently end in *bach* (brook), *feld* (field), *holtz* (grove), *wald* (wood), and *born* (spring), thus indicating their origin ; e.g. Bergerbach, Elberfeld, Holzbach, Sponholtz, Tannwald, Paderborn.

161. caementorum. sc. *caesorum lapidum*.

tegularum. The French *tuile*, whence *Tuileries*.

materia. " Building material."

subterraneos specus aperire. When the Emperor Julian (the Apostate) was passing through the territory of the Alemanni, a deserter informed him that the enemy had concealed themselves in a great number of subterranean caves with intricate windings, out of which they might rush upon his troops at any moment. (Ammian. Marc. xvii. 1 foll.) Cf. Xenophon, *Anab.* iv. 25.

aperire. = *fodere*.

hiemi. Dative.

fallunt. " Escape notice " = λανθάνουσι.

quod quaerenda sunt. i.e. because it would require some considerable time to find them.

Sagum. A Gallic word ; the modern French *chagrin*, English *shagreen*, *shag*. In Latin it regularly means the soldier's heavy cloak, and is often used metaphorically as opposed to *toga*, the garb of the civilian or *pékin*.

maculis pellibusque. Hendiadys = *maculatis pellibus*.

brachia ac lacertos. *Brachium* is the forearm ; *lacertus* is the arm from the elbow up. There is no word in Latin for the arm as a whole.

ad delicias muliebres. " For the finical tastes of women."

162. coniugales deos. These among the Romans were Iupiter, Iuno, Diana, Venus, Hymenaeus, etc.

denuntiant. " Solemnly declare."

sic vivendum. Sc. *esse*, depending on *denuntiant*.

spectaculorum. Tacitus here, as in so many other places, glances at the demoralization of Roman society, heightened by the contrast which it presents to the purity, simplicity, and virility of the Germans.

XXV. GAIUS SUETONIUS TRANQUILLUS.

163. damnosior. "More wasteful."

a Palatio Esquilias usque. i.e. *usque ad Esquilias.* The celebrated gardens of Maecenas were on the Esquiline (Hor. *Sat.* i. 8), and Nero now joined them to the imperial precinct. (Tacitus, *Annales*, xv. 39.)

transitoriam. "Passage-way." So the Forum of Nerva at Rome was called Forum Transitorium, as being a passage-way between the Subura and the Forum Romanum.

incendio. Mentioned by Tacitus in the passage of the *Annales*, cited above.

cultu. "Adornment."

in quo . . . staret. Such that a Colossus 100 feet high could stand in it. Pliny (*H. N.* xxxiv. 7) gives the height of this Colossus as 120 feet, and says that it was the work of one Zenodorus. It represented the sun god.

porticus triplices miliarias. i.e. three porticoes, or rows of columns, each 1000 feet long.

rura insuper. Cf. Tacitus, *Annales*, xv. 42.

164. unionumque. The name *unio* was given to any large pearl (*margarita*) when set as a solitaire.

tabulis eburneis versatilibus. Panels of ivory that slipped aside and let flowers fall upon the guests.

fistulatis. So in the amphitheater, concealed pipes sprayed the spectators with saffron-water.

albulis. Water impregnated with sulphur was called *albula aqua.* Near Tibur (modern Tivoli) were a number of sulphur springs, known as Albulae, which made the place the Saratoga of the Romans. Of these several still remain, and are resorted to by invalids as of old. The modern name is Bagni di Tivoli.

165. super fiduciam imperii. "Beyond the credit of the Empire."

equitis Romani. Cf. Tacitus, *Annales*, xvi. 1 foll.

gazae. A word derived from the Persian through the Greek γάζα.

The palace of the Caesars, to which Nero added in so remarkable a manner, was begun by Augustus upon the site of the house formerly owned by the great orator Hortensius, on the Palatine Hill, — a quarter already the most fashionable in Rome. The palace erected by Augustus (a comparatively modest structure) was dedicated by him in 26 B.C. In the year 3 A.D., this was destroyed by fire. A public subscription, in which no person was allowed to contribute more than one *denarius* (about twenty cents), raised a great sum of money for the rebuilding of the palace, with the result that a much more magnificent structure was erected. To this Tiberius added a new wing, and Caligula so added to it as to fill with various edifices the whole space between the *domus Tiberiana* and the Forum. Nero's addition overlooked the valley in which the Colosseum was afterwards built. See the very interesting chapter on the subject in Lanciani's *Ancient Rome*, pp. 106–133 ; and Middleton's *Remains of Ancient Rome*, vol. i. pp. 158–219 (London, 1892).

in amphitheatro Tauri. A stone amphitheatre built in 30 B.C. by Statilius Taurus, a distinguished guard of Augustus.

in Septis. The Septa (neuter plural) was a name used to designate a number of enclosures in the Campus Martius, in which the people were collected by tribes or centuries at the time of the elections (*comitia*) to vote. Each enclosure was originally called *ovile* (a pen or sheep-fold), but in imperial times the whole site was regarded as a single structure, and finished off in marble, surrounded by porticoes and elaborately decorated. Augustus used the place for wild beasts, shows, etc. (Suet. *Aug.* 43).

edidit. The technical term for giving a show ; whence the person so giving it is styled *editor*.

ex utrāque regione. " From every district." Italy has been divided by Augustus into eleven *regiones*.

missilia variarum rerum. The expression *missilia rerum* occurs again in Suet. *Aug.* 98 and *Nero* 11. See Peck's note on the former passage. *Missilia* is here to be regarded as a noun, and the expressions *missilia rerum* to be compared with the *tabularum picturas* of *Aug.* 75.

cum obsonio. *Obsonium* or *opsonium* (ὀψώνιον) is literally anything that is eaten with bread, either fish or flesh, but also applied to relishes and dainties, e.g. figs, olives, and even salt (Pliny, *H. N.* xxxii. 87 and xv. 82). The pure Latin word is *pulmentarium*. See Saalfeld, *Küche und Keller in Alt-Rom* (Berlin, 1883).

contra se. i.e. on the opposite side of the table.

codicillos. " Letters-patent."

extra ordinem. Out of the regular order (*cursus honorum*) in which persons of senatorial rank were advanced from office to office.

Africanarum. Sc. *ferarum*. " African animals " ; e.g. tigers, lions, panthers, buffaloes, etc. At some of these imperial *venationes*, an extraordinary number of wild animals were hunted and killed. Under Caligula, 400 bears were put to death in a single day ; under Claudius, 300. Nero had 400 tigers fight with bulls and elephants. When the Colosseum was dedicated by Titus, 5000 animals perished to celebrate the event. Fierce beasts were frequently chained together, and thus rolled together in the bloody sand in a death struggle. See Magnin, *Origines du Théâtre*, pp. 445–453, and Lecky, *Hist. of European Morals*, vol. i. pp. 278–282.

Troiae decursione. The so-called *ludus Troiae*, which was an equestrian sham fight exhibited by boys of patrician families. See Vergil, *Aeneid*, v. 553–603. .

chrysocollā. Pliny (*H. N.* xxxiii. 5) says that Nero used to strew the track with green sand whenever he appeared himself as a charioteer of the "Green" faction (*factio prasina*).

Commisit et subitos. "He also matched improvised fighters"; i.e. a "scratch" band. In this sense, *subitus* is opposed to *expertus*. The word *subitarius* is also used.

e Gelotianā. Sc. *domo*. The *domus Gelotiana* was an addition to the imperial palace made by Caligula, who purchased a large and handsome house from one Gelotius, and made it a sort of training school and quarters for his jockeys, grooms, pages, etc. The house stood near the Circus, and through it the emperor could pass unobserved to his place among the Greens. Many *graffiti* have been discovered on the ruins which still remain of this building.

maenianis. A *maenianum* was a balcony which projected from the upper floor of a house or other building and overhung the street. The name is said to be derived from that of C. Maenius, censor B.C. 318 (Fest. s.h.v.).

166. aulicis. From *aula* (*regia*), the court.

in verum nepotem. i.e. the son of his own son Drusus.

εἷς κοίρανος ἔστω, etc. A quotation from Homer, *Il.* ii. 204, where it is put into the mouth of Odysseus.

Latiarem Iovem. Iupiter Latiaris, the Latin Iupiter, worshiped especially at the Feriae Latinae.

167. simulacrum . . . iconicum. A statue of exactly the same proportions as the subject; a portrait statue. So, also, *effigies iconica* (Pliny, *H. N.* xxxiv. 4).

magisteria sacerdotii. "The chief places in the priesthood." Those who took precedence of their fellow priests were called *magistri*. These offices were probably held for life (*perpetua*), but temporarily (*vicibus*) under Caligula. It must be remembered that these apparently sacred offices were largely political in their nature, and were sought for the honor they conferred by men who had no religious belief whatever. Thus Iulius Caesar was *pontifex maximus*, though little better than an atheist himself.

generatim per singulos dies. i.e. flamingoes on one day, moor-fowls on the next, peacocks on the next, etc.

ceteros ordines. "Persons of other classes."

equitem. Generic singular = *equites*.

decimas. A word meaning the gifts bestowed upon the people (Cicero, *De Officiis*, ii. 17 ; Suet. *Galba*, 15). It probably gets its significance from the fact that in the early days of Rome, victors and persons in luck generally used to give a tenth part of their gains to Hercules. (Macrob. *Sat.* iii. 12 ; cf. Livy, v. 21).

equestria. The first fourteen rows in the theater assigned to the *equites* by the Roscian law.

paegniarios. From παίγνιον, a plaything.

168. a calvo ad calvum. Literally "from baldhead to baldhead." Presumably a baldheaded man stood at each end of the line ; hence the expression signifies all of them, — "the whole outfit."

169. Atellanae. A species of native comedy usually acted by amateurs.

verbosum in historiā. Livy's history was in 142 books.

respondere. The technical term used of the official opinions on points of law given by the great jurisconsults, and having the force of a judicial interpretation.

praeter eum. For *praeter se*. When the words of another are quoted in the *oratio obliqua*, the exact use of the pronoun is occasionally neglected. This is especially true of the later Latin writers. For instances, see Val. Max. v. 1, 3 ; *percontabatur an ea quae ad aures* EIVS *pervenerant dixissent;* and Eutrop. vii. 11 ; *cum tanti se non esse dixisset ut propter* EVM *civile bellum commoveretur.* A second instance in Suetonius is probably to be found in *Nero*, 31, but the reading there is disputed.

XXVI. PUBLIUS AELIUS HADRIANUS.

170. Ego nolo Caesar esse. The verse is the popular trochaic dimeter based upon accent and not upon syllabic quantity. Thus, *égo, láti-, scýthi-, culi-* are to be regarded as trochees, though properly they are pyrrhics, $\smile\smile$.

171. tabernas. In earlier Latin, *taberna* meant "shop." Later it takes on its modern restrictive sense "tavern."

popinas. An Oscan form, the *p* representing the Latin *q*. Hence, *popina* would have been in a pure Latin form *coquina* (*coquo*). The word meant properly "cook shop," or "eating house," where ready cooked food was sold, and is hence distinguished from *caupona*, a place devoted to the sale of drinks ; but practically there was little difference, so that *popino* means a debauchee. See Macrobius, *Sat.* vii. 14.

Animula, blandula, vagula. This beautiful verse has always been the despair of translators. The latest attempt at rendering it into metrical English is that contained in *Cottabos* for 1894. The nearest approach to the spirit and grace of the original is found in Pope's famous paraphrase, beginning : —

> " Vital spark of heavenly flame,
> Quit, oh quit this mortal frame.
> Trembling, hoping, lingering, sighing,
> O the pain, the bliss of dying ! "

rigida. "Unyielding." In this short verse of five lines, there are three ἅπαξ λεγόμενα (*vagula, blandula, nudula*), while *pallidula* occurs in only one other place.

XXVII. TESTAMENTUM PORCELLI.

172. In the MSS., the *testamentum* has prefixed to it the words INCIPIT TESTAMENTUM PORCELLI.

M. Grunnius Corocotta. Grunnius is from *grunnio*, "to grunt"; Corocotta suggests χοῖρος; but editors cite Porphyrius, who says that in India the hyena is called by the natives κοροκόττα. Now the word hyena (ὕαινα) is properly the feminine form of ὗς, "a hog," given to the hyena because of his bristling, hog-like mane. Hence a sort of connection is established between the name *corocotta* and a pig. Several ancient writers (e.g. Ælian and Pliny) use the word of an Indian or African animal.

Magirus. Gk. μάγειρος, meaning both "a cook" and "a butcher"; both meanings here uniting, unfortunately for M. Grunnius.

solivertiator. Haupt regards this word as = *fugitivus*, because of the following words : *fugitive porcelle;* but we should in this case have a very pointless tautology. For *solum vertere = fugere*, see Cic. *Pro Caec.* 100 ; Petron. 81 ; and Juv. xi. 49. The word is a ἅπαξ λεγόμενον.

dirimo. Colloquial present for future.

puer. The attendant slave, — a kitchen helper.

ut hunc porcellum faciam cruentum. The true nursery-tale way of putting it, — "so that I can make this little pig all bloody." A delightfully horrible sentence, and well adapted to give the small Roman a delicious shiver.

sub die XVI Kal. Lucerninas. All editors have given up this expression in despair, as the Kalendae Lucerninae are nowhere else named. It is possibly a joke to denote the time of the year just preceding the season when the days begin to grow short and the evenings long, — "the month when we begin to use candle light."

Clibanato et Piperato. From *clibanus* (κλίβανος), an earthen or iron pot (Apic. vii. 5); and *piper*, pepper.

clamavit ad se. An archaic use of the verb, retained in the plebeian Latin. It has here the sense simply of *vocare*, as in the Romance forms of the same verb *chiamare, llamar, chamar*. Haupt cites Martial, i. 49 ; *veniet tibi conviva clamatus*, i.e. *vocatus*.

dimitteret. Here in its legal sense "renounce," "bequeath" ; cf. line 29.

173. **Verrino Lardino.** From *verres*, a boar, and *lardum*, bacon.

do lego dari. Legal amplification. "I give and bequeath" ; cf. *dabo donabo* below.

Veturinae. Probably formed from *vetus* like the ordinary proper name Veturius.

Laconicae siliginis. This wheat is mentioned in Pliny, *H. N.* xviii. 10.

Quirrinae. Possibly formed to suggest χοῖρος (as if Χοιρίνη), as Salmasius suggested ; but better from *quirrito*, " to queek " (see p. 16, line 55, of the poem on the nightingale). Hence we have written it *Quirrinae* rather than *Quirinae*, which last is preferred by Haupt.

votum. " Wedding," or "betrothal" ; cf. the Codex Theodosianus, iii. 5, 7. *Si pater pactum de nuptiis filiae inierit et . . . ad vota non potuerit pervenire, id inter sponsos firmum ratumque permaneat,* etc.

dabo donabo. Words continually coupled together usually omit the connective *et*; cf. *comminus eminus, sursum deorsum, prima postrema, huc illuc,* etc.

sutoribus saetas. i.e. for their waxed ends.

rixoribus. Probably the same as *rixatoribus*, "brawlers." One MS. does, in fact, read here *rixatoribus.*

capitinam. A word found only here and of unknown meaning. Possibly it is a plebeian equivalent for *caput* in the sense of *cerebrum*, so often used by the Latin writers as the seat of wrath, hot temper, etc. ; cf. Horace, *Sat.* i. 5, 21, given on p. 90, *cerebrosus prosilit unus;* and *Sat.* i. 9, 11, *O te, Bolane, cerebri felicem.*

surdis auriculas. Because a pig's sense of hearing is very keen.

bubulariis. Others here read *botulariis*, but this would be anticipating the *isiciariis*, which does not differ in meaning. Render "butchers."

isiciariis. From ἰσίκιον, a dish of collops ; whence also the Latin *insicia* and *insicium*, "force meat." The form *insiciarius* is elsewhere used.

pueris vesicam. To inflate and tie to the end of a stick, as boys do in modern times, using it to give their companions harmless blows of tremendous sound.

ungulas. Here to be rendered "claws" for comic effect; cf. Plaut. *Pseud.* iii. 2, 63.

nec nominando coco. "The cook who deserves no mention"; "the unspeakable cook."

popiam et pistillum. "His ladle and pestle." *Popia* = the Gk. ζωμήρυσις.

de Tebeste usque ad Tergeste. "From Dan to Beersheba." Apparently a proverbial expression. Tebeste or Theveste was probably a city of Numidia (Orelli, *Inscript.* 3575). Tergeste is the modern Trieste.

liget collo de reste. i.e. *liget reste ex collo.* The same construction with *de* is found below in line 40: *bene condiatis de bonis condimentis*, and appears to have been common in the language of cookery ; cf. Apicius, iv. 2, iv. 5, vii. 2, viii. 8 (Haupt).

ex litteris. A use of *ex*, also common in Apicius, and presumably formulaic in Roman cook books ; cf. Apicius, iii. 15: *apium coques ex aqua nitrata;* id. iv. 1, iv. 2, v. 1, vii. 4, and often.

consules vitae. An unusual meaning of *consul* = *consulens*, but paralleled in Vopiscus, *Firm.* 3: *Iovem consulem;* and Apuleius, *De Mundo*, 25.

nuclei. *nucleus* (*nuculeus*) is the diminutive of *nux;* it may possibly be used here with *piperis* in the compound sense of *pepper-corn.* See Apicius, viii. 7, where *nuclei piperis* are included in the seasoning of pork.

in medio testamento. Perhaps we should read here *in meo testamento* with our MS.

Lardio. From *lardum*, "bacon." See *Verrius Lardinus* above.

Ofellicus. From *ofella*, dimin. of *offa*, a chop or cutlet.

Cyminatus. From *cyma*, a young cabbage.

Lucanicus. From *lucanica*, a kind of sausage meat much liked by the Lucanians; cf. Cicero, *Ad Fam.* ix. 16: *solebam antea delectari oleis et lucanicis tuis;* Martial, xiii. 35. Its composition is given by Apicius, ii. 4.

Tergillus. From *tergilla*, a rind of pork; a word found only in Apicius, iv. 3, and the *Gloss. Philox.*

Celsinus. A name that suggests the dish called by Apicius (viii. 7) *porcellus Celsinianus.*

Nuptialicus. The significance of the name is not clear. Haupt suggests that it refers to some preparation of pork used at wedding feasts (*nuptiae*), pork being, next to fish, the dish most favored by the Romans. Salmasius conjectures *Botulicus* from *botulus.*

signavit. These seven pigs all sign the will as witnesses, though in line 2, the pig who makes the will says that he is unable to write a will with his own hand, and so has to dictate it, — a slight inconsistency on the part of the author.

Explicit. A word found in later Latin at the end of books, probably for *explicitus* (*liber est*), but here for *explicitum* (*testamentum est*); cf. Mart. xi. 107, 1.

Clibanato et Piperato. See above, line 15.

feliciter. A word of good omen placed at the end of books and other writings. St. Jerome says (*Epist.* 28, 4): *Solemus completis opusculis ad distinctionem rei alterius sequentis, medium interponere* EXPLICIT *aut* FELICITER *aut aliquid istius modi.*

It is to be noted that though the general form of a Roman will is observed in the *Testamentum*, and although the seven witnesses carefully sign, such a will as this would be invalid as no heir (*heres*) is mentioned in it, there being only legatees (*legatarii*). Hence the burlesque is probably not the work of a lawyer.

XXVIII. AULUS GELLIUS.

176. illam talem. "Such a shrew as that."

foris. Abl. of place; *foras*, acc. of direction.

saturā Menippeā. Menippus was a Cynic philosopher who lived about 60 B.C. The works embodying his teaching were cast in satirical form. They are all lost, but some fragments remain of Varro's *Saturae*, written in imitation of him.

minimo. The special names of the fingers are: *pollex*, thumb; *index*, or *salutaris*, forefinger; *medius, infamis*, or *impudicus*, middle finger; *minimo proximus*, or *medicinalis*, ring finger; and *minimus*, little finger.

quas. "Which (operations)"; by attraction to ἀνατομάς.

pergere ac pervenire. Gellius is extremely fond of using pairs of words, generally with alliteration, which together mean little, if any more, than either would mean alone. The fondness for this usage is still more strongly developed in modern German, and may also be illustrated from prayer-book English.

177. Democriti. A celebrated philosopher, born at Abdera, in Thrace, about 460 B.C., who, with Leucippus, was the founder of the Atomic Theory. His writings covered a wide range of mathematics, grammar, music, and philosophy.

178. Archytas. A distinguished philosopher of the Pythagorean school, a contemporary of Plato. He was a practical mechanician as well as a theoretical mathematician. His wooden flying dove was one of the wonders of antiquity.

Favorinus. A philosopher of Arles who lived during Hadrian's reign.

Milo Crotoniensis. A famous athlete who was victor twelve times in the Olympian and Pythian games. He is mentioned by Herodotus, iii. 137.

Olympiade. The period of four years between the Olympian Games. As the latter were held in July, any year B.C. belongs half to one year and half to the next of an Olympiad. The record of victors at Olympus began in 776 B.C. but this system of reckoning was apparently first systematically adopted by Alexandrian writers in the third century B.C.

Arion. A celebrated Greek bard and musician of Methymna, in Lesbos, who spent most of his life at the court of Periander. Of his life, little is known beyond the story here given. A fragment of a hymn ascribed to him, but really belonging to a later period, is contained in Bergk's *Poetae Lyrici Graeci*, p. 566.

179. Periander. Tyrant of Corinth, 625 to 585 B.C.; commonly reckoned among the seven sages of Greece. He was a patron of literature and art, but harsh in his rule and cruel in his private life.

orthium. The *carmen orthium* (νόμος ὄρθιος) was a sort of dithyrambic ode, without, however, any antistrophe or refrain, usually sung to the lyre or flute, and pitched in a very high key. The tune seems to have been a very familiar one among the Greeks, as may be inferred from the passage in the *Knights* of Aristophanes, 1279, with which compare Herodotus, i. 24, where we first find it mentioned, and Aristotle, *Probl.* 19, 37.

XXIX. CHRISTIAN HYMNS.

182. Veni, redemptor gentium. This hymn has been paraphrased by J. Frank in one of the noblest German hymns, " Komm, Heidenheiland, Lösegeld."

Geminae gigas substantiae. The "giants" of *Genesis*, vi. 4, were in legend of two natures or substances, being sons of the angels who came down and united with the "daughters of men." " In the double substance of the giants thus born of heaven and earth, Ambrose sees a reference to Him who in like manner was of twofold nature, divine and human" (Trench).

Egressus eius, etc. Cf. the Nineteenth Psalm.

183. Dies irae. This magnificent hymn, of which the best known verses are given in our text, is said to have first appeared in a missal made at Venice about 1250, and is one of the five "Sequences" of the Roman Church, having its place in the *Missa in Commemoratione Omnium Fidelium Defunctorum*. Its proper title is *De Novissimo Iudicio*, "On the Last Judgment." The text established by the Council of Trent is slightly different from that of the older missals, and a still different version appears on a marble tablet of uncertain date in a church of the Franciscan Order at Mantua. On the probable authorship of the hymn, see Mohnike, *Hymnologische Forschungen*, vol. i. pp. 1–24.

No more impressive specimen of ecclesiastical Latinity exists. Its stupendous theme finds an apt expression in the stately language, and in the solemnity of the verse with its triple beat, which, as Guericke says, makes the innermost soul tremble as with three blows of a hammer. In modern literature, it plays an important part, being introduced, for instance, with thrilling effect by Goethe in his *Faust;* and in music it has received interpretations from the genius of Palestrina, Haydn, Cherubini, and Mozart. Though it defies translation, it has been many times rendered into English, the versions of Crashaw, Macaulay, Lord Lindsay, Roscommon, Williams, Drummond, and in our own country of the late General Dix, being the best. Perhaps the most successful representation in English of the spirit of the original is found in the paraphrase of a portion of it by Sir Walter Scott, at the end of the *Lay of the Last Minstrel*, beginning:

> "'That day of wrath, that dreadful day,
> When heaven and earth shall pass away,
> What power shall be the sinner's stay?'"

In German there are versions by Herder, Fichte, and Schlegel, among others. See *Fifty Versions of the Dies Irae* in the *Dublin Review* for 1882.

Teste David cum Sibyllā. Some read here *teste Petro*, referring to 2 Peter iii. 7–11, while others, who object to the insertion of a heathen Sibyl into a Christian hymn, have altered the whole line to *Crucis expandens vexilla* (Matt. xxiv. 30). But the thought of the line is evidently "both Jew and pagan bearing witness." For the witness of David, cf. Psalms xcvi. 13; xcvii. 3; xi. 6; as for the heathen testimony, cf. Vergil, *Ecl.* iv. See also Lactantius, *Inst. Div.* vii. 16–24.

185. Ut iucundas cervus undas. A reminiscence of the beautiful psalm beginning, "Like as the hart desireth the water brooks, so longeth my soul after thee, O God."

INDEX TO THE NOTES.

[THE REFERENCES ARE TO THE PAGES OF THE BOOK.]

254